For Sophie Co... ...llie Norp.

At Merlin thanks to Noelle Moran, Aoife Barrett, Chenile Keogh, Julie Dobson and Tony Hayes. Additional thanks to Eoin Murray and to the obliging staff of the Gilbert Library in Pearse Street.

PARTY NATION

Ireland's General Elections
The Strokes, Jokes, Spinners and Winners

PARTY NATION

Ireland's General Elections
The Strokes, Jokes, Spinners and Winners

Damian Corless

MERLIN
PUBLISHING

First published in 2007 by
Merlin Publishing
Newmarket Hall, Cork Street,
Dublin 8, Ireland
Tel: +353 1 4535866
Fax: +353 1 4535930
publishing@merlin.ie
www.merlinwolfhound.com

Text © 2007 Damian Corless
Editing, Design and Layout © 2007 Merlin Publishing

10-Digit ISBN 1-903582-71-7
13-Digit ISBN 978-1-903582-71-8

A CIP catalogue record for this book is available from the
British Library.

10 9 8 7 6 5 4 3 2 1

Typeset by Artwerk Design
Cover Design by Artwerk Design
Printed and bound by Creative Print and Design, Britain
Cover photographs courtesy of Artwerk Limited and
McCarthy Photography

Contents

Acknowledgements vi

Introduction – The Drivel is in the Detail............................... ix

Political Party Family Tree xi

Top Ten Elections... xii

1918 Vote For A Sober Peace... 1

1921 All Eyes On Carsonia 7

1922 The Alphabet Of Miseries... 13

1923 They Had Not The Military Strategy Of Niggers........ 19

1926 A Cheap Music-Hall Jingle – Picking A
National Anthem.. 25

1927 Act One – I Hope The Time Will Come When
People Like That Will Be Denied Citizenship....................... 29

1927 Act Two – Tearing Down Posters And Beating
Fianna Fáil Workers 35

1932 I Dare You To Shoot Me.. 43

1932 An Irish Speaking Colony – Reviving The Language
Through Public-Private Partnership.. 59

1933 The Ignorant And Sentimental Vote............................ 63

1937 A Low Turnout Of Priests... 71

1938 The Elephant Plays A Mouth Organ 81

1943 A Shortage Of Pencils 89

1940s-1950s The Complete Ignorance Of English
– Hoax Letters To Taoisigh.. 97

1944 The Baby At The Christening And The Remains
At The Funeral 103

1947 We Have Too Many Sissies In This Country – The
Struggle For An Irish-Speaking Ireland 109

1948 This Country Will Be Doomed 113

1951 The Emigration Of Girls... 119

1954 The Centipede In The Ditch 125

1957 None Of The Above.. 133

1950s-1960s Could You Find A Girl Around
14 Years Of Age As A Pen Pal For Me? 139

1961 The Oh-So-Quiet Election.. 145

1965 Staggering Behaviour.. 151

1969 Queer Fellows In The Engine Room........................... 159

1973 He'll End This Election As MP For Scunthorpe 166

1977 Promises, Promises, Promises....................................... 173

1981 Was Your Mother A Nun?... 185

1982 Act One – Small-Footed Women 201

1982 Act Two – Car Crash Government.............................. 209

1987 A 32-County British Ireland 219

1989 A Hospital Trolley Is Just A Bed With Wheels 231

1992 The Wince Factor... 237

1997 Some Sort Of Handshaking Marathon 249

2002 You Have A Great Chance Of Getting A Vote
If A Dog Bites You 263

2003 From Time To Time I Smoke It Myself – The Ups
And Downs Of A Rezoning Windfall 283

2005 Fuck It, We'll Say No More – Freedom Of Speech
In The Dáil Chamber 287

2007 Somewhere, It Had All Gone Horribly Right 293

Selective Glossary 305

Introduction

THE DRIVEL IS IN THE DETAIL

If politics is showbiz for ugly people, a general election is the festival spree where all the performers take their show on the road. This book rates the entertainment value provided by Ireland's political caste over the course of 29 campaigns from 1918 – which spawned the first Dáil Eireann – to the present day.

The early elections detailed here were no barrel of laughs. To a greater or lesser extent, all were subdued by the shadow of the gunman. Nevertheless, each contest from 1918 to September 1927 was uniquely pivotal in the formation of the Irish body politic. In terms of entertainment value, the first blockbuster election was that of 1932, with much of the colour injected by Fianna Fáil's newly-arrived fun-loving mouthpiece, *The Irish Press*.

Style, as much as substance, is the focus of this book. In many campaigns, style has been the only substantial difference separating rival tribes descended from the same family tree. The former high-office holder, Padraig Flynn, spoke for more than himself when he reflected: "All that pseudo-intellectual stuff about ideals, and why you do it, that's all clap-trap."

Over the course of almost a century some themes have come and gone, while others have remained strikingly constant. The Red Scare tactic had a particularly long innings, featuring in almost every election from the 1920s right up to 1997 when Fianna Fáil suggested that the Democratic Left element of the Rainbow Coalition harboured a vestigial Soviet-inspired impulse to sabotage the farming sector.

Other issues which we think of as recent pop up across the

decades. The illegal dumping of household waste was a major problem in the 1940s, with air-raid shelters a favourite tipping ground. Drink driving comes up time and again. In 1957, for instance, Ireland's publicans argued that drink drivers were being scapegoated for the fact that a proportion of motorists will always be "mentally prone" to having accidents, whether drunk or sober.

Hospital overcrowding is another recurring theme. During the 1937 general election, a report stressed that keeping patients on stretchers and temporary beds "must not be allowed to continue". During the campaign of 1932, the management of one caring institution were accused by a judge of abusing patients by feeding them watered-down milk.

The decentralisation of civil servants from Dublin is another hardy perennial. In 1969, Fianna Fáil's Justice Minister from Mayo, Michael O'Morain, unveiled plans to relocate 1,700 staff to Castlebar. They budged not an inch. In 1982, Charles Haughey promised that the decentralisation of 400 Post & Telegraphs workers to Waterford was ready to go "full steam ahead" as part of a larger relocation. "This is not an election gimmick," he stressed.

The most consistent thread running through this series of snapshots is the amount of sheer guff which flies around at election time, a great deal of it heroically preposterous. Everyone knows this to be true as a general principle, but here, over the next 300 pages or so, the drivel is in the detail.

Damian Corless

2007

THE MAKING OF OUR POLITICAL FAMILIES

IRISH PARLIAMENTARY PARTY
Founded 1882 by Charles Stewart Parnell to win Home Rule under an English Monarch. Wiped out by Sinn Féin in the general election of 1918. Dissolved 1918.

LABOUR PARTY
Founded in 1912 by James Connolly, James Larkin and William O'Brien as the political wing of the Irish Trades Union Congress. Did not contest the elections of 1918 and 1921 to allow voters a clear-cut choice on the national question. The disastrous consequence was that Labour neglected to woo an electorate of mostly first-time voters forming the political habits of a lifetime.

MONARCHICAL SINN FÉIN
Founded in 1905 by Arthur Griffith to win Home Rule under an Irish Monarch. The party was one of the motive forces behind the 1916 Rising.

REPUBLICAN SINN FÉIN
At the Sinn Féin Árd Féis of 1917 the party raised its sites from Home Rule under an Irish Monarch to winning a 32-County Irish Republic. After a landslide victory in the 1918 general election, its MPs refused to take seats in Westminster and assembled as the illegal Dáil Eireann.

TREATYITE SINN FÉIN
In December 1921, a Sinn Féin delegation led by Michael Collins signed a Treaty with the British, granting a 26-County Free State. Dáil Eireann – effectively a Sinn Féin private members' club – approved the deal by 64 votes to 57. The pro-Treaty majority became the Provisional Government of the Free State.

ANTI-TREATY SINN FÉIN
Led by Eamon de Valera, a large block of Sinn Féin TDs opposed the Treaty in furious Dáil debates. In 1922, the political frictions ignited into civil war. Those fighting on the anti-Treaty side were dubbed Irregulars.

FIANNA FÁIL
In 1926, three years after defeat in the Civil War, Eamon de Valera resigned as leader of Sinn Féin and founded Fianna Fáil, meaning Soldiers of Destiny. The anti-Treaty Sinn Féin policy of not taking seats in the 26-County partitionist Dáil was abandoned. Fianna Fáil began 16 years of rule with victory in the general election of 1932.

CUMANN na nGAEDHEAL
In early 1923 the TDs of pro-Treaty Sinn Féin AKA the Government Party, changed their name to Cumann na nGaedheal, meaning League Of The Irish. Led by WT Cosgrave, the party governed the Free State until defeat in the general election of 1932.

FINE GAEL
Following its second general election defeat in the space of a year, in late 1933 Cumann na nGaedheal merged with the right wing National Centre Party and the even more right wing Blueshirts. The new party called itself Fine Gael, meaning United Ireland.

PROGRESSIVE DEMOCRATS
The Progressive Democrats were founded in 1985 by Desmond O'Malley following his expulsion from Fianna Fáil for "conduct unbecoming". O'Malley was ostensibly banished for refusing to back Fianna Fáil's policy of denying access to contraception. The real reason was his enmity towards party leader Charles Haughey. He was joined by another anti-Haugheyite, Mary Harney, when she too was expelled from Fianna Fáil some months later.

Top Ten Elections

TAUTOLOGY

1977

A full-blooded, good-humoured, mid-summer election, with a twist in the tail. The ruling coalition of Fine Gael and Labour reckoned they had the contest sown-up thanks to a juggle of the constituency boundaries. However, having conspired successfully to keep the young people of Ireland from voting in the previous campaign of 1973, Fianna Fáil in opposition now went all out to engineer a youthquake. Frank Dunlop, Eoin Ryan and Seamus Brennan wooed the pop kids and Fianna Fáil buried the ruling coalition under a shock landslide. (9/10)

1981

The first of a gripping trilogy of ill-tempered campaigns within 18 months, where Good and Evil were pitted in starker relief than at any time since the 1930s. The challenger for the title of Taoiseach was Garret Fitzgerald, billed by Fine Gael as Garret The Good. The incumbent was Charles Haughey of Fianna Fáil, billed even by some of his own party colleagues as the Devil incarnate. Republican hunger-strike candidates threw a spanner in the works. (9/10)

1982 (February)

Having snatched victory in the 1981 contest, Fitzgerald's Fine Gael-led coalition inflicted fiscal self-harm with a budget which penalised women with small feet. Fought in the dark depths of mid-winter, during a period when one retiring Minister pronounced the country "very nearly ungovernable", this was a bleak, dirty and compelling campaign. The star performer was Fianna Fáil's Pat O'Connor Pat O'Connor, a man so committed to the electoral process that they named him twice. (9/10)

1982 (November)

Charles Haughey's grotesque, unbelievable, bizarre and unprecedented GUBU administration was hauled before the electorate kicking and screaming after nine months of car-crash rule. Just before the election, Labour's leader Michael O'Leary dramatically jumped ship and joined Fine Gael. U2 weighed in with an endorsement of Garret The Good. Fianna Fáil's Albert Reynolds claimed to have secret tapes which "proved" that Fine Gael had tried to smear Charles Haughey. (9/10)

1932

In the ten years since the establishment of the Irish Free State, Cumann na nGaedheal had ruled on a ticket of law-and-order. The party led by WT Cosgrave oversaw the establishment of firm civilian control of the military, and the founding of an unarmed police force, both at a time when other young democracies were falling under a totalitarian yoke. However, as the 1932 campaign got underway there was an excited sense that Cumann na nGaedheal's work was done, and that Fianna Fáil's day was about to dawn. (8/10)

1987

The election of 1987 was the last great campaign before the dismal scientists of the spin-doctoring profession suffocated the life, colour and spontaneous gombeenism out of the process. Garret Fitzgerald and Charles Haughey squared up for the last time. The Progressive Democrats entered the contest for the first time. Sinn Féin claimed to be the victims of Irish apartheid, the Labour Party were accused of promoting "childsex", and Unionist candidates promoted reunification with Britain. (8/10)

1927 (September)
After a strong showing in the general election of June 1927, the recently-founded Fianna Fáil seemed well-placed to oust the ruling Cumann na nGaedheal party. Following the murder of Justice Minister Kevin O'Higgins and his government's near defeat in the Dáil, WT Cosgrave called a snap election. He then lost a second Minister when JJ Walsh of the Department of Posts & Telegraphs mutinied and went missing in action. (7/10)

1969
The Labour Party came out of the closet, admitted it had Left-ish feelings and declared that 'The Seventies Will Be Socialist'. For the first time, the opposition tried to make political capital by hinting that there was more to Charles Haughey's wealth than first met the eye. Fianna Fáil branded themselves The Party Of Reality, Fine Gael pitched themselves as The Party Of Sanity, and an independent candidate complained to the Pope about shabby treatment by RTE. (6/10)

1965
Fine Gael's traditionalists and modernisers fought a civil war over the party's manifesto. The Taoiseach, Séan Lemass, was pelted with eggs. Incandescent with rage following an April Fool's prank, Lemass lost the run of himself and branded *The Irish Times* an enemy of the people. (6/10)

1923
The general election of August 1923 was the first to take place in the new political entity of the Irish Free State. It was also the first since the Westminster election of 1910 to take

place under something approaching 'normal' conditions, although that 'normality' was disrupted on a daily basis by shootings, bombings, kidnappings, raids, jailbreaks and bank robberies. (6/10)

AND THE BOTTOM THREE

1921
There was no polling in the newly-partitioned South of Ireland. Sinn Féin took 124 seats uncontested. (0/10)

1951
Fianna Fáil insisted that there was only "one issue", which was "do you want coalition or do you not?" As if to make the point that current issues were of no relevance, de Valera campaigned in Mayo on Fianna Fáil's record of keeping Ireland out of the long-ended Second World War. (1/10)

1957
Joe Larkin of Fianna Fáil in Dublin pushed the boundaries of overstatement to the outer limits early in the campaign when he insisted: "The coming election is one of the most important and critical that has ever taken place here." The opposite was the case and everyone knew it. (1/10)

1918

VOTE FOR A SOBER PEACE

The Incumbents: The Irish Party at Westminster.
Slogan: Home Rule.
Promise: Self-government within a British framework.
The Challengers: Sinn Féin.
Slogan: Brits Out!
Promise: A 32-County Irish Republic free of Britain.
The Mood of the Country: Unneighbourly.
Prediction: A Sinn Féin win, followed by crisis.
Result: A Sinn Féin walkover.
Entertainment value: 3/10.

Victory Before The Opening Of A Single Ballot Box

In December 1918, just weeks after the guns of World War One fell silent, the people of the United Kingdom of Great Britain and Ireland went to the polls for the first time since 1910. The campaign took place during the great Spanish flu pandemic which killed up to 50 million people worldwide, wiping out 280,000 victims in Britain and Ireland. *The Evening Herald* speculated that the flu was actually swine fever caught from eating "bad bacon".

The general election scheduled for 1915 had been a casualty of the war which was to end all wars. If a week is a long time in politics, the eight tumultuous years since the 1910 poll represented the passing of aeons during which all had changed utterly. The general election of 1918 was to be decided by a new generation of voters, with a new outlook, in a new world order, under new voting rules.

Going into the election, Irish nationalism was represented by the fusty members of the Irish Parliamentary Party (IPP) who sat as a minority grouping in the Imperial Parliament at Westminster. The main plank of the Irish Parliamentary Party's campaign was the pledge to finally deliver Home Rule for Ireland. For half a century the IPP had been pressing for the return to Dublin of an Irish Parliament, which would provide Irish solutions to Irish problems while bowing to London on broader matters of Empire. The IPP had landed one hand on its Holy Grail four years earlier in 1914 – when the Home Rule Bill finally made it through Parliament – only to see their legislative victory snatched away by the eruption of slaughter on an industrial scale.

Putting it up to the old timers of the Irish Parliamentary Party were the young firebrands of Sinn Féin who'd thrown in their lot with the rebels of Easter 1916. For these upstarts, Home Rule was an idea whose time had come and gone. Sinn Féin had originally set its sites on the establishment of a duel monarchy with Britain, with an Irish High King sitting as head of state above the restored Irish Parliament. However, the upheavals of the Rising and the British repression which followed galvanised the mood for a clean break. In October 1917, Sinn Féin declared itself a Republican party in pursuit of a fully independent all-Ireland state as set out in the 1916 Proclamation of Independence.

Under the new dispensation proposed by Sinn Féin, the party's candidate for first President of an Irish Republic would have been Eamon de Valera, who was the senior surviving commander of the Easter Rising. De Valera held United States citizenship, which is widely believed to have saved him from joining the other commanders in front of a firing squad. When he stood for re-election in 1918 – having been elected MP for East Clare in a 1917 by-election – De

Valera was aged 36. Other relative young guns standing for Sinn Féin included WT Cosgrave (38), Kevin O'Higgins (26) and Michael Collins (28). Just months before the 1918 election, John Redmond, the leader of the Irish Parliamentary Party, had died at the age of 62. The IPP replaced him with 67-year-old John Dillon.

If there was a clear generation gap between the two parties pitching for the Nationalist/Catholic vote, a seismic generational shift had also taken place which made the body of voters in 1918 radically different to that of 1910. Under a new Electoral Act, the numbers on the 32-County voting register had shot up from 700,000 in 1910 to almost two million in 1918. For the first time, all males over 21 had the vote. For the first time too, women over the age of thirty were granted a say in the democratic process.

The Ulster Temperance Council took out a series of newspaper adverts seeking to mobilise the maiden female vote against the scourge of male drunkenness. In the United States, women had agitated so successfully against alcohol that the 18th Amendment, which would usher in the Prohibition Era, was just weeks away from becoming law. In Ireland and Britain the prohibitionists took their aim at the soldiers marching home from the trenches, to households where their womenfolk and children awaited with shelves to be put up and drains to be unblocked.

In one advert, the Ulster Temperance Council declared: "Women, whose vote is feared because no one knows how the women will vote, can save the soldiers if they will – and the soldiers will thank them for it. They do not want a drunken demobilisation. They do not want the few that cannot resist temptation to disgrace their comrades. WOMEN OF IRELAND, VOTE FOR A SOBER PEACE. Persuade candidates to act against the manufacture and sale of drink until after demobilisation is complete."

Another All-Ireland advert placed by the Ulster

Temperance Council suggested that the Great War which had left nine million dead might just be the curtain-raiser for worse things to come. The headline asked: WHICH IS THE WORST EVIL?

War takes men from work. Drink takes men from work.

War sends men to be murdered. Drink sends men to do murder.

War kills men by the thousands. Drink kills babies by the thousands.

War ruins business. Drink ruins business.

War makes widows and orphans. Drink makes widows and orphans.

War makes cripples. Drink makes madmen.

War destroys food. Drink turns food to poison.

War never did anything but evil. Drink never did anything but evil.

War destroys men's bodies. Drink destroys men's and women's souls.

The advert continued: "Thousands of Irishmen have laid down their lives; more thousands have been maimed and blinded, to put an end to war – for this is to be the last War. To what end, if the men who have saved us from slavery to the Kaiser are to be handed over to the worse slavery of drink? Men and women of Ireland – demand an Armistice from Alcohol!

War is the enemy of man and the arch enemy of women and children. Let every woman with a vote refuse support to every candidate who will not work actively for Prohibition in the next Parliament."

It finished with the instruction: WOMEN – VOTE SOLIDLY AGAINST DRINK.

Many of the candidates and most of the electorate going into the election were unknown quantities, but there was no mistaking which way the straws were blowing in the wind. Three weeks before polling day, the Unionist *Irish Times* observed: "Sinn Féin is full of confidence and seems to be full of money." The paper further noted: "The National Parliamentary Party is marching towards its Waterloo. Sinn Féin's victory at the polls has been made certain before the opening of a single ballot box."

There were allegations (many of them unsubstantiated) that friends of Sinn Féin had had chummy chats with would-be opponents, giving them the opportunity to reconsider whether they really needed the stresses and strains of a life in politics. Whether intimidation was widespread or not, there were other reasons why Sinn Féin won 26 of their seats unopposed. Where it was abundantly clear that a Sinn Féin candidate was going to romp home, the IPP and other parties simply decided not to waste good money chasing a lost cause. It was widely accepted that the Irish Parliamentary Party had lost the election before a vote was cast. What no-one had foreseen was the extent of the IPP's wipeout at the hands of Sinn Féin.

Before polling day, *The Irish Times* predicted that Sinn Féin would win as many as 60 seats, with the IPP holding on to 25 at very best. In the event, Sinn Féin would take 73 of 105 Irish seats, leaving the IPP with six MPs and a ticket to nowhere. Sinn Féin's candidates stood for election promising that they would not take their seats at Westminster, but would instead set up a separatist Irish Parliament. Before polling day, *The Irish Times* ruefully predicted that the inevitable Sinn Féin victory spelled disaster for the country. The newspaper reflected: "From that hour, of course, [Sinn Féin's] real difficulties begin. It will be compelled to substitute some sort of policy for the present orgy of mere emotion, and from the first day of the new scheme of abstention, will take a heavy toll on Ireland's agricultural and commercial prosperity."

Speaking at a Parliamentary Party rally in Wicklow, DJ Gogan said that if the Irish people gave victory to Sinn Féin, they would bring disgrace on themselves and earn the contempt of the free nations of the world, of which there weren't too many. He maintained that the United States was already "disgusted" with the Irish people for spending the Great War squabbling amongst themselves. He charged that Sinn Féin had already made the big mistake of siding with Germany in the war, and he wondered aloud how many more blunders the party would make if given an electoral mandate?

Gogan didn't have to wait long to find out. Just weeks after receiving the Christmas present to end all Christmas presents with its electoral landslide, Sinn Féin's newly-elected MPs assembled illegally in Dublin as Dáil Eireann. By that act of defiance, they lit the fuse on thirty months of struggle that would become known as the War of Independence.

1921

ALL EYES ON CARSONIA

The Incumbents: Sinn Féin in the illegal Dáil Eireann.
Slogan: A 32-County Irish Republic free from Britain.
Promise: Boycott the partitionist Southern Irish Parliament.
The Challengers: None.
The Mood of the Country: In the South – Brits Out!
Prediction: Sinn Féin walkover in the South.
Result: Never in any doubt.
Entertainment value: 0/10

Bad News For Monaghan Hospitals

In the previous general election of 1918, Sinn Féin had been
assured of victory before a single vote had been cast. Only
the scale of that victory had been in any doubt. Three years
on, in the general election of 1921, even the scale of the
Sinn Féin victory was known in advance. Sinn Féin
candidates stood unopposed in 124 constituencies while
candidates from Trinity College Dublin took the other four
of the 128 seats, also uncontested. The carve-up meant that
there was no actual polling in the South.

The country had effectively been partitioned the previous
year, with the British making provision for a Northern
Ireland House of Commons in Belfast and a Southern Ireland
House of Commons in Dublin. The 1921 elections were to
fill the seats of those counterpart Parliaments. The seats in
the Northern Parliament were contested amid much

violence and intimidation, but the Southern House of
Commons was stillborn. Following their electoral walkover
in May 1921, the 124 TDs of Sinn Féin sat illegally in the
Second Dáil of their own making.

After its humiliation at the hands of Sinn Féin in 1918,
the Irish Parliamentary Party had disintegrated. In advance
of the 1921 election the IPP's last leader, John Dillon, noted
ruefully that the heavy hand of British repression had made
it virtually impossible for any Nationalist to oppose Sinn
Féin.

In the months and weeks before the electoral non-event
in the South, the entire country was in a state of turmoil.
Patrick Moloney, the youngest son of PJ Moloney, the Dáil
Deputy for South Tipperary, was shot dead in a gun battle
with members of the Crown police force, the Royal Irish
Constabulary. In Tralee, the young mother of a three-month-
old baby was shot dead when she opened her front door to
investigate a commotion on the street outside. On Dublin's
Grafton Street bombs were thrown at policemen on the beat,
injuring women and children doing their shopping. From
Rome, Pope Benedict XV dispatched a missive urging
"English as well as Irish to calmly consider ... some means of
agreement". The British had been angling for a Papal
condemnation of the Irish terrorists and were furious when
Benedict effectively conferred a parity of esteem between the
gunmen and His Majesty's Government.

As the nominations were being finalised, *The Evening
Herald* led with the headline EVENING EXECUTION. The
report began: "Tried by military court, condemned to be shot,
and executed within 25 hours of his arrest, in Cork Barracks
– that was the fate of a man named Patrick Casey, announced
in a sensational communiqué issued from General Military
Headquarters in Dublin last night.

This is the second occasion on which the death sentence
has been carried out without the public being aware of its

imposition, the previous case being that of Cornelius Murphy, Rathmore, Co Kerry, who was shot in the same barracks on February 1."

The newspaper added the name of Patrick Casey to a list headed EXECUTIONS DURING THE PAST SIX MONTHS. Beneath the headline was a roll-call of 20 names, beginning with that of Kevin Barry, an 18-year-old medical student hanged at Mountjoy Jail for his part in an ambush on a military lorry. Hundreds of people had gathered outside the prison in the hope of forcing a reprieve, but Barry became the first rebel to be executed by the British during the War of Independence.

Against this backdrop of vicious skirmishing between Republicans and the British forces, voters in the Dublin Metropolitan District had been living under a state of curfew for over a year. Armed troops patrolled the streets with orders to shoot anyone crossing their path between midnight and five am. Looking on the bright side, Dublin Corporation's Electric Lighting Committee reckoned that the curfew would save it £19,000 a year on the cost of street lighting. In the run-up to the election, a horse and trap travelling after dark on Dublin's Gardiner Street was fired on by police, killing the horse.

A leading medic blamed the military clampdown on a range of public activities for a general breakdown in the health of Dubliners. He'd personally diagnosed the ill-effects in his own middle-class patients, and colleagues confirmed that rich and poor alike were also suffering. He told the press: "In all cases I have come to the same conclusion – that their complaints may be traced to close confinement indoors, the curtailment of their ordinary amusements, and the restrictions of faculties for obtaining fresh air." Another doctor concurred, saying: "In the cause of hygiene, common sense and common humanity, the curfew ban should be lifted."

While the police had their hands full with shootings and bombings, they still found time to issue a warning urging shopkeepers to be on their guard against ordinary decent criminals. The authorities were particularly worried that "cross-channel swindlers" were operating along the East Coast under cover of the turbulent civic conditions. A senior officer pointed out: "The whole aim of the swindler is to puzzle or perplex the shopkeeper or his assistant – often a girl." According to police intelligence, many of the swindlers' con-tricks were as old as the hills, involving various sleights of hand and the passing of counterfeit money. The authorities had come across a lot of suspicious activity where strangers had tried to pass off "spurious" five pound notes. Unhappily for the conmen, the strife-torn economy was in such a depressed state that few shopkeepers had the change of a fiver to give them.

With the election in the South a foregone conclusion, all eyes were on 'Carsonia', as the fledgling Northern Ireland was disparagingly known. The Dublin-born lawyer Edward Carson had been the driving force behind the formation of the Unionist laager. On the eve of polling in the North, in his capacity as 'President of the Republic', Eamon de Valera gratuitously urged the voters of Carsonia to: "Vote tomorrow against war with your fellow countrymen."

In the event, six Sinn Féin candidates were elected to the Northern House of Commons, including Michael Collins for Fermanagh/Tyrone and the imprisoned Arthur Griffith for Armagh. When the numbers were crunched, however, the Unionists romped home winning 40 of the 52 seats. One newspaper reported that: "Throughout the campaign, Orange terrorism was rampant over large areas and especially in Belfast. On polling day, organised 'Partition' bands used the most violent means of preventing their opponents from voting. In Belfast especially, the elections were a farce."

Gangs of 'Ulster Specials' stood guard outside many

polling stations, protecting the democratic process from disloyal voters. One newspaper reported that: "Mr William Coote MP, speaking at a Unionist meeting in Cookestown, said that the 'Loyalists' of Tyrone had made it plain that for every Loyalist shot in any village in the county, there would be three prominent Sinn Féiners shot." A 13-year-old girl was shot in the head by Loyalist gunmen as she made her way home from a Nationalist rally.

By the time the Second Dáil convened following the May non-election in the South, the illegal Sinn Féin administration had already made big strides towards wresting the levers of power from the British bureaucracy. During recent decades, the British had dampened down dissent by pumping generous subsidies into Ireland's local authorities. The result was that the country's parish pump politicians had never had it so good, with local chieftains dispensing State-funded patronage and jobs in their cushy fiefdoms. The puritan reformers of Sinn Féin took a very dim view of what they regarded as widespread gombeenism. Many local authorities propped up clusters of small-time hospitals, which the Sinn Féiners regarded as bad medicine. The visionaries of a new Ireland were even more disapproving of the county workhouses, which they blamed for destroying morale and weakening the will of the people to better themselves.

Some months after the election, the Dáil sent an inspector to investigate whether the sick and the needy of the underpopulated county of Monaghan really warranted four hospitals and a workhouse. The inspector reported back that Monaghan County Council was carrying far too much deadwood and that the workhouse could go, along with the hospitals in Carrickmacross, Clones and Castleblaney. It was decided that the hospital in Monaghan town itself was more than adequate to meet the needs of the whole County.

1922

THE ALPHABET OF MISERIES

The Incumbents: Slightly more than half of Sinn Fein.
Slogan: We now have the freedom to achieve freedom.
Promise: Secure a 26-County Irish Free State.
The Challengers: Slightly less than half of Sinn Féin.
Slogan: No sell-out!
Promise: Oppose the partition of the island.
The Mood of the Country: Give peace a chance.
Prediction: A vote of confidence in the Treaty.
Result: A vote of confidence in the Treaty.
Entertainment value: 5/10.

Knoutings, Licence, Murders, Nerve Strain

The previous general election of May 1921 had taken place against a backdrop of bombings, gunfire, and sporadic mayhem. The general election of June 1922 also took place against a backdrop of bombings, gunfire and sporadic mayhem, but this time between two different sets of belligerents. A year earlier, Irish freedom fighters had been battling British forces in the War of Independence. In June of 1922, although nobody wanted to even whisper the dreaded words 'Civil War', Irish freedom fighters were killing and maiming each other over how much freedom was enough freedom.

Two months after the May 1921 election, the British had agreed a truce with the Irish rebels, opening the way for negotiations on what was to become the Treaty. In London in

December of 1921, a Sinn Féin delegation led by Michael Collins had signed an accord with representatives of the British government. By then Ireland had already been effectively partitioned, and a Unionist-dominated Parliament in Belfast was already well advanced with its mission to abolish democracy in the North.

Democracy in the South was having troubles of its own. The Irish public had been denied the chance to vote in the previous general election of 1921, as Sinn Féin had taken 104 of the 108 seats in the Southern Irish House of Commons without a contest. The Sinn Féin deputies had then refused to sit in the partitionist Parliament devised by the British, and had instead assembled as the illegal Second Dáil.

Now, going into the June 1922 general election, Sinn Féin found itself in the unique position of being both the party of government in Dáil Eireann, and the party of opposition. The President of the party, Eamon de Valera, was vehemently opposed to ratifying the Treaty signed by Collins, which fell short of delivering a 32-County Irish Republic. Collins maintained that the Treaty offered "the freedom to achieve freedom" and a majority in his party took the same pragmatic view. De Valera was defeated when the pro-Treaty members of the Dáil approved the deal with Britain by a slim margin of 64 to 57. De Valera's faction, known as the anti-Treatyites, spent the early months of 1922 agitating against the pro-Treaty members of their own party who had now taken the role of the Provisional Government of the Free State.

The British insisted that before they would withdraw from Southern Ireland, the Provisional Government must secure popular approval for the Treaty. Fearing an escalation of the existing antagonisms between old comrades, the two feuding sides of Sinn Féin hatched a gentleman's agreement that the Treaty would not be overtly an issue in the general election of 1922, although the world and his wife knew that it would be the only issue.

Just before polling day the Provisional Government broke the gentleman's agreement and put up posters warning that the grim alternative to accepting the Treaty was a return to war with the world's mightiest Empire. The message to the electorate was: "You can get the Republic for all Ireland through the safe and sure method of the Treaty or you can try another round through the alphabet of miseries.

> A – *Auxiliaries*.
> B – *Black and Tans*.
> C – *Commandeering*.
> D – *Deaths*.
> E – *Executions*.
> F – *Fatalities*.
> G – *Gallows*.
> H – *Hangings*.
> I – *Internments*.
> J – *Jails*.
> K – *Knoutings* (Whippings).
> L – *Licence* (Disregard of the law).
> M – *Murders*.
> N – *Nerve Strain*.
> O – *Oppression*.
> P – *Persecution*.
> Q – *Questioning*.
> R – *Raids*.
> S – *Spies*.
> T – *Threats*.
> U – *Usurpation*.
> V – *Vandalism*.
> W – *Wails*.
> X, Y, Z – *The final horrors which words cannot describe*."

The public was already on board. The Dáil had decided to

allow non-Sinn Féin candidates stand, and the electorate responded by giving the Labour Party, the Farmers Party and Independents 40% of the total vote between them. Every one of the non-Sinn Féin candidates elected was pro-Treaty, with the result that the electorate gave a resounding thumbs-up to the limited British concession of a 26-County Free State. The pro-Treaty side of Sinn Féin now assumed a legitimate grip on power, under the twin executives of Arthur Griffith and Michael Collins.

Gun-Runner Sues IRA

While the two halves of Sinn Féin were taking potshots at each other in a row that would soon escalate into a full-blown Civil War, a former gun-runner was suing the IRA in a dispute over money. In addition to establishing a parallel system of local government, Sinn Féin by 1922 had also set up a parallel legal system. Shortly before the election, cutlery manufacturer Séan O'Shea took a case in the Republican District Court against the Adjutant-General of the IRA stationed at Beggar's Bush Barracks. O'Shea claimed that he was owed £226 by the IRA for arms and ammunition which he'd delivered to the Irish Volunteers prior to the Easter Rising of 1916.

He claimed that the arms and ammunition had either been used-up in the Rising, or had been destroyed while in the possession of the Volunteers. As the successor body to the Volunteers, he said that the IRA was responsible for paying off the money owed. He itemised the equipment he'd supplied as fifty .25 automatic pistols at 51 shillings and six pence each, 200 .22 revolvers at 10/6 each and 10,000 rounds of .22 ammunition at a cost of ten shillings per 1,000 rounds.

The IRA was represented in court by its book-keeper Séan McGarry TD. He insisted that the money wasn't owed to O'Shea, because the munitions in question had been worse than useless. The IRA's contention was that in 1915, O'Shea had met up in Birmingham with Michael O'Rahilly, the rebels' Director of Arms. The pair managed to buy £1,000 worth of arms on their trip, but O'Rahilly said that £4,000 worth would have served the cause much better. At this point the conversation turned to how much easier the gun-running business would be if arms could be made in Ireland. The IRA suggested in court that the cutlery craftsman O'Shea had taken this idea on board, and had manufactured an amateurish batch of arms at a forge in the Leitrim village of Ballinalee, and then tried to pass them off as imported.

O'Shea swore that he had paid good money for the consignment in England and was entitled to recover his outlay. He said that for all the "big risks" he had taken during his gun-smuggling days, he'd only made a profit margin of 7.5%. He claimed that he'd imported the weapons in an unfinished state and his intention had been to finish them off. But before he could get to work on them, the authorities seized 500 bayonets in the North Wall area of the city and he was hauled into Dublin Castle for questioning. With "G-Men" at the end of his street, members of the Volunteers had whisked the guns and ammunition from his home for safe keeping.

On behalf of the IRA, Deputy McGarry said that there had been a lot of bad guns going around before the Rising, and they were so shoddy that they couldn't be shifted to wannabe insurgents at any price. A court reporter wrote: "People looked on them with contempt; they also looked so tiny. There were several defects in them and a change of temperature would make them go off. They had too many of these weapons when Mr O'Shea's consignment arrived."

While this glut of unsuitable weapons from other sources suggested that O'Shea may indeed have acted in good faith, the Republican Court found in favour of the Republican Army. The judge dismissed the case on the grounds that O'Shea could provide no proof of delivery.

Sitting in parallel to the new Republican apparatus, were the centuries' old courts of the British administration. Shortly before polling day the Right Honorable Recorder of Dublin addressed the grand jury at the opening of the City Sessions. Bombings, shootings and bank-robberies were making the headlines on a daily basis, but the Recorder drew special attention to an epidemic of stolen bicycles. He was reported as saying: "Nothing could be a greater menace to the public than this practice which was growing unfortunately. The vast number of respectable, hard-working people found it essential to use bicycles and nothing could be more intolerable than they should have their property made away with, when it was left aside even for a few moments."

Bicycles also featured in another grave reflection from the Recorder. "His Lordship referred to the important question of the reckless driving of motorcars and cycles through the crowded streets of the city. It was a practice that would have to be stopped. In England people were fined for driving at 12 mph, but here in Dublin at any time of the day or in any place, they might see machines travelling at 20 mph or more. He called attention to the matter in the hope that something would be done to put a stop to this practice."

Two days after this stern warning went out to the motoring public, 22-year-old John McEntaggart found himself standing trial on a charge of manslaughter. It was McEntaggart's misfortune to have knocked down and killed John Willis while driving on College Green at a speed which witnesses put as high as 25 mph. It was his further misfortune that the man judging his case was The Recorder himself.

1923

THEY HAD NOT THE MILITARY STRATEGY OF NIGGERS

The Incumbents: Cumann na nGaedheal led by Cosgrave.
Slogan: Law and order.
Promise: Restore stability after the Civil War.
The Challengers: Anti-Treaty Sinn Féin led by De Valera.
Slogan: Sinn Féin will abolish the murder gangs.
Promise: Not take their seats in Dáil Eireann.
The Mood of the Country: War weary.
Prediction: A Cumann na nGaedheal win.
Result: A Cumann na nGaedheal win.
Entertainment value: 6/10.

Some Drums And Instruments Broken

The general election of August 1923 was the first to take place in the new political entity of the Irish Free State. It was also the first since the Westminster election of 1910 to take place under something approaching 'normal' conditions, although that 'normality' was warped on a daily basis by shootings, bombings, kidnappings, raids, jailbreaks and bank robberies. The Civil War had officially ended three months earlier with the defeat of De Valera's anti-Treatyites, also known as 'The Irregulars', but the Free State Army and police were still engaged in aggressive mopping-up operations. On the night before polling day, voters in the centre of Dublin were roused from their slumber by sustained bursts of machine gun fire at 3 am.

Since the previous election of June 1922, the two chief executives of the new State, Arthur Griffith and Michael Collins, had both died within days of each other. Collins perished when his motorcade was ambushed by Irregulars, while Griffith was credited with working himself to death for the cause. Their joint leadership was now merged in the prim and proper person of WT Cosgrave who became President of the Executive Council of the Free State. The party of which Cosgrave assumed the leadership was variously known as the Government Party, the Ministry Party and the Treaty Party. In advance of the election it took the name Cumann na nGaedheal, meaning League Of The Irish. As the party of peace, stability and law and order, it curried support amongst the propertied classes such as farmers, businessmen and the professions.

Making electoral capital out of its two recently deceased martyrs, Cumann na nGaedheal unveiled a "temporary cenotaph" to Griffith and Collins at a ceremony on the lawn of Leinster House. Adding belt to braces in its bid to spur the voters to support the fragile democracy, the Government Publicity Department declared that polling day would be a public holiday "to facilitate the citizens of Saorstat Eireann in performing their civic duties". When the day arrived there were queues outside many polling stations before they opened. After performing their civic duties, many voters headed for the seaside to enjoy the August sunshine.

With the pro-Treaty wing of Sinn Féin now rebranded as Cumann na nGaedheal, the defeated anti-Treatyites decided to contest the election as continuity Sinn Féin. This infuriated many in Cumann na nGaedheal who felt that the Free State was the legitimate legacy of Sinn Féin's struggle for freedom. De Valera's faction put forward 87 candidates on the proviso that none of its elected TDs would take their seats in the Dáil. The party's manifesto stated that: "The Sinn Féin candidates in this election stand as they have stood in every election since 1917, for the unity and untrammeled independence of Ireland."

The Free State government took strenuous measures to make the campaign trail a hazardous place for the Sinn Féin candidates. Of the 87 standing on the De Valera ticket, 64 were prevented from pressing the flesh by reason of being fugitives from the law or in jail. When De Valera attempted to address an election rally in Ennis, Co Clare, troops supported by an armoured car moved in to capture him. They fired a volley of shots over the platform to stampede the crowd, and De Valera saw out the rest of the campaign under lock and key.

The newspapers were overwhelmingly hostile to Sinn Féin, but their enmity didn't prevent them from taking the party's money. In one large advert, De Valera's party set out some of its election promises, stating: "Sinn Féin will abolish the murder gangs and secure the life, liberty and property of the people ... Sinn Féin will reform the present burdensome and expensive legal system ... Sinn Féin will abolish the censorship of the press ... Sinn Féin will stand by the Republic constitutionally proclaimed by the representatives of the people in January 1919."

On the eve of the election, WT Cosgrave finished his campaign in Waterford, where he received a rude reception, but not from the anti-Treatyites of Sinn Féin. Waterford was the home of John Redmond, the late leader of the Irish Parliamentary Party. Many in the city thought of Cosgrave not as the hero of the Civil War which had preserved the Treaty, but as one of the damnable Sinn Féiners who had swept Redmond and his party from power in 1918.

As Cosgrave addressed his meeting, revolver shots went off. He told his listeners: "Don't mind them. We have met that sort of thing before." Asked if the Irregulars still posed a serious threat to the Free State, he said "they had not the military strategy of niggers". The Cumann na nGaedheal bandwagon then moved onto the streets of the town centre, where a number of bands were playing. Cosgrave's minders asked the bandsmen to take a break, as the leader of the nation was about to address his people. But some of the musicians declared themselves to be Redmondites and they kept on playing. When members of the public began jostling and jeering Cosgrave, his escort fired shots in the air to put manners on them. This provoked scuffles "in the course of which blows were exchanged and some drums and instruments broken".

The following day there was a scuffle at a South Dublin polling booth where grocer's assistant Thomas Tynan was arrested on a charge that he had "accosted voters, taking from them their cards and marking them as to how each individual was to vote, thereby obstructing the voters at the polling booth". He was swiftly hauled before a judge, where his lawyer argued that since Tynan hadn't attempted to personate any of those he'd interfered with, there was no case in law to answer. The judge agreed and threw out the case.

In the Wicklow village of Glendalough, voting proceeded without incident until around noon, when a group of men armed with rifles descended on the polling station and insisted on helping out the Free State soldiers on guard duty there. The freelance militia refused to disperse until forced to, when the Army sent in reinforcements to relieve them.

An old woman in a shawl approached the presiding officer of a Dublin polling station and complained that she could only make out one name on the ballot paper. On that basis, she'd given the only legible candidate her Number One preference. However, she wanted to work her way down the paper and asked the official to give her some guidance. When he said it was against the rules, she put her ballot in the box with just the one tick on it.

In Thurles, an illiterate man had the names and details of the 15 candidates on the paper read out as he made "a careful and protracted selection" of his options. After deliberating at length, he told the presiding officer that he wanted to vote for Eamon de Valera, whose name was not on the list. In Kilkenny, an elderly woman insisted on voting for Doctor Daniel Mannix. Officials politely explained that Doctor Mannix was not a candidate in her constituency nor in any other, since he was fully occupied with his job as the Catholic Archbishop of Melbourne, Australia. On hearing this, the woman said that if she couldn't vote for the Archbishop she would vote for no-one, and she walked out.

When the votes were counted, the Sinn Féin 'on-the-runs' had done remarkably well, upping their number of seats by eight to a total of 44.

1926

A CHEAP MUSIC-HALL JINGLE
PICKING A NATIONAL ANTHEM

The Soldier's Song became Ireland's national anthem largely by default while the architects of the Free State wrestled with more pressing matters, like quelling the natives of bandit counties such as Sligo and Leitrim. In this regard at least, *The Soldier's Song* is a truly fitting anthem for Ireland, an embodiment of that native spirit that says: "Ah sure, it'll do."

The Soldier's Song was composed in 1907 by Peadar Kearney and Patrick Heeney and was later adopted as the marching song of the Irish Volunteers. It became one of the theme tunes of the Easter Rising and reached a wider audience in late 1916 when it was published as sheet music in New York.

Established in 1922, the Free State got by without an official national anthem for a while. However, in 1924 Sean Lester, the Director of Publicity at the Department of External Affairs, urged the government to pick a tune because "pro-British elements" were taking advantage of its absence to sing *God Save The King* at public functions. Lester tactfully suggested to the cabinet that while *The Soldier's Song* was "excellent as a revolutionary song", it was his opinion that "both words and music are unsuitable for a national anthem". He proposed holding a competition to pen new lyrics for Thomas Moore's melody, *Let Erin Remember The Days Of Old.*

Ruling out a competition, the government unofficially decided to have two anthems, with *The Soldier's Song* to be played on home ground and *Let Erin Remember* at State occasions on foreign soil. However, the *Dublin Evening Mail* picked up on the idea of a competition and put up the handsome sum of 50 guineas for the best new lyrics to Moore's melody. The stellar judging panel for the song contest was made up the author James Stephens, the playwright Lennox Robinson and the living legend William Butler Yeats. When Yeats and his fellow judges declared that not one of the entries was "worthy of fifty guineas or any portion of it", the *Mail* asked readers to pick a winner from six of the lyrics.

If the votes of the *Mail*'s readers had counted, Croke Park on match days would now reverberate with the opening lines: *"God of our Ireland, by Whose hand/Her glory and her beauty grew/Just as the shamrock o'er the land/Grows green beneath thy sparkling dew."* But the media-led campaign fell on deaf ears and the new State muddled on with two anthems. That this couldn't go on was highlighted by a Dáil farce in early 1926 when a question was tabled asking the President of the Executive, WT Cosgrave, to reveal the true identity of the country's national anthem. The inquiry was tabled by Osmonde Esmonde, a member of Cosgrave's own party.

Cosgrave ducked the question by passing it on to the Minister of Defence, Peter Hughes. Esmonde complained to the Ceann Comhairle: "I sent in this question in order to get a definite assurance from the Head of the Executive as to what the national anthem is. I find that it is put down to the Minister for Defence as if it were an army matter, whereas it is a matter that affects everybody outside the army. I think I should have been consulted."

In an intervention worthy of Sir Humphrey Appleby in *Yes, Prime Minister*, the Ceann Comhairle replied: "I think I can solve the problem. The President of the Executive Council is not responsible as a matter of fact or policy for an answer as to what is the national anthem. The Minister for Defence can be asked a question regarding tunes played by military bands. The question on the Paper is therefore to the Minister for Defence in regard to tunes played by military bands. If the Deputy desires to investigate any problem in regard to the national anthem, he cannot ask a question of the President. The President cannot be asked to define what is the national anthem. It is not part of his functions."

Esmonde persevered: "Then I desire to ask the Minister for Defence whether he is aware that at two recent State functions army bands have played two different tunes purporting to be the national anthem, and that the prevalent uncertainty in this matter is often a cause of confusion and irritation, particularly in connection with international sporting events; and whether he will state what is the national anthem, or, if the matter is not finally settled, what tune should be provisionally accepted as such pending a final decision?"

Defence Minister Hughes responded: "I am not aware that at recent State functions army bands have played two different tunes purporting to be the national anthem."

With Esmonde now starting to lose his cool, he eventually dragged out of the Minister that the army considered The Soldier's Song to be the more official of the two songs. That same month, July 1926, the National Executive of the Free State formally adopted The Soldier's Song as the national anthem for all State occasions, home and away. For some, this was an affront to good taste on a par with granting retention planning permission for an illegal dump. The anthem's critics came out in force in 1933 after Peadar Kearney sued the State for ripping him off. As the Dáil agreed to buy out the copyright from Kearney and the late Patrick Heeney for £980, Deputy Frank MacDermot branded their composition "a jaunty little piece of vulgarity" that was "unworthy" of representing the Irish people in song. He complained: "It does not serve any useful purpose to have a cheap music-hall jingle instead of some splendid and moving Gaelic melody as a national anthem."

General Richard Mulcahy didn't think there was much point in replacing *The Soldier's Song* "until we have raised the standard of music and musical construction in the country". Deputy Richard Anthony favoured more urgent action because: "Anyone with the most elementary knowledge of music ... could not for a moment suggest that the music of *The Soldier's Song* is either inspiring or even musical."

He continued: "The whole thing is an abomination to anyone who knows anything about music. I have hopes that some musician and some poet will collaborate one day and give us a national anthem something like the Marseillaise."

In the mid-1990s, with the North in thaw, Taoiseach John Bruton felt it was time to take another look at the suitability of *The Soldier's Song*. His concern was not so much the tune's sludge-like consistency, as its undiplomatic reference to roughing up the "Saxon foe". The Taoiseach told the Dáil: "I am having the position regarding the required procedures for the commissioning and putting in place of a new anthem checked to see if any exist and I will advise as soon as the relevant information is available."

No more was ever heard of the matter.

June 1927

I HOPE THE TIME WILL COME WHEN PEOPLE LIKE THAT WILL BE DENIED CITIZENSHIP

The Incumbents: Cumann na nGaedheal led by Cosgrave.
Slogan: Hearts and heads up!
Promise: Mend the economic fence with Britain.
The Challengers: Fianna Fáil led by Eamon de Valera.
Slogan: Time for a change.
Promise: A self-sufficient, Irish-speaking island.
The Mood of the Country: Better the Devil you know.
Prediction: The government to be returned.
Result: The government returned.
Entertainment value: 4/10.

A Menace To Society

Going into the general election of June 1927, the pro-Treaty brotherhood of Sinn Féin had been in power for five years. Having absorbed some additional TDs from the conservative side of the political spectrum, and taken the name Cumann na nGaedheal, the governing party now found itself faced with an energetic new rival.

A year previously, Eamon de Valera had resigned as leader of anti-Treaty Sinn Féin in order to found a new national movement to represent the plain people of Ireland and deliver his personal destiny as Big Chief of the young nation. Where Sinn Féin TDs had boycotted Dáil Eireann following the previous general election of 1923, de Valera made clear that his new Republican party, Fianna Fáil, had its sights set on parliamentary power.

The differences between the sitting government and the new challenger were striking. Where the resolutely populist Fianna Fáil would cast its net in the gene pool of the disenfranchised, Cumann na nGaedheal had evolved from the top down. The organisation led by WT Cosgrave had been a cluster of pro-Treaty Dáil deputies before it was ever a party. From the outset, Fianna Fáil put great store on building a grassroots machine around the parish pump. Cumann na nGaedheal, in stark contrast, tended to field candidates from the great and good of society.

Where Fianna Fáil from the start treated politics as a deadly serious full-time business, it was a criticism of the rival party until well into the 1960s that half its TDs could be found on any given weekday plying their trade down the Law Library. Where the supporters of Fianna Fáil mustered to the mirage of a 32-County, Irish-speaking Ireland with a square deal for the small man, Cumann na nGaedheal's 'Vision Thing' didn't look much beyond upholding the peace and maintaining the status quo. One of Cumann na nGaedheal's founders, Richard Mulcahy, noted frankly that his party was a coalition of strange bedfellows, and that its former Sinn Féin revolutionaries such as himself did not always make a snug match with what he called "the Ballsbridge complex", an early evocation of "the Dublin 4 set".

With the newly-formed Fianna Fáil threatening to take its seats and vigorously oppose the government, Cumann na nGaedheal faced the very real prospect of being dumped from office. The party had secured less than 40% of the seats in the 1923 election, but had formed a government with ease because the TDs of anti-Treatyite Sinn Féin had boycotted the Dáil. In addition to the challenge of the new Republican party, Cumann na nGaedheal found itself under threat from publicans. In its bid to establish what has been called a

Republic Of Virtue, Cumann na nGaedheal had stiffened a range of censorship measures and clamped-down on pub opening hours.

As polling day approached, a cabal of Dublin publicans revolted by producing a circular urging the drinking classes to vote against the government Party and its killjoy Justice Minister, Kevin O'Higgins. This brought a rebuke from their association, which reminded them that they had agreed at their AGM to stay out of partisan politics. Standing for one of the Unionist seats assigned to Trinity College, BC Waller addressed a campus rally and stated that he "opposed the present tendency that the State, or a majority, should decide what should be read, learned or drank". A section of the crowd responded with "onions, small packets of flour and eggs of ancient lineage and overpowering odour". According to the *Irish Independent*: "Accuracy of aim was an attribute of the hostile element."

The break with Britain in 1922 had damaged economic relations with Ireland's biggest market by far, and the Free State in 1927 was suffering the consequences. Cumann na nGaedheal accused Fianna Fáil of damaging the morale of the country by drawing attention to this fact. The government's slogan was "Hearts and heads up!" While the business class of Cumann na nGaedheal were all in favour of mending the economic fences with England, Fianna Fáil nurtured the fantastical notion of a go-it-alone future for the Free State. Dismissing Fianna Fáil's economic fantasia, WT Cosgrave said: "The only moral to be learned from this document is that a fool when he gets loose on figures is dangerous, but a dishonest man when he gets loose on figures is a menace to society."

Not only were Fianna Fáil dishonest, said the government, but they were also unreconstructed terrorists with twitchy trigger-fingers. Justice Minister Kevin O'Higgins told voters: "If you want to put in control the people who burned houses, blew up bridges and wrecked railways, you can do it next Thursday week." A Cumann na nGaedheal advert was headlined: MR DE VALERA WHO BURNED YOUR HOUSE YESTERDAY COMPLAINS TODAY OF THE SMELL OF PETROL. Again blaming Fianna Fáil for lowering the morale of the populace, the copy line continued: "If you think more petrol is a cure for 'The Decline', support the Fianna Fáil candidates."

Not only were Fianna Fáil dishonest, and unreconstructed terrorists, said the government, but Cumann na nGaedheal implied that the only people who would consider voting for the newcomers were Grade A morons. It was reported that WT Cosgrave turned up in the Carlow conurbation of Haketstown to endorse the candidature of DJ Gorey. According to the pro-government *Irish Independent*, "an excited looking individual" shouted "Up Dev!" at the pair. The candidate, Mr Gorey, instructed two policemen to: "'Bring that gentleman over here so that the people can get a good look at him.' When this was done, waving his arms about, the man began to execute a sort of dance, much to the amusement of the crowd. 'Look at that horror,' said Mr Gorey, pointing at the dancing figure. It is people like that who want to rule the destinies of this country. Can you look at that man and not be moved? I hope the time will come when people like that will be denied citizenship'."

Not only were Fianna Fáil dishonest, and unreconstructed terrorists, and the Party of Fools, said the government, but they were potential women-beaters too. The pro-government press reported that after she spoke at a Cumann na nGaedheal meeting on Dublin's O'Connell Street, Mrs Collins-O'Driscoll was "followed by a crowd of young men and women and an attempt was made to molest her. As the hostile crowd was closing in on her near the Parnell Monument, the intervention of a number of her supporters was the means of saving her and enabling her to get away safely by tram".

Not only were Fianna Fáil dishonest, unconstructed terrorists, the party of fools, and women-haters to boot, said the government, but De Valera's party was also responsible for putting about false rumours. Under the headline A WARNING TO VOTERS, the *Irish Independent* reported: "With a view to injuring the Government candidates, by inducing Government supporters to stay at home on polling day, an absurd rumour has been widely circulated in Dublin that the votes of electors who stay at home will automatically go to the Government. This is, of course, totally without foundation. Voters should clearly understand that the only votes which will count are those actually registered by electors themselves on polling day and that voters who stay at home not only do no good to the cause they believe in, but incur the risk that they may be personated and their votes used against the candidates they favour."

On the morning of the election, Fianna Fáil took out press adverts declaring FIANNA FÁIL WINS TODAY. The forecast proved to be premature, but the party of dishonesty, terrorism, fools, women-haters and falsehoods did remarkably well and put Cumann na nGaedheal on notice that their days were numbered.

September 1927

TEARING DOWN POSTERS AND BEATING FIANNA FÁIL WORKERS

The Incumbents: Cumann na nGaedheal led by Cosgrave.
Slogan: Ireland in peace, not pieces.
Promise: Protect the nation from Fianna Fáil chaos.
The Challengers: Fianna Fáil led by Eamon de Valera.
Slogan: A 32-County Irish-speaking Republic.
Promise: Protect the nation from CnG dictatorship.
The Mood of the Country: Unsettled by the Minister's murder.
Prediction: The government to be returned.
Result: The government returned, narrowly.
Entertainment value: 7/10.

The Dumps Are Harmless

The Cumann na nGaedheal government had been returned to office in the general election of June 1927, but the real success story of that contest had been the strong showing of Eamon de Valera's newly-founded party, Fianna Fáil.

Shortly after the June poll, on Sunday, July 10, Justice Minister Kevin O'Higgins was on his way to mass in the Dublin suburb of Booterstown when he was spotted by three IRA men who were apparently on their way to a Gaelic football match in Wexford, armed to the teeth. O'Higgins, the government's strong-man and a hate-figure for anti-Treatyites, perished in a hail of bullets in what seemed to be an opportunist assassination.

Already suffering something of a persecution complex following its lukewarm endorsement in the general election, the government reacted to the killing of O'Higgins by rushing through a Public Safety Act which re-introduced a measure of martial law. Cumann na nGaedheal also pushed through an Electoral Amendment act obliging all Dáil deputies to take the Oath of Allegiance to the English Crown.

The government's intent behind the Electoral Amendment Act was that it would cause a rupture between Fianna Fáil's deputies and their grass-roots supporters. To take the Oath would be to effectively accept the terms of the Treaty. For De Valera and his new party, this would represent a 180 degree U-turn from the position of 1922 when they plunged the country into Civil War in rejection of the deal. The government's plan to damage Fianna Fáil didn't work. De Valera's deputies took the Oath, deriding the ritual as "an empty formula" of words, but without inciting a grassroots revolt.

De Valera's condemnation of O'Higgins' murder as "a crime that cuts at the root of representative government" signalled his determination to make the strategic shift from the gun to the ballot box. With Fianna Fáil now active in the Dáil chamber, the prospect arose for the first time that Cumann na nGaedheal could be ousted from power.

Immediately after taking their Dáil seats, Fianna Fáil began horse-trading with prospective coalition partners, and in the middle of August it seemed that De Valera was about to topple the government by joining forces with the Labour Party and the small National League Party. On the morning of August 16, the nation was gripped with great excitement as the opposition tabled a motion of no confidence in the minority administration of WT Cosgrave. Adding up the numbers, it looked as if the government would be defeated by a single vote.

However, when the time came for the big showdown, the National League's John Jinks had gone missing in action. A frantic search of Leinster House failed to locate the Sligo TD. The vote was sensationally tied and the government was saved on the casting vote of the Ceann Comhairle, Michael Hayes. The rumour-mill went into overdrive and newspapers in Ireland, Britain and even the United States reported suspicions that Jinks had been kidnapped in a government-inspired plot. When Jinks reappeared he told reporters: "I was neither kidnapped nor spirited away. I simply walked out of the Dáil when I formed my own opinion after listening to a good many speeches. I cannot understand the sensation nor can I understand the meaning or object of the many reports circulated. What I did was done after careful consideration of the entire situation. I have nothing to regret for my action. I am glad I was the single individual who saved the situation for the government, and perhaps, incidentally, for the country."

Another version which quickly gained currency was that Jinks had been waylaid before the crucial vote by two fellow Sligomen of an anti-Fianna Fáil bent. It was said that the ex-Unionist MP Major Bryan Cooper and the future *Irish Times* editor Bertie Smylie had poured drink into Jinks and persuaded him that his constituents, who included many ex-British Army servicemen, would not appreciate him putting the 1916 rebel Eamon de Valera into power. According to one story, Cooper warned Jinks that customers affiliated to the British Legion would boycott his auctioneering and grocery businesses if he brought down the government.

When Jinks returned to Sligo, his sack of fan-mail included one telegram proclaiming him 'Ruler of Ireland', while the Cumann na nGaedheal administration was quickly dubbed the 'John Jinks Government'. Hoping to turn the instability factor to his advantage, and with Kevin O'Higgins newly martyred to the cause, WT Cosgrave challenged the voters as to whether they really felt it was wise to install

Eamon de Valera as leader of the Free State just five years
after he had started a war against it.

Cumann na nGaedheal attacked Fianna Fáil with
newspaper adverts headlined: WHAT MISTER DE VALERA
HAS COST IRELAND. The copy told readers: "He wilfully
caused a Civil War over what he now calls an 'empty formula'
– a Civil War which cost the country £30,000,000 as well as
the lives of hundreds. Vote for Cumann na nGaedheal. The
party that gives you peace today not promises of peace in the
indefinite future – after another war!"

Another Cumann na nGaedheal advert again played on
the fear that De Valera was hell-bent on wrecking the hard-
won peace of the past five years, insisting that: FIANNA
FÁIL PROPOSES TO ESTABLISH THE PERFECT
PEACE …

- By enlisting its gunmen in the people's army.
- By smashing the Treaty.
- By destroying the Constitution.
- By having another round with England.
- By punishing Ulster by sending Mr Frank Aiken
  northwards with his 'army' to bring in the Six
  Counties by force.

THE GOVERNMENT HAVE GIVEN PEACE TO THE
COUNTRY, FIANNA FÁIL WANTS TO MAKE PIECES
OF THE COUNTRY.

Caught off guard, Fianna Fáil replied with charges that
the snap election was a waste of taxpayers' money and an
attempt by Cumann na nGaedheal to seize power in
perpetuity. Fianna Fáil further charged that the government
was paying for its campaign with "English gold" – an alleged
slush-fund of £150,000 donated by the Tory media magnate,
Lord Beaverbrook. The Party took out adverts asking: "DO
YOU STAND FOR DICTATORSHIP OF CUMANN NA
nGAEDHEAL?"

Fianna Fáil asked the rhetorical question: "Why did the government put the country to the expense and inconvenience of a general election? There is only one answer. The government wants to establish a virtual dictatorship, to smother independent criticism ... The government has attacked Proportional Representation and clearly intends to replace it by an electoral system that will give it an overwhelming automatic majority."

The government was indeed developing a pain in the neck about Proportional Representation, although some sources place the first outright attack on the system in May 1930 when the Cumann na nGaedheal house organ *An Réalt* (*The Star*), claimed: "One of the factors which has delayed normal political development in the Saorstat is our bad electoral system." Objecting that the excessively egalitarian process which militated against strong parliamentary majorities had been "thrust upon the country by the British", the writer argued: "The main objection to Proportional Representation is that it inevitably operates in such a way as to be undemocratic."

After Fianna Fáil's assumption of power in the general election of 1932 the positions of the two largest parties on Proportional Representation would be reversed. Once installed in office, it was De Valera's Party which favoured abolishing Proportional Representation in favour of the British first-past-the-post system which promised to keep Fianna Fáil in power for ever and ever. Presented with this option by Fianna Fáil at referenda in 1959 and 1968 the Irish public said thanks, but no thanks.

During the campaign, the government pressed Fianna Fáil to surrender its dumps of illegally held arms. Rejecting these calls, Fianna Fáil's Séan Lemass told a meeting: "The dumps are harmless. If nobody goes near them they are dangerous only if there is hate between Irishmen, and in that case it does not matter if the arms are concealed in a bog or in a barracks in Dublin. All danger from the dumps will be removed when the causes of ill feeling between Irishmen are removed."

It was not just Fianna Fáil which argued that a second general election in the space of weeks was unnecessary. JJ Walsh, the Minister for Posts And Telegraphs, went missing shortly after his party leader called the poll. Stories began to emerge that the Minister had stormed out on his party. Cumann na nGaedheal released a damage limitation statement saying: "The public are advised not to pay any attention to any alleged interviews of conversations with Mr JJ Walsh published by political opponents in his absence. It is quite true that Mr Walsh has had to take a prolonged holiday, due solely to the state of his health. The mean campaign of misrepresentation that has been launched against him in his absence is beneath contempt."

However, the stories persisted and Cumann na nGaedheal finally had to admit that the rumours of Walsh's mutiny were indeed true. Party member Barry Egan told a meeting in Cork: "Unfortunately Mr JJ Walsh has not been in good health recently and I have received a telegram from him asking me to announce to my Executive his resignation."

Alongside the resignation story, *The Irish Times* ran a report written by "A Dublin gentleman". The gentleman wrote of an encounter in a Paris hotel, saying: "I thought that the shape of the back of the head of the man in front of me at the counter was familiar and when he spoke I knew it was JJ Walsh. I gripped him by the right arm and said 'Isn't the world very small?' He looked around and with a sort of a gasp said: 'What in the name of God brought you here?'"

Walsh told the nameless gentleman that he hadn't yet formally resigned as Minister because under the Constitution he had to remain in the post until his successor was in place. However, once that was done he intended to resign "from everything" because the Cumann na nGaedheal government was moving to "the reactionary Right" while his own political leanings were to "the progressive Left". He said he'd explained his position in a letter to the government.

His cabinet colleague Ernest Blythe dismissed Walsh's principled objections as an afterthought. Blythe charged: "Mr Walsh went for a holiday on the Continent on the eve of the general election apparently for no better reason than that he had his tickets bought before the dissolution. His letter is in the nature of an excuse for his irresponsible action. If Mr Walsh had desired a serious discussion on the issues he raises, he would doubtless have put off his Continental trip and debated them face-to-face with the electors."

On polling day itself, Fianna Fáil activists complained of police harassment under the guise of the recently introduced Public Safety Act. In the Dáil, one speaker complained: "In Castleisland and Knocknagoshel, Co Kerry, you had a superintendent that thought it was his duty to commandeer the cars of the Fianna Fáil people in the campaign when they were going to a meeting, and that thought it his duty under the alleged impartial Administration opposite to seize the personation and other papers that were being distributed to conform with the formalities required of people doing personation work during the election. He thought it his duty also when remonstrated with, to arrest people who had been forwarding the campaign in County Kerry on behalf of Fianna Fáil."

He continued: "During the election I saw those 'stewards' in my own constituency, or at least I have reports about them in my own constituency, going out and tearing down posters and beating Fianna Fáil workers. I suppose they thought it their duty to do that, being the servants of the so-called impartial Administration on the other side."

When the votes were counted, Cumann na nGaedheal had improved its position marginally, but it had failed to inflict the electoral damage on Fianna Fáil which it had hoped for. Entering a formal coalition with the conservative Farmers' Party, Cumann na nGaedheal would hold power for the next five years, but the two elections of 1927 had demonstrated that the political momentum was now with Fianna Fáil.

In 1930 the government lost a Dáil vote and WT Cosgrave resigned. However, rather than form a shaky minority government or share office with a coalition partner, De Valera declined to step into the breach. Instead, he chose to bide his time, in the sure knowledge that Fianna Fáil's day would come.

Cosgrave resumed the leadership of a lame duck government.

1932

I DARE YOU TO SHOOT ME

The Incumbents: Cumann na nGaedheal led by Cosgrave.
Slogan: A vote for Fianna Fáil is a vote for national suicide.
Promise: Protect the economy from communist Fianna Fáil.
The Challengers: Fianna Fáil led by Eamon de Valera.
Slogan: Self-sufficiency in food, clothing and building.
Promise: Make Ireland more Irish.
The Mood of the Country: Ready for a change.
Prediction: A close-run thing.
Result: Fianna Fáil win power for the first time.
Entertainment value: 8/10.

Blowing The Feelgood Factor

During its ten years in office, WT Cosgrave's government
had secured the fledgling Free State as a stable democracy –
no mean feat in an era when dictatorship was sweeping
Europe. However, the Great Depression was biting and
Cumann na nGaedheal had nothing to offer except more of
the same belt-tightening to an electorate increasingly restless
for a spot of change. Cumann na nGaedheal could have
maximised their chances of victory by holding the election
close to the 31st Eucharistic Congress which was due to be
held in Dublin in June 1932. Staging the Congress was the
Catholic world's equivalent of hosting the Olympic Games
and plans were already underway to give Dublin a facelift for
the Greatest Show In Christendom.

Instead of timing the election to capitalise on the massive feelgood factor the Congress would generate, the pious WT Cosgrave decided to get the campaign out of the way early, so it wouldn't interfere with the pray-in. The diaries of the writer Ulick O'Connor contains the following passage: "Desmond Gorges regales us afterwards with stories about his 'Uncle Willie', WT Cosgrave, President of the Irish Free State. Apparently he went to three masses every day to make up for polishing off a number of his best friends during the Civil War."

When Fianna Fáil won power for the first time on election day, the glaringly colourful Séan MacEntee proclaimed it a victory for the Catholic voters of Ireland, his point being that Cumann na nGaedheal had been propped up by anti-national Protestants.

A Phantom Ambush

In previous elections the newspapers had been hostile to De Valera, so in 1931 he set up one of his own, *The Irish Press*. In addition to giving Fianna Fáil a mouthpiece, *The Press* brought a new sense of fun and colour to the dowdy world of Irish publishing. One eye-catching *Irish Press* front page headline during the 1932 election campaign blared out the warning WATER FAMINE. On the following line, in much smaller print, was the word UNLIKELY. The report began: "Dublin householders need have little fear of a water famine, despite the abnormally low rainfall since Christmas."

As the election campaign peaked, *The Irish Press* branded the *Irish Independent* A DISCREDIT TO DECENT JOURNALISM, for serving up "fictions" and for "doctoring" one news report in support of a government candidate. The *Independent* had run a story saying that the car of Cumann na nGaedheal's JT Ennis had been fired upon by gunmen in Finglas. *The Press* charged that the *Independent*, "alone in Ireland, reported the supposed ambush as having actually occurred, although it had at its office before 10 pm on the previous evening a declaration by the police authorities that there was no foundation for the story." The *Independent*, it insisted, had "suppressed" the garda denial.

The *Independent* countered that there had been no garda denial of its story, and pointed out that on the day the *Press* was accusing it of bias, the Fianna Fáil newspaper and its editor had been convicted of seditious libel against the State in the courts. The guilty verdict arose from a series of interviews with prisoners who claimed they had been abused in State custody, leading the *Press* to argue that there was "reason to fear" a culture of misconduct within the police. the *Press* retorted that the *Independent* was trying to change the subject, which was just what you'd expect of an organ which had "called upon the British courts-martial of 1916 for the blood of James Connolly and Séan Mac Diarmada".

The Irish Press broadened its attack on the "campaign of vilification and misrepresentation carried out by the Cumann na nGaedheal press" by accusing *The Irish Times* and *The Cork Examiner* of dirty tricks against Fianna Fáil. It claimed that *The Irish Times* had published a statement purportedly from Fianna Fáil's Séan T O'Ceallaigh which was entirely made up. It also alleged that *The Times* and *The Examiner* had made "scandalous misrepresentation of a public man" by publishing quotes from Fianna Fáil TD Seamus Moore in praise of the writer Peadar O'Donnell. This "Fianna Fáil benediction" of O'Donnell was actually a year old, and had been made long before O'Donnell had made "hostile references to the Bishops in his most recent book".

The Press warned its readers of an attempted government stroke in Mayo. A year earlier Mayo County Council had been dissolved by ministerial order for refusing to appoint Protestant Letitia Dunbar-Harrison to the position of county librarian. With the Council abolished, public services in

Mayo had suffered. Close to election day, The Irish Press reported that Ms Dunbar-Harrison had resigned – something she denied. The Press went on to speculate that the government had extracted her resignation so she could be replaced with a Catholic, getting the local bishops and clergy on-side for the election. According to The Press: "It is a matter of common knowledge that the four bishops holding jurisdiction in that county, as well as practically all the priests, feel strongly on the subject, and that on the eve of a general election the transfer elsewhere of Miss Harrison might sway opinion in favour of the Cumann na nGaedheal party." The unfortunate civil servant was eventually transferred to an Army barracks where, as a Senator later noted: "The denizens were too corrupt to be corrupted by a Protestant librarian."

Slush Funds And Air Drops

Senator Connolly of Fianna Fáil said that anti-Irish forces were determined to keep his party out of office by use of a secret fund. Making things worse, he said that one of the subscribers to the slush fund was a descendent of a member of the 'packed' jury which condemned Father Nicolas Sheehy to death in 1766 for a murder he did not commit. It was well-known that the supposed murder victim was seen very much alive after Fr Sheehy was hanged outside Clonmel Courthouse.

Cumann na nGaedheal's John Hearne countered with the damning accusation that De Valera had said: "To Hell with the bishops!" Senator Quirke of Fianna Fáil responded that if the Catholic Church was ever attacked, Dev would be the first onto the field of battle in its defence.

Days before the poll, Fianna Fáil claimed the government had hired an aeroplane to drop defamatory leaflets saying: "The gunmen are voting today for Fianna Fáil. Which way are you voting?" Dev's Irish Press wrote: "This leaflet was, of course, like most of Cumann na nGaedheal's offensive literature, paid for out of ex-Unionist money."

Cumann na nGaedheal lost no opportunity to present Fianna Fáil as the party of the gunmen. Seamus Burke said that if Fianna Fáil were ever allowed to hold the reins of power, the party would open the jails "and let out the murderers". De Valera's *Irish Press* accused Finance Minister Ernest Blythe of scaremongering, when he commented: "If Fianna Fáil get into power we would never be able to put them out, for they would threaten the electors at the point of the gun."

Fianna Fáil's Séan Lemass claimed that if Cumann na nGaedheal were returned to power, they would stay there forever by giving double votes to their wealthy supporters. Lemass told a meeting: "I, for one, am certain that they will include the introduction of plural voting, and if you miss this opportunity that is given to you next Tuesday, you may never get another opportunity of removing these men from office."

The *Press* ran a front page story claiming that 40 Cumann na nGaedheal election workers at the party's Cork HQ had gone on strike when they found that their pay for addressing envelopes had been slashed in half by their ungrateful employers. At the end of the report, the paper carried Cumann na nGaedheal's response that the *Press'* story was made-up rubbish. Elsewhere the *Press* charged Cumann na nGaedheal with making snooty 'flawed pedigree' remarks, reporting that Agriculture Minister Minister Patrick Hogan had said Fianna Fáil were unworthy of office because "you must have breeding to govern".

As The Fat Man Said To His Wife

Dev's new *Irish Press* had a children's page hosted by Roddy The Rover. During the election campaign, Roddy asked his young readers what made them most proud of Ireland. As the

contest climaxed, Roddy could hardly contain his
excitement. He exclaimed: "Today is prize day. What a week
I have had! Reading postcards I was from morning till
nightfall, and shouting out, 'First, second, third, fourth – take
away the first number you thought of', in my sleep. Well now,
ladies first, as the fat man said to his wife when he thought
that the cross dog was on the other side of the gate. Nearly
half the girl competitors wrote in Irish. About one-third of
the boys wrote Irish. One boy, an O'Suilleabhain and a
Gaelic speaker, wrote English because he thought that Roddy
– Ruaidhrí Rodach – wouldn't understand Gaelic. *Grrrrrr!* I
wish I could lay my hands on him. When I had finished with
him he'd know what rhymes with Dingle."

Angela Brennan of Ballinkillen, aged nine, sent Roddy
the following competition entry: "When the Free State and
Northern Ireland are gone forever and we have our own little
island in one again, I'll write you pages why I like my own
country best." Roddy replied: "It is good to know that our
young people realise (what some of their elders forget) that
Ireland is partitioned."

Roddy told his young readers: "To love your own parish
best is the beginning of right feeling. What a grand thing it
is to realise, before it is too late, that the hills around your
home are lovely, and that there is joy in carrying tea to the
folk working in the bog. Mairead Ni Thonnaigh (10) is
proud of her birth at the foot of Croagh Patrick, the scene of
a brave fight in the Irish war. Kitty Hartnett of Croom loves
her country for its martyrs' sake and says: 'I will love it still
better when our great leader Eamon de Valera rules my
native land'."

The Alarming Spread Of Lunacy

SPREAD OF INSANITY trumpeted *The Irish Times*,
reporting that one in every 200 people in the Free State was
a patient of a public mental institution. "In addition, there

are a large number in private asylums, workhouses and hospitals and a large number are hidden away in private homes."

A report of the Grangegorman Inspection Committee recorded "the alarming increase in the spread of lunacy in the Free State". This was discussed at the monthly meeting of the Grangegorman Committee. Possible causes for the epidemic included "alcoholic excess, mental worry, lack of social intercourse and bad housing conditions". Supporting a motion calling on the government to investigate this spreading lunacy, Senator Foran said he'd been informed by a senior medic that "this country has a higher number of lunatics than any other country in Europe".

Elsewhere, the independent farmers candidate John Cuffe applied to hold an election meeting at Portrane Mental Hospital. The Hospital's Committee refused.

Meanwhile, Canon Walsh, chairman of the Waterford Mental Hospital Committee, took issue with remarks by a judge which he called "objectionable and misleading to the public". The judge had imposed a maximum fine of £20 on Johanna Kennedy for selling milk to the Mental Hospital which had been watered down to the level of 37.1%. The judge observed that hospital staff knew in advance that the Food & Drugs Inspector was arriving to test the milk for its cream content, and he wondered what the level of watering down might have been if they hadn't been forewarned. Canon Walsh resented the judge's insinuation that the Mental Hospital was buying in watered-down milk and then diluting it even further for the unfortunate inmates.

The watering down of milk was a nationwide problem, leading to regular court prosecutions. There were also health issues about the milk supply. One newspaper thought it worthwhile to publsh the following hygiene tips for dairy farmers. "When attending to cows in a byre, to ensure clean milk never sweep a dry floor, do not shake up straw before milking, keep cows groomed, keep loose hairs off your clothes, wash hands and vessels thoroughly, don't handle milk cattle roughly, do not smoke or spit."

Led Astray By Two Boys

John Moore, a painter from Carrick-on-Shannon, was found guilty of extracting money from publicans under false pretences. In court, a letter was read out which Moore had been hawking around pubs in the area. It was signed 'OC' (Officer-in-Command). It read: "Dear Friend. We are writing a few lines to tell you that owing to us being wanted by the Guards and Detectives, we are obliged to leave this part of the country. Friend, we have a lot of stuff that we cannot take with us, but as a friend of ours we will give you the chance of taking it. It includes whiskey, brandy, port wine, tobacco, cigarettes and motor tyres. Dear Friend, if you can see your way to taking any of the stuff from this man you can make all the necessary arrangements as to the time of delivery, which will be made any time after 8 o'clock tonight."

Moore was given probation on the grounds that it was his first offence, and that there was no record of any goods having been stolen that matched his bargain list. No action was recorded against the publicans who had parted with cash expecting to get their hands on stolen goods.

In Dundalk on polling day, Daniel Coffey of Newry was arrested for attempted impersonation at a polling booth. He had asked for a ballot paper in the name of Albert Switzer. When he appeared in court, the judge said that it was just not on for the resident of another state to try to influence an Irish election. Coffey said that he had been in the South for the day to work as a driver for one of the candidates. He had been led astray by two boys outside the polling station who told him he had a vote, and gave him a registration number. He was sentenced to two months imprisonment with a one shilling fine.

Government's Record On Affordable Housing "Shameful"

The Communist candidate for North Dublin, J Troy, attacked the government's record on housing as "shameful". He quoted official figures which showed that the number of people in the Free State who had to eat, cook and sleep in a single room was 140,061. This figure concealed other scandalous realities. One thousand two hundred and seventy families lived ten to a single room. Two hundred and ninety-seven lived 11 to a room. One hundred and ninety lived 12 or more to a single room. According to Troy's figures, the Cosgrave government had built only 2,000 houses per year during their decade in office.

Dublin City architect Horace O'Rourke called for the 'censorship' of Dublin's architecture in order to guard against the capital becoming a third-rate city in appearance.

Missing The Boat

With the Great Depression biting hard, American Dean Farrell had been out of work for two years and was standing in a New York breadline when a friend recognised him and offered to get him a job as a railroad engineer in Virginia. Arriving on the New York wharf, Farrell handed over his luggage to a porter and borded the liner, *St Louis*, which was about to sail. He awoke the next morning to find the ship, unexpectedly, out of sight of land. Some days later the liner docked at its first port of call, Cobh. *The Irish Press* speculated that the post in Newport would be filled by the time he got back to the States.

Degrading And Tyrannical Wedding Blackmail

In their Lenten pastorals during the election campaign, the Catholic bishops condemned the "modern craze for amusement". They singled out improperly supervised rural dances, dangerous movies and the custom of giving drink and money to costumed 'straw men' at rural wedding receptions.

The Bishop of Kilmore called on the forces of law and order to intercept anyone going about in disguise. He warned his flock: "This innocent custom has degenerated into something unlawful and degrading. The visitors demand drink in a threatening and pretempory manner. They get, through fear and under threat, sometimes more than they should, consistently with temperance, or, that they may be got rid of quietly they are given money instead. For this they get drink at the nearest public house. This sometimes whets their appetite for more and they return and demand more drink or more money, and by rough and threatening conduct terrify people into giving." The bishop appealed to young men not to take up this "degrading and tyrannical blackmail". If they'd already taken it up, they should stop straight away.

I Dare You To Shoot Me

Fianna Fáil candidate Ben Maguire was touring Sligo-Leitrim charging that Cumann na nGaedheal was in the grip of Freemasons and ex-Unionists. However, when Maguire was injured in a car crash, his Cumann na nGaedheal rival Deputy Pat Reynolds sportingly announced that he would do no more canvasing on Maguire's patch until he was back in the fray.

Further along the campaign trail, Reynolds got wind of treachery by a supposed supporter of his. One Sunday, after addressing a meeting, the TD drove to the home of ex-policeman Joseph Leddy, who was having dinner with his family. Reynolds entered and confronted Leddy, saying: "You ****! You're out canvassing against me."

Leddy replied: "I never went canvassing against you. I always figured on giving you my number one."

But there was no calming Reynolds, who repeated: "You're out canvassing against me. I'll kill you, you ****!" Reynolds tried to hit Leddy. He felt that Leddy owed him his loyalty, because he'd helped sort out a state pension for the ex-policeman. Leddy told Reynolds to get out of his house "or I'll shoot you". Reynolds unwisely replied: "I dare you to shoot me." As he left, Reynolds threatened: "You ****! I took a wrong oath to get you that pension, and by **** I'll see you broke of it."

Threatened by Reynolds with the loss of his livelihood, Leddy grabbed his shotgun. Reynolds' bodyguard, who was armed with a pistol, warned Leddy: "There are more guns than yours." At that, Leddy blasted both men. A third man who tried to wrench the shotgun from Leddy got a puck in the face for his troubles. Leddy went into his kitchen and dispatched one of his children to fetch a priest. The dying Reynolds called weakly to "Joe" (Leddy) for help, but Leddy stayed in the kitchen, pacing up and down with his shotgun.

At his arrest hearing, Liddy asked to be taken to Sligo jail by uniformed guards, saying that he'd been roughed up by the detectives holding him in custody. The garda superintendent was dismissive, saying "prisoners do make these statements".

One newspaper stated: "The arrested man is married and has a family. It is reported locally that a sister of his was in a mental home."

Reynolds' widow took his Dáil seat in the postponed poll.

Drowning While Temporarily Insane

As the election campaign gathered pace, a court case lifted the lid on the bizarre goings-on in a Mayo school. Norah Molloy, a former teacher at Lisduff National School, Kiltimach, claimed she had lost her job through a conspiracy hatched by other teachers, the parish priest and a school inspector.

Molloy said that relations had once been good between herself and the school principal, Bridget Egan, and another teacher, Margaret Egan, who was Bridget Egan's sister-in-law. Molloy told the court that both Egans had been absent a lot.

Margaret Egan had missed 46 days in one period but Molloy was sure this wasn't down to illness. She knew this because the two were next-door neighbours. In 1926, after a falling out with the two Egans, Molloy had reported these long absences to a school inspector.

The reason she reported the pair was because they were trying to force her out of the school. She said that the school clock had been set fast by the headmistress, so that pupils of hers arriving in on time were being marked late and therefore absent on the roll, making her look like a teacher lacking control. There were other irregularities. On one occasion the principal moved six of Molloy's pupils to a more advanced class, reducing the numbers she had to teach and making it look like she was surplus to requirements. She said that the principal also encouraged pupils in her class to stay away from school, in a further attempt to put her job on the line.

Meanwhile, her next-door neighbour Margaret Egan had also tried to do her down. Molloy said that when she gave the pupils sweets, Margaret confiscated them and threw them on the floor under the desks. Margaret Egan had also bad-mouthed her to the pupils.

Called in to referee, the school inspector advised both sides to let bygones be bygones and get on with their jobs. The warring parties shook hands and agreed to bury the hatchet. However some months later Molloy discovered that the Egans were plotting behind her back and had levelled complaints against her for creating insubordination in the school. This was despite the fact that the principal had never raised these complaints with her.

Things came to a head when Molloy got a letter from the Department of Education giving her the sack. She wrote back accusing the two Egans of conspiring against her, and asking to be allowed keep her job on probation. The next Monday she turned up to teach, but a garda sergeant barred her entry. He said he was acting on the instructions of the parish priest and school manager, Canon Gallagher. For the next week the police stood guard outside the school.

Molloy agreed in court that she had refused to stand up when Canon Gallagher visited the school, but this was in protest at the fact that he deliberately blanked her in the street, directing his eyes to the ground. She would have no hesitation in standing up for the Canon if he would recognise her. Molloy's brother, the Reverend Luke Molloy said that the Canon had dragged him into the dispute by refusing him permission to say Mass in the local chapel when he was home on leave. Subsequently the Canon did let him celebrate Mass in the church, but that was on a weekday and only on account of a special occasion – his father had just died and it was his funeral. On another occasion when he'd tried to see the Canon, he was "received on the doorstep".

At this point the already sensational trial took a tragic twist. Margaret Egan killed herself. Her body was found in five feet of water in the River Pollagh. A rope around her neck was tied to a heavy stone. Her sister told the inquest that Margaret had been unwell for some time and was depressed at the prospect of appearing in court. The county coroner recorded the cause of death as "asphyxia due to drowning while temporarily insane".

Back in court, Margaret Egan's name was struck off the list of defendents. The school principal, Bridget Egan, took the stand and blamed Norah Molloy for starting the bother by refusing to mark the disputed attendance rolls. She said that when conducting oral lessons, Molloy kept shouting to her children at the top of her voice and encouraged them to read their stories as loudly as they could. The untenable level of noise pollution spilled throughout the entire school.

The principal said that when she'd promoted six children out of one of Molloy's class, Molloy had herded them back. When the principal spoke to her, Molloy told her to mind her own business. During prayers, Molloy's pupils kneeled down, but their teacher did not. The headmistress warned Molloy that she would get in trouble for teaching the children disobedience.

Molloy said that she stood for part of the prayers because she thought they went on too long for kneeling. She admitted that she'd shortened the examination of the pupils on their catechism.

The headmistress said matters became worse and she complained to the school manager Canon Gallagher. The principal said that Molloy generally interfered with the discipline of the whole school. A letter was read out from the headmistress to Canon Gallagher complaining that Molloy's bad discipline was making the pupils "sulky and disobedient". Molloy denied that she was soft on discipline, saying she'd placed some of her pupils on their knees as a punishment.

The principal denied that anyone involved in the school had ever tried to get rid of Molloy. She admitted that she had confronted Molloy, saying Molloy was after her job. This was after she'd learned that Molloy had applied to succeed her as principal when she retired.

She admitted that the six children she'd promoted out of Molloy's class had not been examined to see if they were suited to a higher grade. She explained that if she had gone to Molloy's class to examine them, Molloy would have insulted her.

"I suppose I was wrong," she conceded when pressed. "I did not follow the rules."

Canon Gallagher said that he'd kept out of the dispute as he didn't want to get mixed up in fighting between teachers, especially women ones. He denied that he had "boycotted" Molloy in the street. Molloy was not very approachable after the friction began with the Egans, and he didn't want to run the risk of a rebuff, which might account for him not shaking hands with her. He admitted that he may have touched her on the shoulder at a children's Mass, but he denied that he hustled her. As regards Molloy's brother, the canon said: "He said I prevented him saying Mass when his father's remains were in the church. That is untrue because he did not ask me. If he had, he would have got permission." He added that matters of Canon Law were for the Bishop to deal with, and not a public court.

Schools inspector Henry Morris told the court that his honest report on Molloy found her guilty of gross, persistent and deliberate insubordination to her superiors. He'd found that the deceased Margaret Egan had started the quarrel, keeping it up and working up among the pupils and others a conspiracy of hate against Molloy. He'd recommended that she be fined £25 or £30. He said that the headmistress had come best out of his inquiry, although he'd found her guilty of making false entries in the roll book and of promoting children out of Molloy's class without examining them. He'd recommended that she be reprimanded.

Bridget Egan's lawyer called the charges "cruel and abominable" but she was found guilty of being party to a conspiracy, and Norah Molloy was awarded £1,000.

1932

AN IRISH SPEAKING COLONY

REVIVING THE LANGUAGE THROUGH
PUBLIC-PRIVATE PARTNERSHIP

Daniel O'Connell said of the Irish language: "I am sufficiently utilitarian not to regret its abandonment." The Liberator believed that for his people to take their place amongst the nations of the Earth, they must liberate themselves from a language of the dispossessed. Almost a century later, having been dealt a mortal blow by the Great Famine, the language was being maintained on life-support by the coming men of Official Ireland.

The academic Myles Dillon sensed more to their bedside vigil than unconditional love. Decades after Independence, he noted: "This policy of compulsory Irish was launched in 1925 and it was inspired, I've long suspected, by the purpose in the minds of the few that pressed for it, of using the language as a means of transferring power – or rather authority. At that time all the cultural institutions of the country, except the National University, were in the hands of the Protestants ... All that must be changed. A new administrative class was to be established and the language was one of the means used."

Gaeltacht Park in Dublin was to be a physical statement of that changeover.

At the birth of the Free State, Dublin was in the grip of a

housing crisis. A 1913 inquiry had reported that 60,000 slum-dwellers were in immediate need of re-housing, but ten years on little had changed. However, in the lead-up to Independence Dublin Corporation had begun entering into public-private partnerships with co-operatives called Public Utility Societies (PUS) in its bid to fast-track new social and affordable housing. This relationship between the public authority and the private sector blossomed with the encouragement of WT Cosgrave's cash-strapped Free State government.

The 1932 Housing Act belatedly defined a PUS as any company that satisfied the Minister that its objectives were entirely philanthropic and ran projects that included the provision of homes for the working classes. That was the theory. In practice, the bottom line was profit, with each scheme custom-built to milk every available grant, rebate and remission going.

Instead of advancing the building of social housing, as their charter required, some PUS societies simply piggybacked on Corporation estates, buying up ready-to-go land on the edge of the new developments which had been serviced with water and sewage at the public's expense.

These border strips were designated Reserved Areas by the Corporation after an idea which may have been lifted from Russia's Catherine the Great. Legend has it that when Catherine gave foreign dignitaries the grand tour of her realm, her sidekick Field Marshall Grigori Potemkin would have fake villages built along the route so as to create an illusion of prosperity. Similarly, in 1920s Dublin the societies were incentivised to build grand houses along the main thoroughfares, forming an elegant fence around the matchbox estates of the poor that was easy on the eye.

In theory, the Corporation had the societies on a tight leash, since any breach of compliance could be penalised by withholding the tax breaks and other perks. In practice, there is evidence that the builders had the authorities in their pockets. The plans for one scheme in the Drumcondra suburb of Dublin stipulated that an access road into an estate should run from A to B. The society decided to put up extra houses where the road should have been. The Corporation let it be.

Enthusiastic developers of the day included the Christian Brothers Past Pupils Union PUS, the Tram & Omnibus PUS and Celtic PUS, but none showed greater enthusiasm for their cause than the one which styled itself An Gaeltacht, trading as Nua Gaeltacht Atha Cliath Teo. The aim of the group was to found "an Irish speaking colony" in the heart of the English Pale.

In 1927 An Gaeltacht secured a 150 year lease on two prime acres in Whitehall on Dublin's northside, which was then on the edge of the city limits. The first step was to build ten fine houses for the ten well-heeled individuals who came up with the scheme. After that, the rest of the houses would fly up as likeminded gaelgeoirs flocked to swell the colony. However, in 1929, having built their own grand houses, the members of the society solemnly pleaded that there was no way they could afford to complete the roads which they'd promised to build under the terms of their lease. Most obligingly, the Corporation took back the bothersome lease and legitimised the *fait accompli* by handing back ten individual, obligation-free leases.

Having let the members of An Ghaeltacht off the hook, the Corporation was left to build the roads itself. While putting them in, it began developing some adjoining lands for housing. In response, Sean O'Cuill of An Ghaeltacht fired off an angry letter objecting to the neighbouring development, insisting that the ten culturally pure households had been given assurances that non-Irish speakers would not be allowed to contaminate their colony.

O'Cuill got no satisfaction. When the development was officially christened in 1932, its given name was Gaeltacht Park, although the title was never anything more than aspirational.

The vision that inspired Gaeltacht Park flickered on, and on September 26, 1968 the country's self-proclaimed 'first Irish language hotel' opened its doors in Dingle, Co Kerry. Guests were obliged to register in Irish, relax in Irish, eat in Irish and sleep in Irish.

Posterity does not record the date of its closure.

1933

THE IGNORANT AND SENTIMENTAL VOTE

The Incumbents: Fianna Fáil led by Eamon de Valera.
Slogan: To all decent citizens a frugal living in their land.
Promise: Free the country from the residual British yoke.
The Challengers: Cumann na nGaedheal led by Cosgrave.
Slogan: A quick reprieve from the madness of Fianna Fáil rule.
Promise: Save the nation from Bolshevism and pauperism.
The Mood of the Country: Combustible.
Prediction: An enhanced Fianna Fáil majority.
Result: Fianna Fáil win an enhanced majority.
Entertainment value: 5/10.

A Dangerously Insane Experiment With Autarchy

Between 1923 and 1932, the Cumann na nGaedheal
government had dedicated itself to calming the ripples of the
Civil War period. The transfer of power to Fianna Fáil in
1932 was generally smooth and peaceful at first, but as De
Valera began to implement the more radical elements of his
election manifesto, old wounds began to re-open. The
unbanning of the IRA and the release of prisoners who'd
fought on the losing side in the Civil War provoked a
reaction which led to the formation of the Blueshirts as a
countervailing force which was pledged to protect "free
speech" from IRA thuggery. It remains open to debate
whether the Blueshirts were a fascist movement or, as some
would suggest, more of a fashion movement.

De Valera also made good on his promise to stop paying

perpetual annuities to landlord Britain, sparking an Economic War which would last until 1938. Britain retaliated by placing an embargo on Irish exports, damaging the farming and business interests that supported the less anti-British Cumann na nGaedheal. With the political temperature soaring, De Valera called a snap election in January 1933 hoping that the swift and decisive delivery of his election promises would be rewarded with more seats. Cosgrave said he welcomed the snap election, insisting "this desperate gambler's throw has not found us unprepared".

Not everyone was prepared to suffer the faction-fighting which was bound to scar a full-blooded election campaign, and reports emerged from Clare that Fianna Fáil and Cumann na nGaedheal activists had come to an agreement that a contest there wasn't worth the trouble it would bring. In order to avoid "expense and turmoil" all concerned would prefer if the deputies who'd sat in the last Dáil were returned unopposed. It was a peaceable but not a practical idea.

During the campaign, Taoiseach Eamon de Valera made no apologies for the hardships caused by the British boycott which he'd provoked. He told the country's producers: "You could not have got out of the rut you were in without having a little shock here or there." Cosgrave told the voters that he would make a deal to restore normal trade with Britain within three days of getting back into office. Cumann na nGaedheal insisted: "Our policy is one of honourable and advantageous peace with our neighbours." Fianna Fáil, on the other hand, would drive the country "through Bolshevism to pauperism". *The Times* of London accused Dev of pursuing a dangerously insane experiment with 'autarchy', which it described as a "fantastic belief in self-sufficiency".

Vote Fianna Fáil! – The IRA Speaks

In a statement, the IRA leadership told voters: "The convention decides to release the organisation from the restriction that prevented it from taking part in elections, and we are recommending our members, and the mass of national opinion that looks to us for leadership, to work and vote against the Cosgrave candidates and their so-called Independent allies. In practice this means that the Fianna Fáil government should be assisted into office again."

Republican enthusiasts targeted a Cumann na nGaedheal rally on Dublin's O'Connell Street, where, according to a newspaper hostile to Fianna Fáil, "disgraceful scenes of organised hooliganism marked the proceedings from start to finish". Missiles were thrown and there were several rushes at the platform where General Richard Mulcahy was speaking. Men were pulled off the Cumann na nGaedheal lorry, which was defended by members of the Army Comrades Association (ACA) wearing a uniform of a blue shirt, which was by now establishing their popular name. The windows of the ACA HQ were smashed and many were injured in the street fighting.

Cumann na nGaedheal's Director of Elections, Liam Burke, said: "I have had definite information that several contingents of the more militant followers of Fianna Fáil were brought in from the country in an organised attempt to break up our meeting."

Taoiseach Eamon de Valera replied: "There is no evidence that the disturbances were prearranged or organised. The suggestion that the government or the police countenanced interference with meetings is, of course, without foundation."

During the disrupted rally, Mulcahy had told the crowd that Fianna Fáil was trying to damage Cumann na nGaedheal by putting it about that Britain wanted Cosgrave's party back in power. Britain, of course, *did* want a Cumann na nGaedheal victory. *The Manchester Daily Dispatch* welcomed Dev's snap election as "an act of political suicide after a life of political debauchery". It hoped the Irish electorate would provide "no corpse reviver". *The Times* of London agreed, saying: "His last budget imposed large burdens on the southern Irish taxpayer. His next, if he is returned, is likely to be catastrophic, but ignorant or sentimental small farmers, especially in the south and west, are probably less amenable to this consideration than to the stream of anti-British propaganda with which the government will certainly endeavour to conceal its past mistakes."

The London *Times* pointed out with some concern that the newly-started Economic War between Ireland and Britain would actually give Dev's government a pre-election bounce, because the drop in exports to Britain would mean more plentiful, and cheaper, pigs and poultry for Irish dinner tables. However, it warned that a vote for Fianna Fáil was a vote for a fleeting fools paradise: "This improvement in the standard of living is clearly temporary. It will continue only until the current stocks are consumed."

Contradicting the London view of the rural voter, *The Irish Times* published a clarification headlined FARMERS NOT BACKWARD. It read: "Mr P Baxter, Cavan, in his speech at the Congress of Cow-Testing Associations in Dungarvan last Wednesday, said that: 'Irish farmers are not so backward as other classes think they are.' This was not made clear in the summary of his speech which appeared yesterday."

In an effort to reach out to the rural voter, Cumann na nGaedheal came up with a novelty approach. Beneath the headline A TALKING FILM, readers of *The Irish Times* learned that: "An interesting electioneering device that has been prepared by Cumann na nGaedheal for the remoter areas is a talking film, which includes a speech by Mr Cosgrave lasting about 15 minutes. This will be submitted to the Film Censor for his approval and it will be sent immediately on tour to smaller places which Mr Cosgrave will be unable to reach." It was first tried out in the open air in the remote area of Howth, Co Dublin, and was a great success. "People around the meeting place were able to remain at the windows of their homes and see and hear the speakers without any difficulty."

A Married Woman, A Lunatic or Idiot

The wife of Cumann na nGaedheal's Ernest Blythe insisted: "The women of Ireland can make or mar the country at the coming election." She was addressing "a largely attended meeting of women at the Mansion House, Dublin, called for the purpose of organising enthusiasm amongst women".

Enthusiasm *for* women was badly wanting in the upper echelons of the public service. During the campaign, HP Boland of the Department of Finance told the Civil Service Commission that the recruitment of more women civil servants was inevitable, but would cause problems. He advised the Commission that: "The number of girls in the Civil Service was increasing and would continue to increase, and women of higher education and capacity would be required to deal with the problems of discipline and control peculiar to them. So many girls were employed in the Land Commission, for instance, that a Minister for Agriculture complained on one occasion that the place was more like a school than a government office."

Shortly after Fianna Fáil's election win, a bill on citizenship began wending its way through the Oireachtas. Page five of the draft document contained the line: "A certificate of naturalization shall not be granted to a married woman, a lunatic or idiot." Not only was the drawing up of legislation a clearly all-male affair, so was the drawing up of advertising copy.

FAT! – blared the eye-catching headline on an advert for Kruschen Salts. The ad read: "When excess fat starts to overtake a woman, her dressmaker will soon detect it. This alteration may be so slight at first as to escape mention, but corpulency will stealthily creep on, gradually crushing out those youthful lines of grace and elegance." Taking Kruschen Salts not only helped a woman stave off corpulency, but also helped "banish painful itching and sickness" and "miserable fullness and flatulency".

In the Dublin courts, a woman gave evidence which the judge took with a large pinch of salt. *The Irish Times* reported: "Mary Keane, an elderly woman of no fixed address, was charged with having deliberately broken a plate glass window in the premises of Messrs Findlater in O'Connell Street. The woman flung a brick through the window. Putting her hand through the hole in the window she abstracted a bottle labelled 'whiskey'. She had just enough time to discover it was water when she was arrested. She told the guard that she wanted whiskey because her heart was weak."

Six Deaths To His Credit And Still Driving A Car

In the days before the election, John Healy from Churchtown in Dublin was charged with drunk driving. A garda Officer had noticed a lorry swerving outside the Mansion House on Dawson Street. It was reported: "He found the defendant, who was at the wheel, under the influence of drink, while there was a woman in the lorry who was also under the influence of drink. While taking the defendant to College Street Station a crowd collected, and the defendant called upon them to rescue him, shouting that he was a captain in the IRA." Healy's lawyer said that his client had been in the British Army in India and had suffered from sunstroke three times, which might have had an effect on his behaviour.

Shortly after the new Dáil convened, the Oireachtas began drawing up new road safety legislation. One deputy argued that proper enforcement was the key to beating drink driving, but he added that motorists would still try to get off on technicalities and that tougher enforcement wouldn't work without a tight legal definition of the word 'drunk'. He explained: "This is a very serious matter. I have one case in my mind where a man has had six deaths to his credit and he is still driving a car."

1937

A LOW TURNOUT OF PRIESTS

The Incumbents: Fianna Fáil led by Eamon de Valera.
Slogan: Don't vote for a plucked turkey.
Promise: Deliver a contented Irish-speaking Ireland.
The Challengers: Fine Gael led by WT Cosgrave.
Slogan: We're not a plucked turkey.
Promise: Be different to Fianna Fáil.
The Mood of the Country: It wasn't meant to be like this.
Prediction: Fianna Fáil to be returned.
Result: Fianna Fáil returned.
Entertainment value: 5/10.

Disillusionment And Despair

After almost five years of economic war with Britain, the
wheels had all but come off Ireland's economy. Fianna Fáil's
programme for self-sufficiency was focused primarily on small
farming and rural living and had no answers to social
scandals such as urban slum living and overcrowding in the
hospitals. It was to be the first general election for Fine Gael.
After Fianna Fáil's decisive victory in 1933, the new
conservative party had formed from a merger of Cumann na
nGaedheal, the Centre Party and the Blueshirts.

However, four years after its foundation Fine Gael had yet
to work up a head of steam, and it entered the contest as the
overwhelming underdog. As the campaign wore on, despite a
prevailing mood of disillusionment and despair, Fine Gael
convincingly lived up to its billing in a Fianna Fáil advert as

a plucked turkey. By holding a parallel referendum on his new constitution, Bunreacht na hEireann, De Valera effectively sidelined all the niggly gripes that Ireland was becoming a hellhole by turning the contest into a straight vote of confidence on the moral authority of his leadership.

With the economy stagnant, there was little to spare in the coffers to 'buy' the election, but the government did cut the price of tea by two pence a pound and shaved a halfpenny off the price of a 4 lb loaf. It was announced that the State's telephone network was to be expanded to cover most of County Wicklow, with new lines to go up from Wicklow town to Arklow, and from inland Rathdrum to the sea at Brittas Bay.

The Irish Times' Political Correspondent predicted that the election would be held on July 6 in preference to July 13. He wrote: "There are two reasons why the earlier date would be more acceptable. There are superstitious people who do not like the 13th and, especially in some of the northern constituencies, that date comes inconveniently close to an anniversary that is still observed, even in the Free State."

In the end, polling day was set even further from the Loyalist walkabout of July 12 than had been anticipated. July 1 was chosen, despite the reservations of some that this date would mean a low turnout as it was traditionally the day on which many Irish workers began their summer holidays. One deputy pointed out that most of the Catholic clergy would be away on their annual retreat and wouldn't be able to vote. This raised questions as to which party, if any, would suffer most from a low turnout of priests.

A Farewell Salute In The Nazi Style

As the summer campaign gathered pace, so did the annual migration to Britain in search of seasonal farm work and perhaps something more permanent. A reporter sent the following dispatch from the west of Ireland: "The early train from Sligo to Claremorris yesterday might reasonably be described as an emigrant train, as it carried another large group of young men and girls from their native west to seek work across the water, following in the trail of many hundreds who have gone before them since the beginning of the year. I am told that they used to shout 'Up Dev!' and 'Up the Republic!' but yesterday they shouted with a somewhat forced gaiety 'Up Sligo!' and their last recollection of their home town as they bundled their new suitcases on the carriage racks was a farewell salute in the Nazi style.

The emigrant specials are now a commonplace in the west. Little of the distress at parting that characterised emigration in former years is now associated with it. Nevertheless, there is something pathetic about the manner in which the younger people, especially the girls, cling to each other's company. Many of the emigrants, ostensibly going for harvesting employment, are really determined to get any sort of a job. As one said: 'We are going for anything we can get.' Asked how he felt about losing his opportunity to cast his vote in the election, he said it did not matter much to him."

A Job-Seeking Joyrider

A Dublin man taking a different form of transport was 21-year-old Thomas Darcy. Under the headline WENT 'JOY RIDING' IN CAR, *The Irish Times* reported that the mechanic from Rathmines had appeared in court charged with stealing a motor vehicle. The owner, William E Callicutt, stated that on the previous Sunday evening his car was taken without his consent from outside the Methodist Church, Charleston Road, while he was at service. Detective Burns said that, when challenged in the stolen car, Darcy tried to make an escape on a bicycle. After his arrest he was initially very disorderly at the station, but he calmed down and made a statement. His defence was that he took the car to go job-seeking in Naas.

The members of the Dublin Port & Docks Board heard of a crime spree in the port where hundreds of boys would gather around docking banana boats every day in the hope of liberating some of the cargo "on the sly". Elsewhere, it was reported that: "Bridget Hannon and Christina Coffey, both married, were charged and remanded in custody for a week, in connection with the larceny of perambulators from outside a cinema. Detective Officer McEvoy stated that 'prams' had been reported missing from various parts of the city. The woman Coffey, he said, had admitted taking 19 'prams' which had been left by their owners outside shops, cinemas and medical dispensaries."

Meanwhile, in Co Clare, Judge EJ McElligott said with deep regret that the current assize would go down as 'The Dirty Assize' because, of the 11 cases before him, seven were cases of indecent assaults on girls under 17. It was reported that: "Another case was against a poor creature for concealment of the birth of her illegitimate child."

The judge told the court: "Irish missions are being sent to China, to nigger countries, to Japan and various other places, but really and truly the young people of Ireland ought to take stock of themselves and see what they could do to improve their own moral relations." The jury found James Egan guilty of a "serious offence" against a girl under 17. However, the jurors made a recommendation of mercy "owing to the immoral state of the county". Judge McElligott said that this plea to go lightly on the offender because everyone was doing it was a shocking and terrible thing to hear coming from a Clare jury, but he would accept their recommendation. He sentenced Egan to five months in prison, but without hard labour.

Labour Party Responsible For Slums Says Top Cleric
Despite broad clerical disapproval of its ever so slightly socialist leaning, Labour ran a moderately successful

campaign in 1937 which would yield five extra seats when the votes were tallied. Labour backed the calls of the Citizens' Housing Council for a ten-to-fifteen year plan to clear the slums of Dublin and build 30,000 new affordable homes. Despite the fact that Labour had never been in office, Canon Hall of Glengeary held the party responsible to a degree worthy of mention for the slum conditions. He argued that, since Labour claimed to represent the working classes, they should have made it their business to get the selfsame working classes up off their lazy arses. Labour, he said, should have taken up the issue of bad housing "as a crusade for the honour of God". But the party had let down both God and their own class, because: "They are not willing to put their backs into this work in such a way as will make their own kind and their own class reap the benefits that the community as a whole wants to offer them."

People unable to escape the slums, in Canon Hall's dim view, were often stuck there through nobody's fault but their own. He explained: "My experience is that, of the number of men available for work, about one-third are capable of giving an adequate return for the pay they get. Two-thirds of these people cannot give a good return – men who are slipshod in their ways and do not have power of production about them. That is one of the sorrowful facts of life. And consequently, when you see a large number of unemployed, you are up against the factor that a great many of them are not able to give an adequate return."

There was another housing crisis sweeping Ireland, landing some people in court. A fine of £5 was imposed on Patrick Brunt, Kevin Street, Dublin, for permitting the Leeds Social Club at the rear of Granby Row to be used for the purpose of an unlawful game – namely 'House'. The arresting officer said that he found between 40 and 50 men playing, with the defendant shouting out numbers. One of the men yelled "House!" and went up to the platform and received

three shillings as a prize. JA Geary of the Chief State
Solicitor's Department said that the game of House was
becoming far too common. He said the guards were being
swamped with complaints from the wives of these men who
were squandering their family's money on gambling.

Hospital Overcrowding Cannot Continue

Responding to a report on overcrowding, the governors of Sir
Patrick Dun's Hospital sought government approval to erect
temporary shelters to house patients. *The Irish Times*
reported: "In order to meet the demands made upon it, it has
been necessary to put up stretchers and temporary beds in
many of the wards, yet in spite of this, many cases are, of
necessity, turned away for sheer lack of space. This, says the
report, is a condition which must not be allowed to
continue."

In the world of childcare, the annual report of the Sick
Poor Institution & Liberty Crèche recorded the number of
child attendance days at 6,822 for the year, a decrease of 497
on the preceding period. The attendance figures were down
owing to several epidemics but it was noted with satisfaction
that with the passing of the winter aliments, the number of
children being dropped into the crèche was again on the up.
A report said: "The crèche fills a great need in Dublin by
allowing parents to leave their children there while they
shop and carry out their work. The children are given clean
clothes and fed and looked after for the day."

Meanwhile, the AGM of the Save The Children Fund in
Stephen's Green heard that the Society's chief work – the
supplying of dried milk and cod liver oil to children in need
– had continued without interruption over the winter.
However, the meeting also heard that there were needy
children at home with their families when they ought to be
institutionalised. Dublin's Lord Mayor said: "In almost every
village of Ireland there are deaf and dumb or blind children

who should be sent to institutions for care, but whose mothers will not let them go." The Mayor held local authorities largely to blame for not coming down harder on parents refusing to give up children with disabilities.

The Illiterate Voter

Just before the Oireachtas dissolved for the election, in a debate on De Valera's new Constitution, the virulently anti-Fianna Fáil Deputy Frank MacDermot tabled an amendment to require that all voters "can read and write". MacDermot, who would shortly pull a spectacular u-turn and join de Valera's party, told the Dáil: "The existence of the illiterate vote is sometimes used as a method of intimidation, because men and women who are perfectly well able to read and write and vote in the ordinary way are sometimes intimidated into declaring themselves illiterate so that they shall vote openly and it shall be known which way they vote."

The Labour Party leader William Norton attacked MacDermot's suggestion, calling it a further punishment on those who had already been failed by the state in the realm of education. Norton argued: "Imbeciles are at present prevented from voting in an election, and Deputy MacDermot would also prevent the man suffering from the disability of being unable to read and write from voting in an election." He said that if people who couldn't read or write were to be denied the vote, they shouldn't be asked to pay tax. He continued: "Under this amendment it would be possible for a released burglar or a ticket-of-leave man to vote, but it would not be possible for the honest man who can neither read nor write."

MacDermot stood his ground, countering: "The person who does not make himself or herself literate is failing in his or her duty to the community. The class is a dying and diminishing class and, so far as my experience goes, the chief effect for a good many years of this illiterate vote at election times has been to cause an undue amount of intimidation to be applied. People who declare openly what side they are voting for are naturally more subject to intimidation than anybody else, and that very democratic system of the secret ballot is made absolutely futile so far as they are concerned. As I say, people who are not illiterate at all are sometimes induced to declare themselves illiterate under threat."

At this point Fianna Fáil's Deputy Eamon Donnelly called for MacDermot to withdraw his amendment, saying: "I have always found that illiterate voters in any constituency are always guided by one great principle. It is the principle which should guide most people, that is, the principle of common sense. It does not follow at all, as Deputy Norton has said that because people may have super-education, they have got all the common sense in the world, and illiterate voters are not so easily intimidated at all as Deputy MacDermot might think. There is ample protection under the Ballot Act for every illiterate voter, and, when an illiterate voter declares how he is going to vote in the polling booth, the agents, the presiding officer and the poll clerk are sworn to secrecy. If they are honourable people they will not come out of that polling booth and say how a particular person voted. As a matter of fact, there is a penalty for it. I think Deputy MacDermot would be well advised to withdraw the amendment. It is hitting a section of the community which should be spared such a blow, and if Deputy MacDermot's experience is that illiterates have been intimidated, and if he had personal knowledge of that sort of thing, it was his obvious duty to look after it at the time. Apparently he did not, and he feels now that all these people should be disfranchised. They would be a very big percentage of the register in some places and a bigger percentage than we might like to take credit for."

With his proposal for striking off illiterates beaten, MacDermot came back with a plan to reward the responsible family man with double voting rights. He accepted that: "We should have to define just what we mean by 'family' and just what we mean by 'head of the family'. The broad question is whether the position of the family in our social life should be recognised by giving extra voting power to the person who carries the family responsibilities."

William Norton wanted to know what would happen if the head of the family wasn't a responsible man but an irresponsible woman. He argued: "You might have a case of a family consisting of an old, infirm mother and a number of sons. The mother is probably incurable and unable to perform any work – even her maternal duties in the home. Three or four sons may be contributing to the maintenance of the household. Deputy MacDermot would give that chronically infirm mother, who is unable to discharge her maternal duties in the household, two votes and the sons' one vote each. There may be a good reason for doing that but I have not heard it."

1938

THE ELEPHANT PLAYS A MOUTH ORGAN

The Incumbents: Fianna Fáil led by Eamon de Valera.
Slogan: Strong government!
Promise: Do the nation's work.
The Challengers: Fine Gael led by WT Cosgrave.
Slogan: This election is a waste of time and money.
Promise: Be different to Fianna Fáil.
The Mood of the Country: Indifferent.
Prediction: Fianna Fáil to be returned.
Result: Fianna Fáil returned.
Entertainment value: 4/10

A Dictatorship Of The People

After losing a Dáil motion by one vote, De Valera called a snap election in the summer of 1938 on the single issue of strong government. Dev declared that: "A government with a precarious parliamentary majority – constantly at the mercy of group combinations in support of sectional interests – cannot do the nation's work as it should be done." As the decades rolled by, and the ideological gap between Fianna Fáil and Fine Gael shrank to vanishing point, Fianna Fáil would time and again appeal to the voters to support strong government over squabbling coalitions.

The surprise election caught the opposition parties off guard. Fine Gael's WT Cosgrave attacked the contest as a waste of money because it would cost the public purse £50,000. He added that it would seriously disrupt the tourist season. He accused Dev of ordering some Fianna Fáil TDs to stay away from the Dáil in order to engineer the government's defeat and manufacture a pretext for going to the country. Labour's William Norton went further and stated that some of the 16 Fianna Fáil deputies who'd contrived to miss the vote had been instead at the Shelbourne Park races. Another Labour Deputy, Archie Heron, charged: "There is no doubt that Mr De Valera is aiming at a dictatorship." Dev responded: "It is a strange sort of dictatorship to go to the people and get their decision. I am quite prepared to say that we have a dictatorship of the people in this country."

During the campaign a new piece of legislation came into force which was intended to improve the working conditions of shop staff by placing tight controls on their hours and duties. However, the Shops Act proved unpopular with shoppers and shop-owners alike. One frustrated customer complained: "This restrictive legislation may have its uses, but frankly, I am getting a trifle tired of it. On Wednesday I had my first experience of the operation of the Shops Act. I wanted two things, a new toothbrush and a tin of photographic fixing salt. So I turned into a neighbouring chemist's shop. 'Could I have a toothbrush?' I asked. 'You could not,' was the reply, and thereupon I learned that this was the first Wednesday on which the Shops Act operated and that one of its effects was to prevent chemists from selling anything other than medicines on Wednesday."

Annoyed at the curbs on their rights to make money, shop-owners decided to field protest candidates under the banner of the Registered Traders Association. A spokesman said: "The government controls hours of trade and at the same time ignores the travelling shop which is a great menace to trading at all times." One travelling salesman prosecuted as a menace to society was John Nicholl of the

Irish Presbyterian Church who was summonsed for selling Bibles door-to-door. In his defence, the court was told that there was nothing in the content of the Bibles which would give offence to the Catholic religion. However, District Justice Goff ruled that door-to-door Bible salesmen are peddlers and that Nicholl was breaking the law by selling scripture without a licence.

Bowing to pressure from the country's retailers, just before polling day the government suspended the new restrictions on Sunday trading imposed by the Shops Act.

I'll Horsewhip The Minister For Finance

The politics of the Civil War were well to the fore of the 1938 campaign, with Fianna Fáil's Séan MacEntee rounding on Fine Gael's Richard Mulcahy for not fulfilling his duty of care to the GAA fans killed and injured by British forces at Croke Park on Bloody Sunday 1920. Branding MacEntee "a coward and a cad", Fine Gael Senator Gearóid O'Sullivan warned the Finance Minister: "If there was any responsibility it was on the British, and, perhaps, on me and Mick Collins. I'll go round every street in Rathmines and repeat that, and if ever I meet him I'll horsewhip him."

Two Fianna Fáil candidates sent letters to Protestant constituents asking for their vote. The notion of Fianna Fáil trying to poach members of the 'ex-Unionist' fold outraged Fine Gael. That party's Ernest Benson quoted a nameless member of Fianna Fáil as saying: "I personally am in favour of storing up sufficient poison gas so that when you get the wind in the right direction you can start at the border and let it travel and follow it."

Fine Gael accused the outgoing Fianna Fáil government of sabotaging its election literature which had been put in the post. Richard Mulcahy told a meeting that his party's material had been found floating on Dublin Bay. He seethed: "We want to kill rottenness of administration of that kind." The

Government Information Service rejected the allegation of
dastardly deeds, with the statement: "The Department of Post
& Telegraphs notifies with reference to the alleged
mistreatment of election literature passing through the post,
that a full inquiry has been made into the matter and that it
has been found that the statement is groundless."

On polling day it was one of the opposition parties which
stood accused of underhand measures after a burst of
excitement in Cork. It was reported that: "Crowds lined the
Ballhooly Road in Cork to watch an exciting chase by a
Civic Guard Sergeant in a commandeered car, after a man
suspected of impersonation. Around 8 pm the man presented
himself at the booth and asked for a voting paper. The vote
in that name had already been cast. Sergeant Sexton and
Guard Finn requested him to accompany them to an address
which he gave. The man agreed but when the party had gone
a short distance he suddenly broke away and ran towards the
centre of the city. The guards gave chase through the crowds.
Sergeant Sexton stopped a passing motorist, commandeered
the car, and drove after the man who took cover in Labour
Party headquarters."

Architecture And Morality
During the campaign Fianna Fáil's Séan T O'Kelly snipped
the ribbon at the opening of a new development in
Tullamore of 146 houses and a swimming pool. He told his
audience: "Our population is not increasing in the way it
should and we shall have to provide houses in sufficient
quantities – if housing is an encouragement, and I think it is
– to encourage more and more of our young people to marry
at an early age, and make the population of this country what
it should be, and what it was less than a century ago." The
swimming pool was of the bracing open-air type. A report
said: "The pond has several springboards and is equipped
with the latest machinery for filtering and cleansing the

water and an inflow from a river in the vicinity that changes the water every four hours."

The new development in Tullamore offered proof positive that the Irish nation could better itself. The writer continued approvingly: "It is most gratifying to learn from the report of the County Medical Officer of Health that the results of the slum clearance policy in Tullamore prove that when people from insanitary dwellings obtain new houses, they keep them in a clean and orderly condition. The changes that have taken place in Tullamore in the conditions of living can be measured by recalling to mind the spectacle of the old, dilapidated, insanitary hovels that have been cleared away."

However, a leading churchman felt that the poor, even given a bite of the carrot, could not be trusted to be on their best behaviour without the whack of the stick. When Reverend G Cooney took the podium: "He suggested that, apart from the rent collector, the Urban Council might appoint a female counterpart to supervise the domestic upkeep of the buildings and ensure that they are kept in a clean and sanitary condition. Many of the new residents who have been slum dwellers will require a little coaching or, perhaps occasionally, a knock of the stick to remind them that it is their duty to care for and preserve the amenities that have been given to them."

As Much Sex Appeal As A Feed Of Parsnips

The cultural landscape of the Ireland of 1938 can be glimpsed from the following excerpt from *The Irish Times*: "An interesting new feature which was much enjoyed in last night's broadcast from Radio Eireann was an item entitled 'On The Road'. It depicted two old ballad singers tramping the road, deploring the changed conditions and the difficulty of picking up reward. Then, as luck would have it, they meet with an old fiddler who, in the days gone by, had travelled the road with them. Old times are recalled and they proceed to sing in the traditional style a number of such well-known ballads as *Follow Me Up To Carlow*, *The Blackbird Of Avondale* and *Michael Dwyer*."

Staying on a musical note, at the AGM of the Musical Society of the Keating Branch of the Gaelic League, the Musical Director, P O'Kelly, reported that the final concert of the season at the Gate Theatre had been acclaimed as "the best Gaelic concert ever presented". A resolution was passed protesting against the inclusion of "jazz and other inferior music" on Irish radio programmes. Another resolution stated that "the employment of alien musicians is inimical to the furtherance of the native music".

At a convention of the Catholic Young Men's Society, CJ Loftus of Tuam argued that the working of the Censorship Act must be toughened up and a system must be put in place to censor publications before, rather than after, they were published.

Not everyone agreed that a new form of super-censorship was what the country most needed. One commentator wrote: "Two or three days ago, while I was driving along Harold's Cross Road I perceived a very striking poster advert for a well-known sports firm. It was a decent, healthy sort of poster depicting a girl with a tennis racket; and a fine, strong lump of a girl she was, with about as much sex appeal about her as a feed of parsnips, yet an attractive girl and an attractive poster. Driving there again today I see that the poster has been removed and replaced by a colourless invocation to buy this particular firm's goods. The next step will be to ban all dictionaries with the word 'woman' or 'girl', or any word that implies the existence of more than a single sex. What a pity they cannot dress us all in the same clothes."

A Leopard That Loops The Loop
Mister MH Mason reviewed the annual report of the Royal Zoological Society of Ireland. Having noted that the food

consumed by the animals included 155 horses, he observed: "The animals at the Zoo are really happy. They have no fear of hunger, nor fear of any other animals that prey upon them. And they usually live much longer than in their wild state." He asked visitors buying monkey nuts to either eat them themselves or feed them to the monkeys only, but not to the flesh-eaters or the fish. He said: "It is delightful to listen to the merry laughter of children in the Zoological Gardens. The elephant plays a mouth organ, and another gives rides to children. There are 13 lions and lionesses, six of them born in the Gardens. There is a leopard that loops the loop, a wallaby whose baby was less than an inch long when it was born, and a parrot that for the past ten years has been asking 'Any water?'"

Only water was the advice to slimmers from *The Irish Times* woman's page. It told readers: "One of the best ways to slim, according to an eminent obesity specialist, is to remain in bed, under a doctor's supervision, for two to three weeks absolutely without food, drinking only water and orange juice. But even though most women desire to be slim, few would go to such lengths to achieve it. Indeed, very few are in a position to afford the luxury of such a treatment. For, though it may not cost anything in food over that period, it does necessitate a domestic upheaval such as few can contemplate."

For When My Teeth Hurt

Crime did not pay for two Englishmen, Fred Johnson and William Smith, who were charged with stealing money from a number for Dublin telephone kiosks, the property of the Minister for Post & Telegraphs. They were seen entering the public phone booths at Berseford Place, Ormond Quay and Botanic Road, in Glasnevin. At Botanic Road they were arrested and found to be in possession of a penny which had been marked by Detective Donegan. At the time of their arrest, both men had in their possession small sums of money in coppers, including the marked penny. One also had a skeleton key and the end of a small broken file.

Detective Sergeant Byrne said that he'd searched a room at 86 Parnell Square where he found three cases, one of which contained a combination anvil and vice, an uncut key, the handle portions of two broken files, one complete file and some copper wire. He brought the case to Mountjoy Station and asked Johnson to open it. Johnson took up a file and said: "Do you know what I use that for?" Johnson then removed his false teeth from his mouth and said: "This is what I have it for – for when my teeth hurt me."

Strong Language At The Toll Bridge

From the southside of Dublin it was reported that: "The demolition of Parnell Bridge has been followed with the deepest interest by the locals since the work began. Every evening a group of experts gathers on the canal bank to exchange views on the progress of the new bridge. The bridge was originally a toll bridge, the tolls being collected (when they were paid) by an old woman called Sally. Legend says that she had a busy time intercepting officers from Portobello Barracks and young men from Rathmines who took a keen delight in trying to evade the payment of the toll dues. When the evasion succeeded, the language which Sally hurled at the defaulters was a source of mirth."

1943

A SHORTAGE OF PENCILS

The Incumbents: Fianna Fáil led by Eamon de Valera.
Slogan: Strong government!
Promise: We have no magic carpet.
The Challengers: Fine Gael led by WT Cosgrave.
Slogan: It's time for a change.
Promise: A national coalition to see out 'The Emergency'.
The Mood of the Country: Largely indifferent.
Prediction: A possible Fianna Fáil defeat.
Result: Fianna Fáil are returned.
Entertainment value: 5/10

Well-Known Fianna Fáil Golfers

With a World War raging, shortages were the order of the day. Politics in Eire had atrophied. Fine Gael's Senator Michael Hayes attacked the Department of Supplies, which he said had "given the people a fuel muddle, a tea muddle, a sugar muddle, a petrol muddle, a potato muddle and a situation in which supplies are plentiful only for the rich on the black market". Knowing that, after 11 years in power, Fianna Fáil would be blamed for everything up to and including the weather, De Valera attempted to buy time with a wartime Electoral Bill that would extend the gap between elections from five years to six. The opposition parties cried foul and the Taoiseach dropped the plan.

It was the second time in short succession that the government had been accused of sharp practice. The Labour

Party charged Fianna Fáil with using its grip on the electoral mechanism to rig the recent municipal elections in Dublin. Labour said that "uncivil" officials had obstructed voters, had closed one polling booth early and had failed to provide enough presiding officers, with the result that votes went missing because the ballot papers were not stamped. Mister Hermon, the Dublin City Manager, rejected the charges. He said that the holding of elections at all during wartime was "a matter for commendation rather than criticism", and he especially praised the manner in which a shortage of pencils had been overcome.

There were calls from several quarters to postpone the election until after the global conflagration ended. *The Irish Times* led the media campaign for the main parties to form a national government along the lines of the one led by Churchill in Britain. Fianna Fáil dismissed these calls as "tomfoolery" and "a stunt". The government's Séan MacEntee said that any coalition formed to evade the legal obligation of holding an election would be seen as fatally weak, nationally and internationally. What was needed, he said, was single party "strong government". MacEntee attacked Fine Gael calls for a national government to include the "best brains" available, be they TDs, academics or businessmen. MacEntee said the country had no need of the brainpower of people who until now had been too proud or too cowardly to put themselves up for election before the people. Referring to a popular children's knick-knack, De Valera remarked that running a national government would be like a child trying to put three grains of shot into three different holes inside a glass covered box.

The Taoiseach said scornfully that *The Irish Times'* proposal for a national government "would make a cat laugh". Fine Gael's John A Costello retorted that Fianna Fáil was like the selfish cat which had been sketched by Kipling as: "A cat that walks by himself, waving his wild tail and walking by his wild lone." Fianna Fáil's grand master of hyperbole, Séan MacEntee, upped the ante, saying: "The proposal would make a rhinoceros laugh." *The Irish Times*, which managed to find a photo of a laughing kitten for its front page, sought to remind its readers of Dev's dictatorial tendencies during his 11 years in office.

It editorialised: "He has no use for any Ministry, or any party of followers over which he has not complete and absolute control … And the iron discipline seemed to extend even to individual relations with deputies of other groups and parties. Fraternisation, even among old friends, was frowned upon. It will be remembered that when Fianna Fáil first entered the Dáil some opportunists, in the hope of creating a better social atmosphere, formed a golfing society, and several successful outings were held – but all the Fianna Fáil members, among whom there were many well-known golfers, remained aloof, obviously under instruction from some high quarters. The society has been defunct for many years."

De Valera was having nothing to do with any form of coalition government, going so far as to state that if the Proportional Representation electoral system brought about a coalition it would bring an end to democracy in Ireland, just as it had in countries on the continent. Much as he was in favour of PR, he said, it was his firm belief that the people should dump it if ever it brought an amalgam of parties to power. In a simultaneous attack on the very notion of coalition, another Fianna Fáiler pointed out that no one had ever seen two drivers on a coach-and-four.

Extra Breast Pockets And Illegal Dumping

Dublin's air-raid shelters were being fitted with gates and locks because they were being used by members of the public as toilets and illegal dumps. One cleaner complained: "They are nothing less than cesspools of filth. It is a mystery to me that they have not caused an epidemic. Almost as soon as we clean them they are almost as bad again. Apart from the stench – created by adults as well as children – many people use them as depositories for domestic refuse."

Responding to a crime spree, the authorities appealed to the citizens of Dublin's inner city to report the theft from unoccupied houses of banisters, staircases, wall sheetings, doors, floors, lead cisterns and piping. Trees were being illegally cut down and lifebuoys and light bulbs stolen from public places. Looking on the bright side with the election in mind, Fianna Fáil's Séan Lemass said the Irish people had the most generous sugar ration in Europe. Whatever government got in, the voters would find that Fianna Fáil had put in place a year's supply of tea, wheat, sugar, butter and turf. Sticking with dietary matters, the python at Dublin Zoo was fed a meal that would have to last it for five weeks: "It was a dead swan from the Sloblands, oil covered when brought in, but clipped and animated for the reptile's benefit."

Weeks before the election the Ministry of Supplies ordered new clothing restrictions, putting a limit on skirt widths and pleats and banning external trimmings such as turned-back cuffs. Cattle dealers and bookies were unhappy with the new so-called 'austerity suit' which only had seven pockets. These special-needs professions appealed to the Minister of Supplies for extra pockets to accommodate the large amount of cash they needed to carry. Their request was turned down. The only derogation granted was to Catholic priests who were allowed an extra inside breast pocket on their waistcoat for carrying sacramental Communion wafers. A tailor told *The Irish Times* that with cotton scarce, most people accepted that an extra pocket this year would probably mean no pockets at all next year, so it was best to go with the restriction. He added that men used to double-breasted suits were suffering the most, saying: "They feel strange in single-breasted suits at first but they will get used to them – they'll have to!"

The Parable Of The Missing Whiskey

Downplaying the fact that the world was at war and that just about every commodity was in short supply, the Finance Minister Séan T O'Kelly argued: "We have only one big political problem, and that is partition." De Valera added that until the Irish language was fully revived, Ireland would only be half a nation. Self-made businessman and Independent election candidate William Dwyer said that Fianna Fáil needed to be voted out because after another term in office all the permanent and pensionable jobs in the land would be in the hands of party cronies. Dwyer thanked the nation's drapers for contributing funds which allowed him to buy 15 tons of potatoes for Dublin's poor, to be distributed by Saint Vincent De Paul. When Fianna Fáil claimed that the Labour Party took its orders from Moscow, Labour's William Norton cast off the attempted socialist slur, saying: "The Labour Party's policy is based on the Papal Encyclicals."

Independent candidate Vincent Rice, who favoured a national government, accused Fianna Fáil of mounting a "whispering canvas" in poor areas to convince voters that a Fine Gael led administration would drag Ireland into the war on the side of Britain. Days later he said the whispering campaign to frighten the "unthinking" poor had become a full-scale war. The independent business candidate, WJ Costelloe, announced that he would make no speeches and hold no meetings. Somewhat optimistically, he said he would instead stand on his record as a manufacturer of raincoats and gloves. The electors decided that he shouldn't give up the day job.

The new Monetary Reform Organisation (MRO) promised easy answers to hard questions. In relation to the country's financial woes, the MRO's devastatingly simple solution was to just print more banknotes. Taking a fierce stand against all things Jewish, such as lending and borrowing, they issued a statement, saying: "We demand that money be issued to end unemployment, poverty, debt and all our present national ills."

Expecting a tight contest, De Valera lectured the Fianna Fáil faithful with the parable of the man who thinks his single vote won't make a difference, so he doesn't bother to cast it. That man, said Dev, is like the guest who goes to a party where everyone on arrival has to pour a naggin of whiskey into a jug in the hall. One skinflint reckons that no one will miss his single naggin of whiskey and he substitutes water. But when the hostess takes out her best glasses and pours everyone a drink, it turns out that there is nothing in the jug but water because everyone made the same selfish assumption. And that, said Dev, is how Fianna Fáil could be left out on their ear.

An Official Taboo On Dance Music

As polling day approached the authorities moved against jazz, also known as 'race' music. One newspaper reported: "An official 'taboo' has been placed on dance music at Radio Eireann. The brake has been applied gradually and the small number of dance music records broadcast recently will be the last to be enjoyed by licence-holders. It is understood, however, that the term 'dance music' will be roughly interpreted as standing for 'swing', 'jive', 'hot' music, or music with a vocal chorus sung by a crooner. Broadcasts of continental dance music, much of which lies outside these classifications, will probably be continued."

When the Dáil reconvened, Labour's Dick Corish praised the "improvement" in Radio Eireann's service as a result of the ban, saying that if the Irish people had been subjected to "crooning and jazzing" for too much longer "we would have had very little music in this country within the next generation". For Deputy Corish, the next improvement needed in the radio service would be to banish "these supposed variety artists" letting down standards on the national airwaves. He argued: "Some of them have been trying to ape British comedians who entertain people on the other side of the water who have not the sense of humour what we have, trying to imitate British comedians who would not be listened to on an Irish stage. I believe that some care should be exercised in the selection of artists of that kind. We have magnificent artists in this country – magnificent violinists and singers and other artists."

Tragedies Of Ignorance

Eighteen people, mostly youngsters, died on Ballymanus Beach, Co Donegal, when a deadly wartime mine was treated as a plaything. One report read: "A tragedy of ignorance is how medical men and soldiers describe the occurrence. It appears that the mine was seen by the youths for some considerable time before it reached the beach, and when it came ashore it was hauled clear of the water with ropes. The men inspected it at close range, at first throwing stones at it and later pulling it with their hands. At least two of the victims are believed to have been in contact with the machine when it blew up, and parts of their bodies were later found in the sea. Not one of the gathering on the beach escaped."

There was more ignorance afoot when Taoiseach Eamon de Valera was made privy to the unreported details of a sordid case going through the High Court. Dublin man Cyril Griffith maintained that he'd been coerced into a loveless marriage through a fear of criminal prosecution, jail, scandal and bad publicity. Griffith, who was 19 at the time he married, said he'd been forced into wedlock with Margaret Hayes by a "gross fraud" perpetrated by her and her mother. The man's lawyer wrote to the Taoiseach outlining the case, in the hope that Griffith would be left in peace by the State to marry a woman he loved without the threat of blackmail.

The solicitor said that his client had met Margaret Hayes only once, on the Hill of Howth, before he found himself being hustled into a shotgun wedding.

Some time after their lone encounter, the girl and her mother arrived at Griffith's father's shop. The girl was pregnant and she named Cyril as the father, much to his surprise. The solicitor wrote: "When the boy's father came on the scene, and heard what was alleged, he there and then insisted on his son marrying the girl. After the marriage, and after twins were born, who did not survive birth, the girl admitted to a priest and to others in writing that the allegation that her husband was the father of the children in question was false."

After the woman's admission, the young couple stopped living together. The Vatican granted an annulment and Cyril eventually met a woman he did actually want to marry. However, when he mentioned his wedding plans to his solicitor, he was warned that he would be committing bigamy because a Papal annulment was not the same as a civil divorce. The legal eagle wrote to de Valera, who consulted with his officials and sent the reply that the State wouldn't be in a hurry to prosecute his client for bigamy, no matter what the outcome of his day in court.

Polling day arrived with petrol in short supply. Bus services were curtailed and many cars were off the road, so extra schoolhouses and libraries were converted into voting centres. An elderly voter arrived into a Dublin centre chanting the mantra: "God bless De Valera." The man explained to officials that he was illiterate. When the list of candidates was read out to him he gave his first preference to a Fine Gael candidate and his second to an independent.

1940s-1950s

THE COMPLETE IGNORANCE OF ENGLISH
HOAX LETTERS TO TAOISIGH

The two main parties of liberated Ireland emerged from the same Sinn Féin gene pool, and they shared a vision that one day their partitioned island would be healed into a 32-County Irish-speaking paradise. For those who cared to examine the matter closely, the obstacles seemed pretty insurmountable, but since the prospect of an Irish-speaking Ireland was one of the founding myths of the new State, it was afforded a generous and widespread suspension of disbelief.

Although no workable plan was ever found for reviving Irish as the spoken tongue, it was not for the want of looking, and the National Archives contain reams of unworkable ones. One, which was clearly the product of a great deal of pooled thought and effort, was sent to Taoiseach Eamon de Valera in 1947 by a committee of clerics. Entitled A *Youth Movement To Save Irish*, the document proposed that at the end of the school day the nation's children would gather themselves in military-type units called 'Meitheal', to speak extra-curricular Irish. The authors wrote: "Each Meitheal is required to hold a Meitheal meeting for at least half-an-hour twice in each week ... Nothing but Irish must be spoken."

Led by a 'Ceann Mheithle' each unit of this elaborate kiddies' hierarchy would be part of a 'Buidhean' (company) directed by a 'Cinnire' and all the companies in a parish would form a 'Gasra' under a Ceann Ghasra. This nationwide grind movement would be called 'Cullacht na n-

Oglaoch' and would, with "God's help and cooperation", make Irish "the general language of the youth of Ireland".

To openly dissent from the patriotic aim of achieving an unachievable Irish-speaking Ireland was to invite taunts of "West Brit" and "traitor". Rather than risk that sort of flak, some conscientious objectors decided to subvert the revival project by becoming more Irish-loving than the Irish-lovers themselves.

Stored today in the National Archives, two of the most detailed schemes sent to Taoiseach Eamon de Valera in the 1940s for reviving the language are transparent hoaxes, although they may not have appeared so by the barmy standards of the day. One, drawn up by Walter Smithwick of Kilkenny in 1943, addresses issues such as the lack of advertising in the native tongue and the problem of postal addresses in English.

To spur the revival, Smithwick sent the Taoiseach a list of "Practical Suggestions". He argued that "all advertisements must be in Irish without any translation". He felt it allowable that a temporary derogation could be made for "Garda notices of the loss or theft of dangerous drugs", "notices from English firms looking for workers" and "notices from abroad looking for heirs to American estates". He also maintained that if road signs and shop signs were made conform to "standard types", they could be used as tools to promote the Irish language. He explained: "There should be a standing order that the letters of the notices should not be less than a given size, thus bringing the word before the eye as well as furthering the knowledge of the language."

Proposing that society's betters should set a good example for the lower orders, he wrote: "An appeal should go out to all lawyers, doctors and business people to change their names into Irish." He urged that after a grace period of one year "the Post Office should be empowered to refuse delivery of letters where the names of the town and county are not in

Gaelic". All English newspapers would be banned under the scheme, except those which published Irish language editions. Amongst polite society, gambling with playing cards was widely regarded as a distraction of scoundrels and wastrels. Smithwick suggested that the backs of these cards should carry illustrations "devoted to Irish culture". He added: "Monopoly [And] Snakes & Ladders should be in Irish and all other languages prohibited absolutely."

Two years later in 1945, Francis McConville of Clontarf in Dublin sent the Taoiseach an even more radical proposal which he hoped would achieve "the complete ignorance of English" within decades. In a lengthy and detailed document, he wrote: "Only by ensuring that a fresh generation cannot speak English will it be possible to eliminate it as the dominant language." McConville explained: "The solution involves the conversion of the existing primary day schools into primary boarding schools, staffed with Irish-speaking teachers who will impart instruction exclusively through the medium of Irish, and with Irish-speaking domestics who will look after the material well-being of the pupils outside school hours and will provide for their wants as those wants would be otherwise provided for in their own home."

The State's existing schools would be expanded into internment camps for the nation's children. Compulsory purchase orders would be slapped on surrounding buildings which would be commandeered for dormitories. McConville said that the scheme didn't entirely involve breaking up families, because parents would have visiting rights. He wrote: "The children would still be close to their parents' homes and would readily be seen at suitable times and at regular intervals by the parents. One can readily visualise the results: children at five or six years of age being introduced to such a school and leaving it at, say, 15 or 16 or 17 years of age unable to speak a word of any language but Irish."

The process would involve pain for some, he conceded, but in a good cause: "Quite a number of pupils – aged, say, ten to 13 years – will be so far through a course of education through the medium of English that a change over to complete instruction in Irish will embarrass them. It will adversely affect some. But it must be borne in mind that the restoration of the Irish language is warfare, and wars connote casualties." He added: "Opposition to the restoration of the language should be made a matter of treason against the State."

He continued: "In the foregoing suggestions I have absolutely ignored the questions of cost because I have assumed that such questions will not be allowed for one moment to influence the issue. The restoration of the Irish language to its rightful place is comparable to a war – a war for the restoration of lost territory – and wars, to be won, must, as we know, be conducted with a reckless disregard of expense."

Thanking McConville for his proposal, de Valera's Departmental Secretary regretted that the Taoiseach "is of the opinion that it would be impossible to get public agreement to a scheme of the magnitude outlined by you".

A decade later, in March 1956, Fine Gael's John A Costello was Taoiseach at the head of the State's second Inter-Party government. He received a letter posted in Spain and addressed to "Excellence John Costello, President of the Republic". It read:

Excellence,

I am very interesting in yuor county's history, and I can't find a good one, a popular one, able to be extended among the Spanish people, and, if it would be possible, to be translated into Spanish language later. I think the beste way to know a people and his History is to rend its own authors with to national judgement. I

*will be very glad and very thanks if your Excellence would send
me one.*

*I am excuse for my audicity because is very know your
generosity. And I carry my audacity until you entreat your
signature on the first page of the book.*

Aurelio Diez Gomez

The Department of the Taoiseach passed on the request to
the Department of External Affairs which recommended
that the Taoiseach send the writer A *History Of Ireland* by
Edmund Curtis. Perhaps detecting the prank, the External
Affairs official reminded his counterpart in the Department
of the Taoiseach that the request specifically asked for the
book to be personally autographed by Costello.

At this point the Taoiseach himself appears to have
smelled a rat, and a request was sent back to External Affairs
to check out the bona fides of Aurello Diez Gomez. The last
correspondence on the matter in the National Archives is
from External Affairs back to the Taoiseach's Department. It
says: "We have been informed by the Ambassador in Madrid
that he regrets he has no information about this man and, as
he lives in a remote part of the country, it would be virtually
impossible to obtain it."

1944

THE BABY AT THE CHRISTENING AND THE REMAINS AT THE FUNERAL

The Incumbents: Fianna Fáil led by Eamon de Valera.
Slogan: A party in coalition has no faith in itself.
Promise: Even more strong government!
The Challengers: Fine Gael led by WT Cosgrave.
Slogan: Fianna Fáil are the party of dictatorship.
Promise: To be less dictatorial than Fianna Fáil.
The Mood of the Country: War weary.
Prediction: Fianna Fáil to get an increased majority.
Result: Fianna Fáil get an increased majority.
Entertainment value: 4/10.

A Hoax Fire Alarm

The opposition had run Fianna Fáil very close in the general election of 1943, but at the start of 1944 the Labour Party split, with the new National Labour Party breaking away on the grounds that the party's Dublin Executive was a "hub of Communist organisation". National Labour branded itself as staunchly Catholic and implacably opposed to all things socialist. Those left in the original Labour Party taunted that the splitters were actually working to a Fianna Fáil agenda.

When De Valera's weak government was narrowly defeated on a Transport Bill, he took the opportunity to call a snap election which caught the fractured opposition off-guard. The Taoiseach said that he'd called the contest as an act of faith in the Irish people, who could repay that faith by acting in the national interest and giving him a bigger majority.

The Taoiseach told the voters that the media, with the exception of his own *Irish Press*, was working to fiendishly thwart the best interests of the country at a difficult and dangerous time. He declared: "I want you to distrust all the newspapers. They have been opposed to us defiantly during all the time we have been working in the national interest." *The Irish Times* was still calling for the formation of an all-party national government to see Ireland through the war. The Taoiseach's response was: "They want instability. They must have some reasons and I leave that for you to guess." His colleague Erskine Childers came straight out with the 'c' word, charging that there was "a conspiracy" to bring down Fianna Fáil.

De Valera said that the main issue of the election was strong government, which only a stable Fianna Fáil majority could provide. Coalition, on the other hand, was a cracked beam which would bring down the ceiling and everything else on top. He explained: "If you want to hold up a mass of masonry with a beam, you would like to get a sound beam, not one that is cracked because it will not stand any strain." A vote for coalition, he insisted, was "a venture into the unknown". Séan Lemass added that: "Coalition government is, at best, a stop-gap arrangement capable only of dealing with day-to-day problems."

As Minister For Supplies, Lemass extended the current tea ration until after polling day, despite a government warning before the snap election call, that it was due to be cut to half an ounce per person per week. In order to conserve supplies of petrol for the storm gathering over Europe – the D-Day landings were imminent – Lemass announced a ban on the use of cars to transport voters to polling stations. Some public transport was still going, and with the arrival of summer it delivered day-trippers from Dublin's seaside resorts back into the city centre where they mingled with crowds attending the final election rallies. One observer wrote: "Jaunting cars, growlers, landaus, brakes and coaches jammed all thoroughfares." A hoax fire alarm brought two fire engines speeding into the middle of a Fine Gael rally at Stephen's Green where they became "jammed" in the throng. When a Fianna Fáil meeting at the GPO ended at just about the same time, hundreds of supporters set off to 'invade' the Fine Gael rally on the other side of the Liffey.

Holidaymakers and party faithful weren't the only ones mobilising in numbers. One report described "the destruction of flowers valued at £30 by a party of women and children who recently entered Herbert Park and proceeded to a systematic uprooting of flowers from carefully laid-out beds. Gardeners and rangers who pursued them received no cooperation from a number of people who had witnessed the occurrence and the culprits escaped. It is believed that the raid was organised with a view to stealing the flowers for sale."

The Last Election Ever Held In Ireland

Labour's William Norton said de Valera's decision to call an election when the Allied invasion of Europe was due any day was "a wanton act of political gamblers" when the country should be stocking up on food and fuel.

The opposition singled out the Taoiseach's repeated and pointed attacks on the proportional representation (PR) voting system as evidence that he planned to abolish it and install himself as a virtual dictator under a first past the post system. *The Irish Times* said: "Proportional representation manifestly is the immediate nigger in the Taoiseach's woodpile." Under PR, it argued, "his dictatorial style is cramped". Fine Gael dubbed Fianna Fáil 'The Party of

Dictatorship'. Labour's William Norton said De Valera wanted one-man government, on the condition that he was that one man. "He wants to be the bridegroom at the wedding, the baby at the Christening and the remains at the funeral," said Norton.

The farmers' party, Clann na Talmhan, said that this might be the last free election ever held in Ireland, because if Dev got in again "he will appoint a dictator and the franchise (to vote) is gone". The party also attacked the "dictatorial whim" of Minister Frank Aiken who had ordered *The Irish Times* to stop using the name Kingstown and only print its approved form, Dun Laoghaire. Hostilities between Fianna Fáil and *The Irish Times* had escalated since the newspaper had called for an all-party national government a year earlier. Now the paper editorialised: "The choice before the electors is plain. On the one hand Mr De Valera is asking for *carte blanche* to give effect to his preposterous policy of a Gaelic-speaking, potato-digging republic, presumably standing in more or less splendid isolation, apart and aloof from the rest of the civilized world, governed by a man who sees in the recesses of his own heart the fundamental wishes of the whole people, and who will brook no criticism or interference of any kind from anybody else. On the other hand, the parties of the opposition – in some respects, admittedly, not particularly a well assorted lot – are standing for the essential principles of democracy."

Fianna Fáil's irrepressible Séan MacEntee had a ready answer to those calling for a national government. According to him, Fianna Fáil already *was* a national government – a one-stop shop successfully representing all sections of the community. He denounced the "secret policy" whispering campaign of the opposition parties. He insisted that the calling of the snap election just a year after the last had "caused dismay in the ranks of the conspirators who found themselves blown up with their own dynamite". He asserted that the opposition, in defeating the Taoiseach in the Dáil vote, had "wantonly dragged down" the man who was the very embodiment of Ireland in the eyes of the world, and all "to secure a party political advantage". By this act of treachery, Fianna Fáil's rivals had sent a signal to the international community that Ireland was led by a man who didn't enjoy the full confidence of his people, and this at a time when Europe was teetering on the brink. With the Allied troops massing to cross the English Channel, the Taoiseach was now giving the voters the solemn opportunity to either make Ireland more safe, or more at risk.

Fine Gael again called on de Valera to participate in a national government if he failed to get an overall majority. He rubbished the notion, saying: "If I am not required to do the work of the country, there is other work I could do." For instance, he said, he could dedicate himself as a private citizen to the task of restoring the Irish language.

A Portion Dealing With Gonorrhoea Is Torn Away

Partially down to the fact that Dublin had become a vacation point for Allied troops based in Northern Ireland, sexually transmitted diseases (STDs) had become so rampant in the capital that nearly all the city's hospitals had opened special wards to cope with the upsurge. *The Irish Times* broke the embarrassed silence on the matter, running the headline DOCTORS WANT PUBLIC WARNED ON VD MENACE. The number of patients seeking treatment at Dr Steevens' Hospital had skyrocketed from 15,184 in 1941 to 25,790 in 1943.

Declaring "a very grave national danger", a top medic told the newspaper: "The first step will be the obvious one of dispelling the secrecy, ignorance and prejudice which surrounds the problem." Somewhat undermining his own case, the doctor declined to be identified. He went on to call on the government to launch a publicity campaign to save the sexually incontinent from "physical deformity, great pain and possible blindness and insanity". *The Irish Times* report chided the government for its inaction. It stated: "The only accessible warning is to be found in the National Library where, on a shelf at the back of the reading room, an *Encyclopaedia Britannica* has a three-page technically-worded reference to the disease, written 34 years ago. There is no reference to preventative treatment, and a portion of the page dealing with gonorrhoea is torn away."

Forced into action, the Department of Health announced a national inquiry into VD. *The Irish Times* had pinpointed the source of the epidemic to "a small number of lounge bars and inferior cafes" in the capital, prompting some members of the Joint Commission of Women's Bodies to call for women police to patrol Dublin's quays. The government declared that an "extravagant publicity" campaign was unnecessary to combat the dangers of VD. A spokesman slammed *The Irish Times* reporting as "misleading" and insisted it was "quite incorrect to say that the only accessible warning in regard to the disease is to be found in the *Encyclopaedia Britannica* in the National Library", although he didn't elaborate on where else information might be found. The President of the Medical Association of Eire, Dr JP Shanley, was the first and only medic to supply a comment on the VD issue using his own name. The only thing he wanted to clarify for the Irish public was that the Association had never discussed VD in any way, shape or form.

1947

WE HAVE TOO MANY SISSIES IN THIS COUNTRY
THE STRUGGLE FOR AN
IRISH-SPEAKING IRELAND

In 1947, a full quarter-century after winning independence from Britain, the great march towards an Irish-speaking rural Utopia had come up against a dead end of poverty, shortages, unemployment, bad housing, emigration, isolation, Hollywood movies and jazz music. The national spirit was flagging and the blame had to lie somewhere. Fine Gael's Patrick Giles was sure he knew where. The Meath TD told the Dáil: "We have too many sissies in this country."

By 'sissies', the ex-Army Captain meant any unmanly male who would prefer soft city living to the rugged, wholesome rural life. He explained: "We have not turned out the product I would like to see. We have not turned out men suitable for country life. Ninety percent of the people should be turned out like that." Giles added: "If there are people who want to go to the city they should have to fend for themselves."

If the sissies polluting the national stock were a problem, they were also a symptom. Giles argued that they were the spawn of teachers who lacked any real commitment to their vocation, and lacked the 1916 spirit. He explained: "In my day they brought the pupils back after hours and gave them lectures on how to be good and noble and, chiefly, to be natural. There were very few sissies turned out then, as was shown by the national struggle from 1916 to 1921 which was carried on by the products of the schools of those days."

It wasn't entirely the teachers' fault. Their morale was low because their belt-wielding hands were bound "with far too many regulations". He said: "I know some teachers need to be tied up by regulations because they have bad tempers, but they are a small minority. The majority are able to deal properly with the children if they are allowed, but they are not. There are many children who need a good spanking very often, but they are not getting it." Any commonsense parent would condone, not condemn, the beatings. On hearing the teacher's reasons for dispensing the punishment, they would say: "You did not give him half enough."

Demoralised teachers and over-regulation were partly to blame for the rising number of sissies, but the real culprit, as ever, was England. As ever too, the only workable solution was the complete abandonment of the English language, which sustained the "slave mind" of the sissy.

For a start, if the Irish people didn't speak English they would instantly be freed from their growing slavery to imported sissy ideas. Giles observed: "If we had an Irish-speaking nation here we need not give two hoots about the cinemas and books that come in from abroad, because we would be able to withstand them. It is because Irish is not the spoken language of the country that these things are liable to do harm."

Deputy Giles found cross-party support for his contention that an Irish-speaking Ireland would solve a lot of problems besetting the country. Deputy Butler argued that compulsory Irish wasn't turning people off; it was those spreading the "propaganda" that it was turning people off who were *really* turning people off. Deputy MacCarthaigh lamented: "If it were a question of compulsory French or compulsory anything else, everybody would be delighted with it. Because it is their own native language they scorn it."

The debate turned to the possible role parents could play in making Irish once again the spoken language of the people, but Deputy McMenamin pointed out: "I am doubtful whether in poor homes, where the mother is busy all day, the children can get any assistance in their studies. When the mother gets up in the morning she has, first of all, to get the breakfast and turn the children out to school. She has then to milk the cows, prepare food for hens and pigs, and get ready meals for the men who are going out to work." Besides, said McMenamin: "I wonder if it is prudent to attempt to teach children two languages in a home of that kind."

Having teased it out further, he decided: "I think it would be better to take the bold step of concentrating on Irish and nothing but Irish." Having concluded that the nation's children should be instructed at home in Irish only, Deputy McMenamin allowed for one exception. Native speaking children in gaeltacht areas should be taught English in the home so that they wouldn't be at a disadvantage when forced to emigrate in search of work.

In 1949, two years after his alert against sissies, Captain Giles was confronted with a new threat on his own doorstep when English impresario Billy Butlin opened a holiday camp at Mosney in his Meath constituency. Giles outlined his objections to this "foreign combine" in an article for the *Catholic Standard* headlined HOLIDAY CAMP AND MORALS.

He asserted: "Holiday camps are an English idea and are alien and undesirable in an Irish Catholic country – outside influences are bad and dangerous." But the bad influences were winning out that year, with Senator Feargal Quinn's father, Eamonn, opening a second holiday camp down the coast in Skerries.

When the government proposed a new tax on amusements, voices were raised for rural Ireland to be given preferential treatment to the towns and cities, with calls for the tax to only apply in the latter. This raised the objection that the "100% Irish" camp close to the town of Skerries would pay, while Billy Butlins' English one out in the middle of nowhere would not.

Unable to prevent Butlin's Mosney from opening, Giles and the bishops secured the concession that a Catholic church would be built right outside its gate, with a chaplain resident to police morals.

1948

THIS COUNTRY WILL BE DOOMED

The Incumbents: Fianna Fáil led by Eamon de Valera.
Slogan: You can't make a chisel out of chips.
Promise: Strong government again.
The Challengers: Fine Gael led by General Richard Mulcahy.
Slogan: The Taoiseach is going daft.
Promise: To end 16 years of Fianna Fáil rule.
The Mood of the Country: Itching for a change.
Prediction: Fianna Fáil to lose.
Result: Fianna Fáil lose. Five other parties in government.
Entertainment value: 5/10.

Slain Gandhi Backs Fianna Fáil

During the previous two elections, held against a backdrop of wartime shortages and a thriving black market, allegations of government sleaze had failed to dislodge Fianna Fáil. However, in 1948, the ruling party faced a new force which pitched itself as younger, more republican, more vigorous and more virtuous. Campaigning under the banner of "Clean Politics", Clann na Phoblachta characterised Fianna Fáil as the party of profiteers and racketeers which had run short of ideas and ideals after 16 long years in power.

De Valera refused to admit that the chips were down, despite defections from Fianna Fáil to the upstart rival. He remarked: "You are told by some of the new parties that they have got some Fianna Fáil members. Of course, most of you have seen a good chisel with chips flying off it. Many a chisel has lost chips, but did you ever see anybody collecting the chips and trying to make another chisel out of them?"

Some of Fianna Fáil's campaigning smacked of the arrogance and complacency of which Clann na Phoblachta accused them. The intrepid Séan MacEntee said the election had been called 18 months early because there was a chance that World War III could break out at any moment, in which desperate circumstance the voters must restore the strong government eroded by two by-election defeats. De Valera threatened the electorate that if they failed to give him a sufficiently strong mandate, they'd be made try again until they got it right. He told the people: "We ask you not to have a second general election to do this." On another occasion, the Taoiseach ruminated: "If we do not get a majority, this country is going to be doomed." This prompted Independent Deputy JM Dillon to scoff: "When a politician announces that if he is not re-elected the country is doomed, it is time for him to ask himself whether he is not going daft."

Clann na Phoblachta accused Fianna Fáil of running scared of the youth vote, by calling the election for a date just two months before a new electoral register would enfranchise tens of thousands. An advert said: "Clann na Phoblachta is a young movement – it is not yet properly organised; it has little or no money; it is not backed by 'big money' interests. All the Fianna Fáil leaders are in receipt of large salaries paid by you. They do their electioneering work in your time with a fleet of State cars and drivers paid by you. Sixteen years of political patronage, of pensions and job-giving, and of license and quota-giving, have given them power in certain quarters. Financial interests, war profiteers and racketeers support Fianna Fáil – and well they might."

The new party's leader, Séan MacBride, accused the government of burying an investigation into an alleged petrol rationing scam involving friends of Fianna Fáil.

Fianna Fáil said it was up to the Gardaí to decide whether they wanted to pursue the allegations.

De Valera attacked those alleging sleaze, charging: "They are damaging the whole community." He continued: "They are charges not merely against the personnel of the government, but charges fundamentally against your nation." The Taoiseach condemned such allegations as unpatriotic in the extreme. He explained: "When we go abroad representing you, we don't want to meet people who will think 'These fellows are a corrupt lot, a corrupt gang, and the less we have to do with them the better'. They will naturally say 'If these are the people the Irish people put in office, the Irish people either have very little judgement or themselves cannot have a very high standard'." He repeated: "If I go to represent the country abroad, or whoever might represent it in my place, he does not want to be pointed to as a member of a corrupt government."

Defence Minister Oscar Traynor added that the sleaze charges were vindictive and unworthy, given that De Valera was recognised as "the leading statesman in the world today". This was confirmed by Mahatma Gandhi from beyond the grave. As *The Irish Press* splashed the news of Gandhi's assassination across its front page, one of its top stories reported that the slain colossus had "recognised Mr De Valera as a man of outstanding vision". As polling day drew nearer, Dev's *Irish Press* carried a series of anonymous essays by soul-searching individuals on the general theme of 'Why I'll Be Voting Fianna Fáil This Time'.

Besmirching Ireland's Good Name

Rising to the challenge of the new party, Fianna Fáil's Seán MacEntee said that during the Emergency years of 1939-45, people who were now in Clann na Phoblachta had worked to overthrow the government and were against the Christian churches. Fianna Fáil said that many of the leaders of Clann na Phoblachta had been in the 'Red IRA' when that body had killed innocents in 1936, and had pressed the government to give the go-ahead for a border campaign against the Six Counties at the outbreak of war in 1939.

In response to this Red scare, the opposition gleefully dug up the fact that de Valera and his lieutenant, Harry Boland, had willingly climbed into bed with Soviet Russia back in 1922. De Valera and Boland had secretly handed over thousands of pounds raised to found an Irish Republic to the dastardly communists, allowing the Russians to pawn a cache of Soviet gems in return. At one MacEntee campaign meeting, fistfights broke out with hecklers yelling at him: "Where's your Russian jewels?"

Aggressive campaigning was a feature of the 1948 election. One fair day in Longford Town, Fianna Fáil's Erskine Childers was orating outside the courthouse through a microphone when a Clann na Phoblachta lorry pulled up provocatively on the opposite side of the street. Noel Hartnett climbed onto the back of the truck and began a tirade, jabbing his finger at the Junior Minister for Local Government. Childers retorted: "This is the sort of democracy we can expect from them. They tried to destroy our neutrality during the war and now they want to destroy freedom of speech."

The din became deafening as the bid for greater volume escalated. When one speaker produced a second microphone, so did the other. When one materialised a third microphone, the other matched him again. The shouting match carried on for an hour and a half, before Childers moved on to his next port of call, leaving Hartnett to carry on speaking for a further hour.

In Kerry, Fianna Fáil complained of a "malicious" attempt to put a De Valera public meeting in the dark after wire or metal was thrown over cables, causing the automatic switches at Ballybeggan Power Station to trip out. At

Listowel the lights also went out just five minutes before the Taoiseach was due to speak. Happily he was running late and wasn't too put out.

About an hour before a Clann na Phoblachta meeting was due to start in Dun Laoghaire, the party's scroll was stolen from the speaking platform and petrol was poured over the five leather chairs assigned to the speakers. When party leader Séan MacBride belatedly rose to speak, he accused the Taoiseach of instructing his "henchmen" to spread lies that there were godless communists in Clann na Phoblachta.

Clann na Phoblachta made the running on the propaganda front with a party political movie entitled *Our Country*. Made in England at Elstree Studios by the Irish Film Unit, the film curiously made no mention of the party's name. Fifty copies went into cinemas and more were distributed to towns and villages with no cinema where they were screened on walls and doors at markets and fairs. The film featured scenes of grinding poverty, prompting MacEntee to accuse the new party of trying to make a name for itself by "besmirching" Ireland's image abroad.

When MacEntee demanded to know where Clann na Phoblachta got the money to make their movie, he already had the answer prepared. He claimed to have in his possession a letter from a priest in England telling him that the movie had been secretly financed by an underground organisation with its headquarters in Belfast, meaning the IRA. He complained that the grocer's assistant in the film was an imposter acting as a "bogus grocer's assistant, pleading a bogus scarcity to a bogus customer who didn't look like she was suffering malnutrition despite the signs saying 'No Eggs' and 'No Bacon'. One element missing was a sign saying 'No Truth'."

Fine Gael accused Fianna Fáil of using the British media to aid its election campaign. Weeks earlier the government had invited the BBC to broadcast what Fine Gael called "an exaggerated and untruthful account of Fianna Fáil's achievements as an authoritative statement of Irish conditions".

Dr Conor Byrne of Clann na Phoblachta said that compulsory Irish in the schools and the practice of teaching through Irish amounted to "the mental murder of the children of the country". To refute this, the language enthusiast Senator Seán O'Donabhain brought five "mentally murdered youths" onto his speaking platform at Fairview to testify that they had survived being taught through Irish.

No Recollection Of Hitting Any Cars

As polling day approached, Walter Pogue of Wicklow was disqualified from driving for life. He had been stopped while steering his truck in a zigzag manner, causing crates to topple off and damage two cars. A policeman flagged him down in the Dublin suburb of Dundrum. In order to establish whether Pogue was drunk, the guard ordered him to get back behind the wheel and drive 100 yards down the road and back. On his return journey, Pogue's lorry swerved across the road and smashed into a car. In court, the defendant said he had no recollection of hitting any cars or losing the crates, and thought that his faulty driving might have been down to nervousness.

When the votes were tallied, the nervousness evident in Fianna Fáil throughout the campaign proved to be well-founded. After 16 years of unbroken rule, Eamon de Valera's party was ousted by a coalition of Fine Gael, The Labour party, Clann na Phoblachta, Clann na Talmhan, National Labour and Independents.

In order to cement the alliance which encompassed former antagonists, the Fine Gael leader Richard Mulcahy stood aside from the post of Taoiseach in favour of his party colleague John A Costello.

1951

THE EMIGRATION OF GIRLS

The Incumbents: A coalition led by John A Costello (FG).
Slogan: Don't condemn us for obeying the law of God.
Promise: To keep Fianna Fáil out of office.
The Challengers: Fianna Fáil led by Eamon de Valera.
Slogan: Coalitions don't work.
Promise: The restoration of strong government.
The Mood of the Country: Destitute and despairing.
Prediction: Fianna Fáil to oust the coalition.
Result: Fianna Fáil oust the coalition.
Entertainment value: 4/10

Coalition Is A Drunken Man

Fianna Fáil had succeeded in making the term 'coalition' a dirty word with Irish voters, with the result that the five-party coalition which took power in 1948 had called itself an Inter-Party Government in an attempt to ward off the stigma of instability. After three years in office, the coalition had notched up some achievements, in particular an effective drive to wipe out tuberculosis. However, cracks increasingly began to show after Health Minister Noel Browne went on a solo run and unveiled plans for a free Mother And Child Health Care Scheme which was denounced by his own party leader, Séan MacBride, as the thin end of the Red wedge. A failing economy and a brace of defections persuaded Taoiseach John A Costello of Fine Gael to call an election for June 1951.

As polling day approached, the outgoing Education Minister Richard Mulcahy accused Fianna Fáil of stooping to the old English dirty trick of "divide and conquer". However, the most dynamic of the five government parties, Clann na Phoblachta, was hopelessly split without any outside intervention. Clann na Phoblachta's Deputy Jack McQuillan revealed the details of a spat between the party's leader, Séan MacBride and the party's Health Minister Noel Browne. MacBride had accused Browne of disloyalty. McQuillan told the press: "In proof of this allegation a dossier was produced at this meeting by Mr MacBride giving an almost word-for-word account of every private conversation between the two men for twelve months. I was aghast that any man would deliberately make a careful note of every phrase used by another man in a private and friendly conversation for the purpose of using it in evidence against him later."

Noel Browne's attempt to introduce State-provided care for mothers and their infants provoked howls of protest from the medical profession, who saw it as an attack on private practice and an attempt to incorporate them into the public service. The medics swiftly got the Catholic Bishops on board their campaign to stamp out the Red threat of 'socialised' medicine. James Fitzgerald-Kenney of Fine Gael told voters that the government had no choice but to resign in order to reject Browne's affront to the Catholic Church. Was the electorate now going to condemn Fine Gael for observing the Law of God? As the lights went out all over Ireland due to enforced power cuts, Kenney's party colleague, Justice Minister Séan MacEoin, blamed "fifth columnists" in the pocket of Moscow for spreading a mood of despair which was clearly not helping the government's satisfaction ratings.

Fianna Fáil, meanwhile, had a field-day, greeting the collapse of the Inter-Party administration as proof positive of what they'd been saying all along – that coalitions just don't work. The latest in a long line of De Valera metaphors for coalition was that of a drunken man: "He staggers forwards and backwards, left and right, and then finds himself flat in the mud." MacEntee charged that for government by consent, the coalition had substituted "government by convulsion". He added: "What one of them says today, another is certain to contradict tomorrow."

De Valera warned voters not to be sidetracked by "false issues" when there was only one issue. He declared: "The issue before the country at the moment is – do you want coalition or do you not? The other questions raised are not issues at all." As if to make the point that current issues were largely irrelevant to the election, he sought votes from the people of Achill, Co Mayo, on his party's record during World War II which had ended six years earlier. He told them: "If Fianna Fáil had nothing else to show from 1939-45, except that we saved our people from the consequences of the war, they would have done a magnificent piece of work."

Irish Workers Sleeping In Relays

With a deeply Freudian typo, *The Evening Herald* reported that the census of 1951 was "the biggest census of copulation ever taken in the State". The population survey recorded that tens of thousands of mostly young Irish people were emigrating each year to work in British factories and labour on the rebuilding of England's industrial cities which had been bombed by the Germans. Before the Dáil dissolved, questions were tabled to Inter-Party Ministers under the heading EMIGRATION OF GIRLS. One Fianna Fáil Deputy suggested that young Irish girls were being lured under false pretenses to England, where they were being led off the straight and narrow.

He asked the Minister for Social Welfare, "if his attention has been drawn to advertisements appearing in the Irish daily newspapers specially drawn up for the purpose of encouraging the emigration of young Irish girls to Britain as student nurses, and whether, in view of the dishonest nature of many of these advertisements, he will cause the Government to take such steps as are necessary to prohibit their continued publication?" The Minister replied that there was no evidence that the adverts had any evil intent, and that in any case he didn't have the legal authority to ban them.

As the election campaign got underway, civil servants were busy completing a report on the scope for "incidents of immorality" amongst the Irish swarming unchaperoned to Britain for work. The study, which landed on the desk of incoming Taoiseach De Valera, reported: "A Catholic welfare officer stated that from her experience 75% of Irish girls becoming pregnant do so by Irish boys. A barman had three children by different Irish girls. A clippie, previously a good Irish girl, got into trouble, and was too ashamed and frightened to take anyone into her confidence. She worked on until one day she collapsed on the bus … [and] died along with her child in hospital. Another Irish girl living with a coloured man had a baby by him." The study told scare stories of Irish girls having their babies adopted by non-Catholic families.

The report cited many instances of married Irish men going to England "in good faith" to seek work. However, it said that the men would then often drop out of contact with their families, and that some wives back in Ireland were resorting to the desperate measure of applying for a police warrant to have their husbands tracked down and dragged back to them. However, it continued: "Many of their wives, fearing scandal and gossip in Ireland, are reluctant to approach the police and write to priests over here [Britain], hoping something can be done. Most of these men are to be found living with some other woman."

The Reverend TT Dinan, an Irish priest based in Birmingham, said he knew of Irish construction workers sleeping "in relays" because they only had access to their beds and tiny flats on a timeshare basis. He remarked regretfully: "They have no home life and are forced to spend their leisure in dance halls and public houses where they meet bad characters." Irish journalists following up the story reported back from England that Irish workers over there had to endure living conditions only slightly better than those of "the negro".

When polling day came, the electorate gave the thumbs down to the bickering five-party government. Settled back into the Taoiseach's Department, De Valera made a speech in Galway saying that Irish migrants in the English midlands were living in "absolute degradation". He urged them to come home to a better life in Ireland, although he was short on the details of how the stagnant Irish economy would facilitate this. His speech raised a storm of protest from English landladies, civic officials and health workers. The Deputy Mayor of Birmingham called it "perfect nonsense and a waste of time. If Mister De Valera thinks we were waiting for him to tell us that there are housing difficulties in Birmingham he has got another thought coming". The Mayor added that if the Taoiseach had "any constructive suggestions" he, and the good burghers of Birmingham, would be "very glad to hear from him".

1954

THE CENTIPEDE IN THE DITCH

The Incumbents: Fianna Fáil led by Eamon de Valera.
Slogan: Strong government.
Promise: To keep out "backroom boys" with "radical policies".
The Challengers: Fine Gael led by Richard Mulcahy.
Slogan: We'll be more effective than a dead mouse.
Promise: To make no promises.
The Mood of the Country: Profoundly depressed and listless.
Prediction: A close run thing.
Result: The second Inter-Party government is voted in.
Entertainment value: 4/10

As Effective As A Dead Mouse

As the election campaign got underway, one newspaper
cheered up the nation with the news that the past year had
been the BEST YEAR EVER FOR LEPERS. The revenue of
the Mission To Lepers had risen to £2,177 for 1953.
However, when Posts & Telegraphs Minister Erskine
Childers made a simultaneous claim that 1953 had been
"Ireland's greatest year" in general, with spending way up on
"the pleasant amusements of life", there were very few takers.
Labour's William Norton retorted that the only ones who'd
had a great year were "the government's friends, the dance
hall proprietors and tobacco manufacturers". Even at that,
the economy was in such a state of shambles that Norton was
probably guilty of overstating his case.

Alongside the abject poverty of the country, there was

the abject poverty of the political thinking. This was reflected in James Dillon's election promise that Fine Gael made no promises but to do their best. De Valera also advised the electorate to set their sites low, saying: "We might all agree that it would be worthwhile to get to the moon or Mars. It is how to get there that is the problem." Despite branding the government's economic policy "as effective as a dead mouse", Fine Gael proposed only "careful changes" to it, leading Fianna Fáil to accuse its rivals of copying its policies.

Fine Gael accused Fianna Fáil of "dishonest propaganda", by putting it about that the opposition party planned to cut children's allowance. Fine Gael said it was Fianna Fáil who had the secret plans, and that the government was preparing to cut the dole once the election was out of the way. Most bizarrely, Fine Gael's John A Costello accused Fianna Fáil of waging a whispering campaign, by broadcasting the lie that Fine Gael planned to attack the Protestant community by rolling back their Constitutional rights.

Fianna Fáil in turn accused Fine Gael of telling voters a pack of lies about Eamon de Valera, by alleging that the Taoiseach had hidden like a yellowbelly in the United States during the struggle for independence, that he'd operated a secret pact with Britain during World War II, and that he was now in the pockets of British financiers. Fianna Fáil warned that in any coalition involving Fine Gael and Labour, the Red tail would wag the dog with Labour dictating "radical policies" orchestrated by shady "backroom boys".

De Valera's latest meditation on coalition was unveiled in Killarney, where he likened multi-party government to something that should be squelched underfoot. He regaled his audience with the following lines: *"The centipede was happy/Until the snail in fun/Inquired which leg came after which?/Which worked its mind to such a pitch/It lay distracted in a ditch/Considering how to run."*

We Have No Beaver But We Hope To Get One

Borrowing a wartime scheme from its London counterpart, Dublin Zoo invited individuals or firms to adopt "lonely animals" by sponsoring their feed and upkeep for a year. An elephant would cost around £200; a lion, tiger or sea lion £100; a leopard or puma £50 and so on. In return, the sponsor could have their name on the animal's cage. The Zoo was forced to make the appeal because attendance revenue was down and the cost of feeding the animals had soared. A Zoo official revealed that one holiday company with a beaver on its logo had made inquiries about adopting one of the water-going rodents. However, he remarked: "At the moment we have no beaver but we hope to get one." The official expressed concern that with horsemeat so scarce and pricy, the Zoo might have to soon start feeding the lions on whale meat.

To some humans, the Zoo animals with a roof over their heads seemed positively pampered. A story came to light of a homeless Cork woman and her two children who were found freezing in the snow with no shelter. An ambulance was called to take the distressed trio to the hospital at Fermoy. However, when they arrived at the hospital they were refused admission and the ambulance was instructed to dump them back in the snow and ice at Buttevant. Defending this hard-hearted treatment, an unflinching Cork Assistant County Manager told the press: "Fermoy is a county hospital, not a county home."

Elsewhere in Cork, Archbishop Lucey put forward a suggestion for boosting the flagging economy and the equally flagging Irish language in one fell swoop. "He proposed a factory or industrial estate in Ballingeary – not one employing a few girls, but one employing men, the daily use of Irish to be a condition of employment, and neglect of the language to entail loss of the job." On polling day in Ennis, Co Clare, a presiding officer delayed the start of the voting until the Rosary had been said in honour of Our Lady, on account of the fact that the Vatican had declared 1954 a Marian Year.

The President of the GAA, Vincent O'Donoghue, neatly dovetailed the topics of the Irish language and Christianity when he demanded that the Minister for Defence forbid the playing of foreign games within the Irish Army. He thundered: "Why not national games for a national army? Why foster so assiduously in an Irish army the games and pastimes and the cult of Imperial England – Ireland's one and only enemy, now as ever?"

The GAA's President next turned his attention to schools and colleges which tolerated foreign games. While he expected no better from "the select group of imperialist colleges whose tradition has been, and still is, openly anti-Irish", he did expect better from those "loud in their Christianity and professing a mild interest in the language revival. They stultify themselves by their excessive devotion to the games cult of a pagan and decadent Britain." Supporting his President, GAA delegate M O'Rourke added: "It would be money well spent to print suitable extracts on the Association's stand against foreign games for wide distribution. [GAA] people sometimes find it difficult to meet the arguments of their opponents."

What Of The Bicycle Menace?
The Irish Association for the Prevention of Intemperance wanted to make drink an election issue. The Association urged voters to pressurise candidates to support a three-point plan.

1. "The taking of blood or breath tests from any motorist who is involved in a road accident."

2. "The total Sunday closing of all licensed premises in cities and towns, and revision of the laws relating to bona-fide traffic." (So-called bona-fide travellers were entitled to

consume alcohol outside the normal opening hours once they had travelled more than three miles from their point of origin. This led to entire town populations passing each other on the roads at night in pursuit of an after-hours tipple.)

3. "The people themselves in any new housing area to be given the democratic right, by their direct vote, to say whether they want licensed premises in their locality or not."

The temperance campaign was not a wild success.

Indeed, for one extremely angry judge, the Fianna Fáil government was fully committed to keeping Ireland sodden with drink. Justice Gleeson in Limerick District Court accused Justice Minister Gerry Boland of using "illegal" means to keep drink drivers out of jail. Boland had instructed the Gardaí not to execute an arrest warrant on a man convicted by the Judge. Justice Gleeson fumed: "This, of course, is by no means the first case of its kind. I have read a statement in the press which refers to what is called a 'settled practice'. Any such practice settled or not, is both illegal and unconstitutional." Giving two forthright fingers to the Judge, Boland responded: "There are cases in which, on reading a petition, the Minister is of the opinion that on full consideration he may deem that the sentence of imprisonment ought not be enforced."

Fine Gael's former Justice Minister James Fitzgerald-Kenney joined the fray, arguing: "If there is one thing more than another in this country that should be put down, it is the reckless driving of motor cars and the slaughtering and maiming and injuring of people on the roads by drunken drivers. If drivers are convicted of this offence they richly deserve the punishment they get and deserve to be put off the roads. But we find in the papers long lists of remissions of sentences and disqualifications imposed by the courts for drunken driving. Mr Boland puts the drunken driver back on the road to be a danger. Mr Boland puts them back in order to get the votes of themselves and their friends for his party. Mr Boland has taken power into his hand that the law does not give him and it is wrong."

Although the term 'road rage' had not yet been coined in 1954, a revolutionary hi-tech device had reportedly been invented to combat the already common condition. Under the headline BRAIN-WAVE SET FOR MOTORISTS, a report said: "A warning device, triggered by feelings of frustration or anger in motorists, could be fitted in cars to help to prevent road accidents. The device would provide a flashing signal or sound a gong to remind the driver that care and control were needed. There is no reason why these warning sets should not be made for highly-strung, hard-driving motorists who are prone to loss of temper."

Another headline asked ARE YOU A ROAD MENACE? The question wasn't for motorists alone. The writer explained: "Cars are not the only offenders. What of the bicycle menace? Dublin alone, sometimes known as 'The City Of The Bicycles', offers some startling lapses of road safety. Defective brakes, lack of rear lights, cycling three abreast, swerving unexpectedly, taking chances in crowded traffic – all play their part in the toll of road accidents."

The Prohibitive Cost Of Childcare

Shortly before the Dáil dissolved, the opposition raised the issue of a 14-year-old boy who had been severely punished with a leather strap by a Christian Brother in Dublin's Artane Industrial School. After receiving his first beating, he was ordered to present his hand for more blows with the edge of the strap. The boy retreated and grabbed a sweeping brush. At this point a second Christian Brother intervened and gave the boy a good hiding, breaking his arm in the process. It was two days before the boy was taken to hospital where the break was set in plaster, and longer still before his mother, who lived nearby, heard what had happened. The school's Superior refused to see the mother, and it was only after eight days, and appealing to her TD, that she was allowed to see her son. Even with eight days' recovery time, his condition shocked her.

The Minister for Education, Séan Moylan, told the Dáil: "I would be as much concerned as the Deputy is, if I thought it was anything other than a very isolated incident, and in one sense what might be called an accident." Moylan pointed out to his colleagues that there was a financial dimension to the affair, explaining: "It would be very difficult to improve the conditions under which schools like this operate, certainly without a very substantial subvention from this House for the upkeep of the schools and for the development of what may be essential and necessary there."

The Education Minister claimed: "I do not know how the edge of the strap is used, but I will make an inquiry into that." He repeated: "This is an isolated incident. It can only happen as an accident." He also repeated that you only get what you pay for, saying: "There are conditions that should be created in all these schools, they are deficient in many things; but that will cost a good deal more money from the State than the relatively small amount that is paid now."

Before the dissolution of the Dáil, a number of independent TDs joined Fine Gael, including Oliver J Flanagan and James Dillon. In Dillon's case, it was a matter of re-joining the Party of which he had once been Vice-President. He had been expelled from Fine Gael in 1942 because of his persistent calls for Ireland to enter World War II on the side of Britain. When the votes were counted, Fine Gael had ten seats more than after the previous election and formed a coalition government with the Labour Party, the Farmers' Party and Clann na Talmhan.

1957

NONE OF THE ABOVE

The Incumbents: Coalition led by John A Costello (Fine Gael).
Slogan: Fianna Fáil is really a coalition!
Promise: To keep out Fianna Fáil.
The Challengers: Fianna Fáil led by Eamon de Valera.
Slogan: To restore strong government.
Promise: Not to strangle the patient.
The Mood of the Country: Australia looks nice.
Prediction: A nil-all draw.
Result: Fianna Fáil returned.
Entertainment value: 1/10.

Too Many Tortured Missionaries

Joe Larkin of Fianna Fáil in Dublin pushed the boundaries of
overstatement to the outer limits early in the campaign when
he insisted: "The coming election is one of the most
important and critical that has ever taken place here." The
opposite was the case and everyone knew it.

There had been previous elections in equally grim times,
when there was little to separate the rival sides in terms of
the difference one would make from the other in
government. Generally, however, those tribal tests were to be
welcomed as a spot of fun and games on a rainswept, lonely
island.

By 1957, however, the nation had slipped into such a
slough of despond that, to many, getting out the bunting
seemed like more bother than it was worth. Throughout the

campaign, Fine Gael and Fianna Fáil resembled Tweedledum and Tweedledee urging the electorate not to mistake them for Tweedledee and Tweedledum.

Fianna Fáil's Kevin Boland accused the "Fine Gael newspapers" of trying to make out that there was no difference between the two main parties, in the hope of lulling the voters into leaving the Fine Gael-led coalition undisturbed. This media suggestion, Boland insisted, was "ridiculous". Other Fianna Fáil figures gave similar warnings that there was a subtle campaign afoot to "confuse" the electorate into seeing the two main parties as interchangeable. Fianna Fáil's Séan MacEntee assured a meeting in Finglas: "There is as much difference in character and national outlook between Fianna Fáil and the parties of coalition as there would be between a lively, vigorous man and a tailor's dummy dressed up in his clothes."

Wittingly or otherwise, Charles Haughey diagnosed Ireland as the sick man of Europe when he said: "Don't let anyone tell you the parties are all the same. Fianna Fáil is different. [Fine Gael] say, in effect, that the patient is eating more than we can afford, so strangle him. That is one answer – it is not the Fianna Fáil answer."

His father-in-law, Séan Lemass, charged that the outgoing government had nothing to offer but "the politics of beaten men who want to pull everything down with them in revenge for their loss of power". He went on to assert that even the strongest supporters of Fine Gael and Labour didn't want to see the two parties back in government together.

Peering into the gathering gloom, Eamon de Valera resembled the faded star Norma Desmond in the movie *Sunset Boulevard*. In that Hollywood classic a young visitor says: "I remember you. You used to be big in the movies." At this, Desmond snaps: "I AM big. It's the movies that got smaller." De Valera tried to transport audiences from the pipsqueak politics of 1957 back to the heroic times of his younger years,

thundering at rallies in Bandon, Lisdowel and Limerick that
no member of Fianna Fáil had taken the Oath to the English
King when the party entered the Dáil 30 years earlier in 1927.
His *Irish Press* took this piece of ancient history and splashed
it across its front page beneath the banner headline WE DID
NOT TAKE THE OATH. Dev travelled back even further in
time, to the Treaty negotiations, for his customary swipe at
coalitions. He said that "the bargaining for place and power
amongst irresponsible minority groups" was "sadly reminiscent
of the scurrying of envoys that went on at another important
juncture in our history".

In response to these ritual attacks on coalition, Taoiseach
John A Costello came up with the inspired retort that all
single parties are actually coalitions, Fianna Fáil included.
He argued: "The present government is at least as strong as
that offered by its opponents who are, after all, like every
single party, only a coalition of sectional interests under a
single name." Having established that fact to his own
satisfaction, the Taoiseach's best shot was an uninspired
appeal to voters to return his government "in the national
interest". He said: "What is required at this historical
moment is a national rally to the parties who have
shouldered the burden of government."

It wasn't much of an inducement, and his opposite
number trumped it with the oldest trick in his book. De
Valera told a meeting in Cork that there was not a day went
by that he didn't keep the idea of a United Ireland fully
before his mind. He said that five-sixths of the national
territory had been successfully liberated, and if that free five-
sixths was made "really Irish" through the efforts of the
people, then "time will settle the other thing".

Fianna Fáil's Seán Brady appealed to the voters not to
leave the coalition in place through apathy. He raised the
fantastical prospect that, returned to power, the least socialist
Labour Party on the planet would try to push through a

radical Red agenda. He said: "Many countries have borne sad witness to the tragic consequences of indifference to elections, and there are too many tortured missionaries to remind us of that fact." Voter indifference could lead to rule by a small minority and "we have lessons enough to know what that means".

Hospital Trolley Dispute

Under policies of self-sufficiency and protectionism the economy had ground to a standstill, and when the entrepreneurial spirit did make a rare appearance at Dublin's Mater Hospital there was an unholy rush to extinguish it. Trader James O'Flanagan received permission to wheel a trolley around the wards, selling sweets, biscuits and other goods to patients and visitors. Local shop-owners had a hissy fit and demanded he be put out of business because he was "an unwarranted encroachment" on their patch. Following protests from the grocers' lobby body RGDATA, the trolley was stopped in its tracks. However, two days later O'Flanagan was back doing his rounds and collecting the signatures of 300 patients and visitors on a petition in support of his initiative. RGDATA sulked impotently that it had no objection to other hospital shops "run by patients for patients" just so long as they didn't operate during visiting hours.

There was another glimpse of the entrepreneurial spirit shining through the gloom when one advertising agency, with commendable lateral thinking, spotted an opportunity to piggyback an Irish product on a red letter day in Africa. At the time, roughly half the population of the Dark Continent was made up of Irish missionaries. The large newspaper adverts featured two black babies in conversation. Baby One: "Teacher says that this is the day that Ghana gets its independence." Baby Two: "My Mammy says that this is the day we get our Clover Skinless Pork Sausages."

For the many hard-pressed housewives who couldn't afford pork sausages with any regularity, one cookery columnist recommended that: "Tripe is a very digestible dish and I can never understand why it always seems a little bit rubbery to me. But the doctors tell us it is, so there you are! Even those who say they don't like tripe might change their minds if its rather anaemic look is disguised." The first recipe given for disguising the off-putting appearance of the tripe involved cooking the cow stomach slowly with lots of parsley and a cow-heel.

The housewives of Ireland put up a number of candidates in the general election. Mary Keating, speaking in support of Mairéad McGuinness, an Irish Housewives independent candidate, said the Dáil would be a better place if there were a dozen or more women TDs elected. Mrs Keating explained that women Deputies practiced in the skills of housekeeping would have a better understanding of the effects of the rising cost of living, and so would be better suited to bring it down. Kathleen Swanton, standing for the Irish Housewives Association, was appealing for votes on the not very populist ticket that Irish embassies abroad were too "extravagant".

There was good news for housewives everywhere from the outgoing Minister for Industry & Commerce, William Norton. He assured voters that rumours of an impending tea shortage were unfounded scaremongering by Fianna Fáil. The country had eighteen million pounds of tea in stock and the price would actually come down before election day.

JL Keogh, Chairman of the Irish Retail Tobacconists Association, told that body's AGM that it had been a tough year for the tobacco trade. Some years earlier a slur had been circulated that "Lady Nicotine", as he called it, was a cause of lung cancer. Fortunately, scientific tests had now "allayed that anxiety". The Chairman said that the only cancer the tobacco trade had to be worried about was "the cancer of cut prices".

At a time of deep gloom and doom, Gilbeys' Wine Merchants were recommending Invalid Tonic Wine as a pick-me-up. Twice as strong as today's wines, at 25.5% proof, the tonic was to be taken three times a day. The first glass was to be downed 30 minutes before lunch, the second 30 minutes before dinner and the third 30 minutes before bed. Gilbeys promised: "You'll feel the benefit very soon."

1950s-1960s

COULD YOU FIND A GIRL AROUND 14 YEARS OF AGE AS A PEN PAL FOR ME?
OVERSEAS REQUESTS TO TAOISIGH

In 1948 Eamon de Valera was ousted from office by a coalition fired-up by the participation of the More-Republican-Than-Thou Clann na Phoblachta Party led by Séan MacBride. De Valera cast off straight away to sail the globe on a ship named Partition, reminding audiences in America, Australia, New Zealand and India of who the real Taoiseach was.

In cities across the United States huge crowds turned out to cheer him. According to one report: "Boston's million Irish smashed parade records of all US cities in honouring Mr de Valera ... half a million marched, half a million cheered." In New York, where he was feted as "the boy from Manhattan who made good in Ireland", he was made an Honorary Citizen of that city – for the second time. In Philadelphia he appealed to his audience for financial aid to help fight "the struggle" against the British "still occupying six of our Counties".

Dev's riotously successful month-long tour awakened an interest in Ireland in a whole new generation of Irish-Americans. What he possibly didn't foresee was that, by connecting so strongly with them, he was setting himself up as Irish-America's very own Jim'll Fix It.

With Dev back in the Taoiseach's office in the 1950s, Mrs Margaret Connolly of Philadelphia wrote to him requesting that he send her a photo album of scenic views of Ballina, to "keep mother fascinated" in her 91st year. Margaret told him: "I hope you understand me asking this favor of you, as I am sure that if such a book is around you would sure get it for me." After some to-ing and fro-ing amongst top civil servants, Ballina District Council eventually sent her three official guides to Ballina along with a dozen postcards.

Shortly before he moved across from the Taoiseach's office to Aras An Uachtaráin, De Valera received the following inquiry dated March 17, 1959. Michael McDonald of Superior, Wisconsin, wrote: "In my boyhood, the most popular song at Irish or Irish American gatherings was *The Wearing Of The Green*. It is many years since I have heard this number. I have discussed this with many others of Irish extraction and all agree that it has not been heard for a good many years. Why?"

Dev's private secretary penned the terse reply: "I am to state that the song you mention is frequently heard in this country. No reason can be advanced for any apparent falling off in popularity in the United States of America."

That same year, 1959, another request arrived addressed to: "Emon DeValery, Premier, Dublin, Ireland." Dennis F Dunlavy from Ohio explained: "I have been confined to my bed for the past three months either at the hospital or convalescing at home, and I am practically learning to walk again. I thought perhaps you would have somebody engaged in the business of selling black thorn canes. My uncle had one with the thorns evenly around the stock about an inch or an inch-and-a-half through diameter. No doubt there are exporters who sell these canes and if you will have him bill me I will be very glad to make payment. I'm sorry to bother you, Your Eminence Premier, but I know no other way of making the approach."

Patricia O'Malley from Montana wrote to Dear Prime Minister (John A) Costello, telling him: "This is the first time I have written a letter to a Prime Minister, so please forgive me if I have made any mistakes in the opening of the letter … I read in the newspapers that you were in New York for Saint Patrick's Day. Was this the first time? How did you like the country and the parade? … Could you send me some real shamrock? … About how many people are there in Ireland? How many square miles in Ireland? What is the largest city? Could you find a girl around fourteen years of age as a pen pal for me?"

The Taoiseach's Department sent young Patricia a booklet on Ireland.

Another schoolgirl, Mary Pierce of Los Angeles, wrote to De Valera to tell him that she had entered an inter-schools "speech contest" on the theme of 'The Irish Horse', but had failed to find any relevant information in her local libraries. She hoped the Taoiseach would be able to furnish some relevant facts. She advised him: "The speech has to be five minutes long so I need lots of information." The eighth-grader continued: "I am also entering an Irish essay contest on Victor Herbert. My mother says I need unusual facts to make the essay interesting. If you have any I would be grateful for these too."

Victor Herbert was the wealthy American music publisher who arranged and published *The Soldier's Song* in New York some months after the Easter Rising of 1916. The files suggest that the Taoiseach had no unusual facts about the man to zest up the schoolgirl's competition entry, but at his Department's request the Irish equine industry supplied her with an essay on horse-breeding.

Horses were to the fore of a hostile letter-writing campaign from England directed at Dev's successor, Séan Lemass, in 1960. Stories had appeared in the British press detailing Ireland's export of live horses for slaughter and sale as food on the Continent.

Mrs Catherine Harber wrote from Lancashire: "As an

Irish woman by birth, I am ashamed that my native country is making money out of CRUELTY. As long as Ireland makes a profit out of cruelty and suffering, she will lose just as much in other ways. I know many people who have boycotted holidays in Ireland and rightly so. One Travel Agency who does £10,000 worth of trade with Ireland has banned it until this shocking traffic is stopped. Ireland will be the loser. In a Catholic country whose Government consists of Catholic men, it is a shameful thing that old horses, after working all their lives, should be exploited in this way and abandoned for slaughter in another country."

Mrs D Shipton of Surrey told Lemass: "It seems you Irish have another vice besides being garrulous and lazy and that is cruelty!!! If there is such a thing as reincarnation I hope you are an Irish horse in your next life, and meet the same horrible fate as these pathetic, worn out horses!!!!?" Another animal lover, Mrs C Coleman-Joscelyne of Harrogate, wrote to inform the Taoiseach that he and his people were a shower of "cowardly skunks".

Not every request to the Taoiseach's Department produced a helpful outcome. The publishers of *John Bull* magazine in London wrote asking Dev if he could supply a photo of himself as a youngster for their weekly series of pen portraits, From My Family Album, together with some biographical details of his beginnings. Dev's beginnings have always been a source of prurient speculation, and were a touchy subject during his lifetime. The request for a photo was turned down, and the publishers were referred to Dev's favourite biography of himself, by MJ MacManus.

Another request which was rejected came from Kathleen Bourke in the United States who had marked her envelope with the four-word address: "The Stationary Office, Ireland." The missive found its way to the Taoiseach's Department. It said: "I am preparing a report for school on your famous country, Ireland, and would apreciate (sic) all 'free' information you could possibly spare … I have yet to learn about your favourite foods and also your famous Irish Sweepstakes. I would appreciate if you would answer as promptly as possible."

Another American, Connie Kumen from Wisconsin, succeeded in getting through to the Taoiseach with a letter addressed simply: "To the Head of the Government, Eire, British Isles."

1961

THE OH-SO-QUIET ELECTION

The Incumbents: Fianna Fáil led by Séan Lemass.
Slogan: Fine Gael offers nothing but windbaggery.
Promise: To prepare Ireland for joining the EEC.
The Challengers: Fine Gael led by James Dillon.
Slogan: Fianna Fáil are on the make.
Promise: To make Ireland an agricultural powerhouse.
The Mood of the Country: Strangely upbeat.
Prediction: Fianna Fáil to beat a fractured opposition.
Result: Fianna Fáil returned with no overall majority.
Entertainment value: 3/10.

An Act Of Personal Treachery

The English press called it the 'Oh-So-Quiet Election'.
Labour, Fianna Fáil and Fine Gael took it in turn to hold
restrained rallies on a podium outside the GPO, prompting
one wag to reflect: "It's no wonder the election has been so
quiet when all the parties share the same platform." Public
meetings and rallies were poorly attended, and with Telefís
Eireann about to go on air in a matter of weeks, *The Irish
Times* detected the end of an era. The paper predicted: "The
next election will probably be fought completely on Irish
television."

It was to be the first general election in Fianna Fáil's
history not to be fought under the leadership of the party's
founder, Eamon de Valera. In late 1958 Dev's sworn enemy,
Deputy Noel Browne, finally confronted the Fianna Fáil

leader with the fact that he was a crook who had swindled his own supporters out of ownership of *The Irish Press*. Fianna Fáil's voting strength meant that Browne's motion of condemnation was soundly defeated. Then, in a bid to minimise the damage in the following day's newspapers, De Valera dropped the bombshell that he was to step down as Taoiseach and stand in the forthcoming Presidential Election. The ploy worked like a dream and De Valera's double-dealings were buried on the inside pages.

Each of the three main parties had changed leaders since the previous campaign, although this didn't necessarily mean a flow of new blood. Séan Lemass of Fianna Fáil had fought in the GPO during the 1916 Rising. Fine Gael's new leader, James Dillon, was touching 60. Labour had elected 41-year-old Brendan Corish as its leader a year earlier, but the party remained terrified that the electorate might mistake it as having a leaning towards socialism. Corish gave a lengthy newspaper interview at the start of 1961 in which there was not a single mention of the 'S' word.

The logic expounded by Fianna Fáil's Séan MacEntee was well up to his usual standards when he asserted that Fine Gael had entered a secret election pact with Labour which would result in the smaller party holding all the power. He added: "This, of course, is how Mr Khrushchev handles the puppet governments of Eastern Europe." In fact, Fine Gael and Labour had fallen out after two coalitions which had gone down the drain, with the result that a Fianna Fáil win was a foregone conclusion.

The Defence Minister, Kevin Boland, was also extravagant in his claims, attacking Fine Gael's new leader Dillon for attempting to stir up a mutiny in the Irish Army during World War II. In fact, Dillon had simply voiced his deep-felt convictions and called for Ireland to enter the conflict on the Allied side. Boland further accused Dillon of saying that the proper place for Irish industrialists was behind bars. To this, he added the colourful, if doubtful, claim that Dillon had said he wouldn't be seen dead in a field of wheat and that he hoped to see the day when wheat, beet and peat would be up the spout.

Fine Gael's Oliver J Flanagan asserted that the principal qualification for getting a public service job in the Ireland of 1961 was membership of Fianna Fáil. He said that one of the first acts of Séan Lemass as Taoiseach was to appoint his own son-in-law, Charles Haughey, as his parliamentary secretary, creating a new post for him paying almost £3,000 a year. Flanagan added that the Irish television service, not even on the air yet, was firmly in the hands of "Fianna Fáil job hunters" out to "get rich quick" at the taxpayer's expense.

The Irish language was compulsory for a range of jobs. When Fine Gael called for a review of this situation, Fianna Fáil's Frank Aiken said that it was unworthy of the party to raise the native tongue as an election issue half-way through the campaign. To do so without giving prior notice was a matter of "shame" and an act of "national treachery".

Ruling out the status of Irish as a fit subject for debate, Taoiseach Lemass said that Fine Gael had made it an election issue "for the first time in history" to their great discredit. He pleaded: "If we roll back down on national aims, where do we stop? The country's economic and social programmes won't be achieved by economic plans alone. They need behind them the driving force of patriotism."

Lemass sorrowfully continued: "In the old days when Fine Gael was led by men like Dick Mulcahy and Ernest Blythe, while we had strong and even violent differences with them, we knew we had all come out of the same school (Sinn Féin), and there were some matters which we left outside our arguments for fear of the damage that might be done to common national purposes." MJ Kennedy of Fianna Fáil maintained that the aim of the restoration of the Irish language had been kept out of party politics since the first

Dáil of 1919. He charged Dillon with "an act of personal treachery" which insulted the memories of Pearse and the men of 1916 and which "brings us back a century in the national advance".

Tranquilize The Adolescents

Irish National Vintner, the magazine of the Vintners' Association, attacked Justice Minister Oscar Traynor for the recent abolition of the *bona fide* trade, which permitted drinkers who had travelled three miles or more to buy a drink outside of normal pub opening hours. Not only did the abolition *not* take drunk drivers off the roads, argued the publicans, it actually generated "more road accidents" besides putting "many traders out of business". The publicans said there was no point in blaming drink for road deaths when some drivers were just "mentally prone" to becoming involved in accidents, drunk or sober.

The article continued: "Lack of consideration, bad roads, badly lighted roads, scooters and pillion riders, cyclists riding more than one abreast and without reflectors – all play a greater part than drunken driving." The publicans claimed that the greatest share of the blame for road accidents lay with careless pedestrians and speed. Having established that pubs were not a key factor in road safety, the publicans then appeared to flatly contradict their own argument when they called for no new licences to be granted along the country's new main roads. This was not an attempt at protectionism, they said – it was purely "in the interests of road safety".

In the interests of safer teen morals, Dublin's Archbishop John Charles McQuaid challenged doctors and psychologists to come up with a distinctly Irish way of telling youngsters about the birds and the bees without telling them *too* much. Naming "the two greatest needs of adolescence" as "temperance and fortitude", His Grace said: "I am convinced that there exists the duty to supply instruction in chastity that is accurate, clear, adequate and supernatural. And it can be done without hurt to sensitivity and without physical details." Properly formulated, he believed, "such an instruction can tranquilize the adolescent".

The Irish Times in election week carried the eye-catching headline DRAPERY BUSINESS NOT FOR SALE. The report read: "Last Thursday we published an advertisement which stated that a drapery shop and premises was for sale, giving the name and telephone number of Mrs Greaney, Main Street, Howth. We are aware now that Mrs Greaney, who carries on a drapery business at Main Street, Howth, gave no instructions whatever for the publication of any advertisement concerning her premises or business or otherwise, nor did she or her husband authorise any person to give such instructions."

A business proprietor from the other end of the capital made the news after he had difficulties casting his vote. The restaurant owner found that his name had been entered on the electoral register as Mister Wimpy.

Situation Disgraceful And Serious

For the entire final week of the campaign a group of American tourists were stranded at Shannon Airport while the pilot waited in frustration for the arrival of $6,000 from his airline to cover fuel and landing charges. When the cash was not forthcoming, the passengers sent a telegram to President John F Kennedy. It read: "103 United States citizens, members of the Erin's Own Gaelic Club in Chicago, are stranded at Shannon Airport since Wednesday. Women and babies ill and hungry. Men face job dismissals. Situation disgraceful and serious. No funds. Please help us."

The plea for help yielded no rescue mission from the White House, but Chicago's Mayor Richard Daley cabled the stranded party to say that he would personally ensure their jobs would still be there when they finally made it home.

After spending a full week in Shannon, the Americans finally arrived back in Chicago on Ireland's election day. The flight touched down at O'Hare Airport where the Ambassador East Hotel had provided complimentary food and drink for a Welcome Home reception. Sadly, the flight which was overdue a week now got in an additional four hours late, and the tired and hungry travellers found that their 200-strong welcoming committee had demolished all the free food and drink that had been laid on for them.

1965

STAGGERING BEHAVIOUR

The Incumbents: Fianna Fáil led by Séan Lemass.
Slogan: No to gimmick politics.
Promise: To keep Moscow out of Irish affairs.
The Challengers: Fine Gael led by James Dillon.
Slogan: Social justice through private enterprise.
Promise: To serve God and mammon.
The Mood of the Country: More buoyant than for decades.
Prediction: Fianna Fáil facing an open goal.
Result: Fianna Fáil win.
Entertainment value: 6/10.

We In FF Do Not Like Gang Warfare

Following three by-election defeats, Taoiseach Séan Lemass called a general election on the basis that strong Fianna Fáil government was needed to save the country from "political confusion". His party colleague Jack Lynch warned the electorate that if they failed to deliver a working majority there would be another election to follow, and then another if required. There was no prospect of an alternative government, as Labour had set its face against going into coalition. Fianna Fáil's Séan MacEntee jibed that Labour's sitting TDs were happy to take their Dáil salaries but not the responsibility of government. Labour, he said, was the Peter Pan of politics, unwilling to outgrow its short pants.

Meanwhile, Fine Gael was a ball of confusion. The party was deeply split over its own election manifesto, entitled

Towards A Just Society, which contained a series of progressive schemes for a joined-up social and economic policy aimed at creating greater equality. At the launch of the manifesto, the old-school party leader James Dillon effectively rubbished his own party's blueprint for a fairer future, saying: "We shall rely on private enterprise. We are a private enterprise party." By that point, however, Fine Gael's new-found social conscience had prompted Fianna Fáil to make some noises of their own in support of greater equality. This gave Dillon the chance to brand Lemass a political Annie Oakley, tooting: "Anything you can do I can do better."

There were occasions when the campaign generated both heat and light. Two nights after bricks were thrown into a Fianna Fáil office on Dublin's Dorset Street, injuring two women, a brace of petrol bombs were tossed through the same door. Party workers put out the blaze with buckets of water and poster paste. *The Irish Press* pointedly employed the term 'Molotov Cocktail' for the projectiles, subtly hinting that the Kremlin's Irish lapdogs were the culprits.

Health Minister Séan MacEntee accused Noel Browne, standing for Labour in Dublin South, of trying to stir up envy, resentment and class hatred. The well-heeled Minister thundered: "If he has anything to say, let him say it about our policies. Criticise those if you can, and leave out how we live and where we live." He continued: "The more aggressive and activist among the doctor's supporters should stop destroying our property. We in Fianna Fáil do not like gang warfare." He accused Labour's "rowdy element" of tearing down 300 Fianna Fáil posters in one night of vandalism. Labour's response was: "We do not have enough workers to put up posters, never mind pull them down."

There was rough stuff at the GPO when the elderly Taoiseach Lemass addressed a rally there. One observer wrote: "The reception for Mr Lemass was quite outstanding

... Mr Lemass was heckled and pelted with eggs, fruit, a bottle and documents at one stage when he was addressing the meeting. Young men in the crowd tried to interrupt him by shouting slogans, and about a half-dozen were taken from the meeting by Gardaí."

At the inauguration of the Ballymun Flats – Ireland's plunge into the future of high-rise living – Minister Neil Blaney warned all voters within earshot against falling for gimmick politics. The classic gimmick, he said, was to promise to set up new bodies which would solve all problems. The proliferation of these gimmick bodies, in turn, would lead to "confused government". His colleague Seán Moore contended that the alternative to Fianna Fáil was "gimmick government" with the Labour tail wagging the Fine Gael dog. In direct contradiction, other Fianna Fáil speakers portrayed Labour as being "totally subservient" to Fine Gael.

Meanwhile, Fianna Fáil's Frank Aiken made the novel suggestion that the arch-conservative Fine Gael leader John Dillon should shove off to Russia, where he would be welcomed by his like-minded Soviet counterparts. Brushing over the fact that he himself had championed Communist China at the United Nations, Aiken asked: "What does Mr Dillon think he has got, to make rigid, centralised planning work that Stalin and Khrushchev haven't got? If he's discovered the secret of making it a success, he can get a fine fat job in the USSR." Aiken said that Fine Gael's new economic plan, which Dillon himself had publicly smothered at birth, would impose a centralised Soviet-style regime on Ireland's farmers and businessmen. He concluded: "I think most of us would like him to try it out on somebody else before he tries it on the Irish people."

Not to be outdone in the hyperbole stakes by Aiken, Fianna Fáil's Michael O'Morain claimed that Fine Gael's skullduggery ran even deeper than that exposed by his party colleague. O'Morain claimed that the rival party had a 40,000 word policy document that they were keeping secret even from their own candidates. Fine Gael counter-claimed that Fianna Fáil was leaning on its "unscrupulous big businessmen" cronies to pressure their customers and suppliers to fund the government party's campaign.

Taoiseach Completely Berserk

As polling day approached, the three main parties united in coalition against *The Irish Times*. Fine Gael's Garret Cooney said the newspaper was allowing itself to be manipulated as "one aspect of the ruthless in-fighting for power in the Fianna Fáil Party between, on one side, Mr Charles Haughey and his father-in-law the Taoiseach, and on the other side the old guard as represented by Séan MacEntee". He saw it as more than a coincidence that *The Times* had called for the old curmudgeon MacEntee to retire just as Lemass was "dropping broad hints to the same effect".

Labour's Proinsias MacAonghusa accused the same newspaper of being "in league with the two conservative parties in blacking out all mention of Labour speeches, Labour policies and Labour activities".

However, the most vigorous and gloriously demented attack came from the Taoiseach himself, who seethed: "*The Irish Times*, which seems to have passed under the control of a group of crypto-Reds supporting Left Wing elements in the Labour Party, has now, for the first time in this country, introduced the Communist tactic of attributing to its political opponents, statements which they never made."

Lemass was responding to an editorial headed STAGGERING. The writer had asked: "Why has Mr Lemass threatened to introduce Prohibition if he receives a majority on April 7?" The editorial went on to criticise the Taoiseach's shock "outburst" against Irish drinking habits, and quoted him as promising: "If I make it on April 7 the boozer will have to go abroad for his drink in the future. He won't get it here."

The Tánaiste, Séan MacEntee, also featured in the editorial, which continued: "Mr Lemass is a seasoned politician, an old hand – as that master of phrase Mr Séan MacEntee might put it – at the game. Why Mr Lemass should raise an issue that bedevilled American politics for over a decade and which proved such a disastrous failure over there, defeats – as Mr MacEntee might say – us." The comment piece predicted that voters would revolt at the Taoiseach's threat to cut off the nation's booze supply. It said: "If we heard Mr Lemass say that he'd decided to abolish St Patrick's Day, in the national interest, it would hardly surprise or agitate us more … What is the purpose? Is it simply pique? We are not informed. We can only guess. May we at this late hour within a week of polling day, beseech Mr Lemass to reconsider his decision."

The STAGGERING editorial had appeared as a prank in the paper's April Fool's Day edition, but the Taoiseach was not amused. His incensed denunciation continued: "Needless to say, the words quoted in this leading article were never used by me. The suggestion is so absurd that, on this occasion, nobody is likely to believe it, but I must expect this tactic to be repeated in some other context before polling day. The Fianna Fáil government liberated the licensing laws and that is our policy. The freedom of the press is a great principle and I personally will fight for its preservation even when it is abused in this fashion."

This was music to the ears of Fine Gael's Gerard Sweetman, who accused Lemass of going "completely berserk". He asked: "Can we continue to trust a man who, so far from seeing a joke, flings out wild accusations of communism against a responsible newspaper? Mr Lemass' reaction is just one more example of the totally irresponsible way in which he has conducted this campaign."

The Irish Press gave blanket coverage to the Taoiseach's hurt and outrage. On April 1 it too had run a health warning that should have carried a health warning. In an article on avoiding back pain, Dr JB Cook warned members of the public against making "elegant-looking dives" off the high-board at swimming pools, as this could cause serious back injury if they entered the water at an awkward angle. He gave an equally strong warning against sustaining whiplash – "the pedestrian crossing injury" – when crashed into from behind while stopped at a zebra crossing. Dr Cook closed by advising readers, the elderly especially, that the best way to stay free of back pain is to make sure never to slip or fall.

Motoring matters besides whiplash were on the mind of Fine Gael's John Donnellan. The Deputy from Galway North East argued that a 30 mph speed limit was suitable for Dublin, but he saw no sense in restricting cars to 30 mph on rural roads as it would slow down drivers in a hurry.

He told the Dáil: "I want to refer to the 30 mph speed limit signs. In the first place, I do not think these signs should be so far away from the main towns. In some cases they are almost two miles outside the towns and in other cases a mile. In the case of some towns, they are quite near. I fully agree with the idea of having a 30 mph speed limit in Dublin but, for the ghost towns between here and the West of Ireland, it is a great waste of time to have a 30 mph speed limit. You could have a 40 mph speed limit for them.

Furthermore, there are too many signs in the country. I do not know whether these signs were erected by private contract or by the county councils in co-operation with the Department of Local Government, but if it was done by private contract then it was a damn good job and a great source of revenue to some individual or some bunch of individuals."

It was Ireland's first television election. On the day of the count, RTE suspended its entire schedule to run an election special. The station borrowed a state-of-the-art computer from Bord na Mona to crunch the numbers coming in from around the country. The data from the space age computer was then chalked up on school blackboards.

1969

QUEER FELLOWS IN THE ENGINE ROOM

The Incumbents: Fianna Fáil led by Jack Lynch.
Slogan: The Seventies won't be Socialist.
Promise: To be the party of reality.
The Challengers: Fine Gael led by Liam Cosgrave.
Slogan: To be the party of sanity.
Promise: To … erm … Nah, sorry.
The Mood of the Country: Vaguely agitated.
Prediction: A Fianna Fáil win.
Result: Fianna Fáil win.
Entertainment value: 6/10.

Fighting To Bring Back The Warble Fly

For the June 1969 election, the Labour Party came out of the closet as a party unashamedly of the Left, rallying behind the war cry: "The Seventies Will Be Socialist." Labour's manifesto said that inefficient farmers should be taken off the land. This played into the hands of Fianna Fáil who denounced them as "admirers of Castro" determined to rob smallholders of their land and enslave them on collective farms. Pitching themselves as 'The Party of Reality', Fianna Fáil taunted Labour's constituency workers that they were the unwitting dupes of godless intellectuals who had never done a day's work in their lives. Nor, added Fianna Fáil, had the godless intellectuals' shadowy puppetmasters.

Styling themselves 'The Party of Sanity', Fine Gael were listless non-starters in the race, and cocky Labour's refusal to enter into a transfer pact with them gifted the contest to

Fianna Fáil before a vote had been cast. This stand-off didn't prevent Fianna Fáil's Micheal O'Morain from sniping: "It has been nauseating during the past 12 months to witness the aged, creaking Fine Gael spinster begging for a marriage with the Labour Party." O'Morain said of the Labour leader Brendan Corish: "He is now like a puppet on a string, jumped and bounced about by the new Left Wing political queers who have taken over the Labour Party from the steps of Trinity College and Telefís Eireann."

On a related theme, Fine Gael's John Kelly accused Labour of seeking to poach progressive thinkers from his party. Attacking Labour's secret string-pullers, Kelly said: "There are a lot of funny noises coming from below (deck) and I suspect they have some queer fellows in the engine room." Kelly's withering judgement on his opponents in Fianna Fáil was: "Their speeches suggest a collection of toothless hillbillies snarling at a Rural District Council in 1900."

Fianna Fáil's Kevin Boland pushed through a change in the constituency boundaries just weeks before the election, in an act described by one opponent as brazen "Kevinmandering". Boland later admitted in an interview that the re-jig had given his party an advantage, however: "Mr Boland said that he had no scruples of conscience about what he had done, and thought that there was nothing wrong with the ultimate result. He had not done it from the point of view of deliberately trying to maximise Fianna Fáil representation, but to try and reconcile boundary disputes between different deputies."

In Dublin, Labour's Conor Cruise O'Brien charged that: "Mr Haughey's mercenaries are about their accustomed electoral task. They are peddling blue cards around the constituency. That is to say, in plain terms, they are leading the people to believe that they will get free medical services individually if they vote Fianna Fáil, and if they do not vote Fianna Fáil these services will be withheld."

O'Brien claimed that many householders in the constituency he shared with Charles Haughey had put Fianna Fáil posters in their windows even though they opposed the governing party. He said: "A startling number of these houses are not Fianna Fáil. The pictures form a sort of protective colouration. People feel it is prudent to appear to support Fianna Fáil, otherwise they risk being discriminated against in respect of certain categories of jobs, and in public services, including medical services."

Fianna Fáil, on the other hand, complained that it was meeting open opposition from elements that had no business getting involved in politics. The party attacked the ESB for allegedly ripping its posters from electricity poles while leaving others undisturbed. A Fianna Fáiler fumed: "To ordinary citizens it seems incredible that the ESB can waste time and money in this way and one can only assume that the autocrats of the ESB have decided that there is some special obligation placed on them to do all they can to hinder the smooth running of the democratic process at election time."

The ESB rejected the charges of bias, replying: "In moving such posters the Board's primary concern is for the lives of election workers. It is possible to be killed by coming into contact with a wire or a fuse on a lower pole."

The most colourful allegation of the campaign was made by Labour newcomer Richard Deasy who accused Agriculture Minister Neil Blaney of "fighting to bring back the warble fly" which would infest the country's cattle herds with its eggs.

In a new twist to Irish elections, the opposition parties started supplying their candidates with off-the-peg speeches outlining central policy on a range of issues. These mass-produced identikit speeches had a blank space for the name of the candidate and constituency, but the newspapers were happy to play along because they were a quick and easy means of filling space. Denouncing this dishonest new "script-party politics", Charles Haughey harangued journalists: "You should be charging for the space they take." He swore that his party would never lower itself into the mass-production game. The very next day Fianna Fáil delivered its first batch of "instant speeches" to the media.

The Parasite Classes Of Irish Society

Auctioneer James Deegan announced on *The Late Late Show* that he would be standing as an independent. He protested that it was undemocratic of RTE to confine coverage to the main parties and wrote two letters of complaint to the RTE Authority, without reply. Another independent candidate, Tommy Banahan, appealed to higher authorities, alerting Pope Paul VI and U Thant, Secretary General of the United Nations, to RTE's lack of fair play. It worked. A couple of days later RTE informed him that the station would run special reports to cover independent candidates under the umbrella category of 'Others'.

Auctioneers and RTE both came under fire from defenders of Irish culture who could see it being swept away by the consumer society. Conrath na Gaeilge lamented that RTE was in an impossible position "because it has a duty to serve the people of Ireland and at the same time must serve the interests of the gods of advertising. This it cannot do." The Irish language body continued: "Our national identity is under fierce attack from the Anglo-American neo-colonialism and neo-imperialism which is attempting to gain possession of Ireland. This involves stamping out freedom – our people's freedom to be full Irish people ... First the national language is destroyed and then the rest of the native culture. Diversity is then swamped in the tidal wave of mass culture ... Since its foundation Telefís Eireann has been assisting in this new conquest."

The Galway Command of the IRA upped the ante with a warning to the Language Freedom Movement that it was to stop agitating to free the people from compulsory Irish. The IRA branded the LFM not so much a movement as "a state of mind – the state of mind of the slave". The terrorist group, which had been virtually dormant for more than a decade, said the LFM represented the "parasite" classes of Irish society: "Slum landlords, ground rent landlords, moneylenders of various kinds, solicitors, auctioneers and brokers." Then came the serious bit: "The IRA will not stand idly by while the fabric of the Irish nation is openly and deliberately attacked by the enemies of the people. It will defend vigorously those who defend our nation and its language, and attack violently and relentlessly those who attack it."

The IRA's enemies list didn't stop with treacherous natives. Days before polling, four farms in Louth and Meath were set ablaze in one night. Three were farmed by Germans and one by a retired British Army officer. The IRA claimed responsibility. Shortly before the arson attacks, the Irish Republican Publicity Bureau had released a statement confirming that it took a dim view of Germans coming over here and occupying farmland.

It said: "We hereby advise prospective purchasers of land, fisheries, buildings or existing enterprises in Ireland, in their own interest, that the Irish Republican Movement is concerned at the amount of such property that has and still is being acquired by non-nationals.

Property acquisition is encouraged by certain Irish estate agents, some of whom even attempt to entice foreign purchasers by advertising offers of Irish property in the press of their countries, but such agents are in no position to guarantee security of tenure."

A Happy Rezoning

The campaign of 1969 was the first in which the opposition tried to make political capital by hinting that there was more to Charles Haughey than met the eye. In the run up to polling day, Haughey was called upon to 'explain' in public how he'd recently had the great good fortune to sell his Raheny home for 20 times what he'd paid for it just ten years earlier. The money he'd received, following a happy rezoning, enabled him that year to buy the Abbeyville stately home on 240 rolling acres with buckets of cash left over.

Haughey told his interrogators: "There is nothing hidden about this transaction. Some of my opponents seem to wish to lower the campaign to a level of personal denigration." Not only was there nothing hidden about the deal, but he had performed a civic duty in accepting the huge windfall from his friend, the property developer Patrick Gallagher. He explained: "The Raheny area has expanded at an astonishing rate. Most of the holdings around me were sold for housing and it became steadily clearer that my land too would have to be made available for housing sooner or later." He continued: "Had I, for selfish reasons of personal convenience, held on to it, it is not difficult to imagine what sort of campaign would then have been waged against me. With great reluctance, therefore, I decided to sell."

As the campaign wore on, and the media and the opposition persisted with the matter, he insisted that the sale between himself and Gallagher was "a private matter". He growled: "I don't think this will help those who brought it up. I have a feeling it will rebound on them."

The Gentlemen In Dublin With Their Bicycle Chains

There were fears amongst Dublin Fianna Fáil candidates that comments by their whimsical Justice Minister, Micheal O'Morain, would rebound on them. Attacking Fine Gael as soft on crime, he said the community must be protected from "the thug, the robber, the flick-knife operator and the gentlemen in Dublin with their bicycle chains". The remark about Dubliners brandishing chains provoked some resentment amongst the peaceable citizens of the capital.

The Minister from Mayo continued: "The Fine Gael spokesmen evidently are unaware of the fact that modern criminals are equipped with fast cars, two-way radios and are on planes out of the country within hours of serious robberies if they are not apprehended. Fine Gael would have the Gardaí chasing these gentlemen on punctured bicycles." Meanwhile, Galway Gardaí had no success in tracking down the enemies who succeeded in puncturing Taoiseach Jack Lynch's Ford Zodiac by laying carpet tacks on the road outside Spiddal.

O'Morain promised to rescue hundreds from the threat of Dubliner thugs with bicycle chains by removing them to the safety of his own county. He announced: "The government decentralisation policy will be pursued with vigour if Fianna Fáil is returned again. The significance of this policy for the people of Mayo should not be underestimated. When we put the Department of Lands in Castlebar, with 1,700 civil service careers on our own doorstep, no doubt our parents and teachers will take full advantage of these new western opportunities that will be available for our boys and girls."

Fianna Fáil were returned again. The government's decentralisation policy was pursued with the vigour applied to many election promises once the polling stations closed.

1973

HE'LL END THIS ELECTION AS MP FOR SCUNTHORPE

The Incumbents: Fianna Fáil led by Jack Lynch.
Slogan: Coalition is a shotgun wedding.
Promise: Strong government in troubled times.
The Challengers: Fine Gael led by Liam Cosgrave.
Slogan: We too can offer strong government.
Promise: To end 16 years of Fianna Fáil rule.
The Mood of the Country: Seething with youthful indignation.
Prediction: Too close to call.
Result: The FG/Labour National Coalition wins office.
Entertainment value: 5/10.

Another Collection Of Rather Similar Irish Men And Women

Four years down the road in 1977, Fianna Fáil would fall over themselves to woo the youth vote. However, in 1973 the party showed the seasoned experience of old-handers to keep the young people of Ireland from having a decisive say in the election. At the time, Fianna Fáil had been in power with just two short breaks for 35 years on the trot, prompting one commentator to note: "They look less like the Soldiers of Destiny and more Dads' Army." The Minister for Posts & Telegraphs, Gerry Collins, might have chosen his words better when he said of his leader Jack Lynch: "We reject the implication that a Taoiseach who has been in office a mere six years is a tired old man."

According to one newspaper story, tiredness was not a problem for one particularly frisky Minister. The members of the Cabinet were under threat from Republican and Loyalist assassins, with the result that they were shadowed everywhere by garda minders. However, some of these bodyguards reportedly felt that they were being overworked by one Minister beyond the compensations of any amount of overtime pay. The report said that at least one Special Branch officer had submitted a complaint to the Taoiseach "about the conduct of one over-amorous member of the Cabinet in his extra-curricular activities". Lynch denied ordering a hush-hush inquiry into the matter.

For this election the voting age was lowered from 21 to 18 for the first time, which meant that over 140,000 new voters were just about to be enfranchised. However, by calling a quickie campaign of just three weeks' duration, Jack Lynch beat the introduction of the new electoral register by a fortnight. Student leader Pat Rabbitte said he was sickened by the move, remarking: "The democratic right of almost 200,000 young people is to be sacrificed in the party political interests of Fianna Fáil."

The National Federation of Youth Clubs signalled its displeasure by announcing "a Youth Rights Sunday during which there will be the distribution of leaflets, collection of signatures to a petition and possibly some fasts". For the first time since the 1950s, Fine Gael and Labour tentatively warmed the sheets of a double bed before the poll, to present an alternative administration under the banner: "Don't Blame The Government – Change It!" Youth clubs, students and school pupils formed a group called 'Youth For Coalition'. Fianna Fáil's salty old Michael O'Morain retorted that: "Coalition government is a shotgun wedding."

David Andrews earnestly maintained that Fianna Fáil really and truly wanted 18-year-olds to have their say, but the party had opted to put the national interest ahead of its own dearest wish because so many grave decisions couldn't wait the extra two weeks. One observer pointed out that the campaign would at least get Fianna Fáil "off the embarrassing hook of where to sit" in the European Parliament. Ireland had just dispatched its first batch of Members of the European Parliament (MEPs) to the EEC and, unsure of where they stood in the ideological scheme of things, the Fianna Fáil party had ended up sitting cheek by jowl with the fascists. Ireland's pioneer MEPs were unelected party nominees. One of them, Labour's David Thornley, admitted: "When I attend a session of the European Parliament, I don't know what I'm talking about half the time."

Fianna Fáil's ritual call for strong government was this time tacked on to the murder and mayhem in the North. Lynch maintained: "This is now essential if a protracted period of political uncertainty and instability is to be avoided." *Hibernia* magazine was having none of it, editorialising: "It is not too difficult to estimate those considerations upon which the result of this general election will have little or no effect, and the first of these is political stability ... From the electorate's point of view there is, in fact, only one question at stake in this general election and that is whether the political power and patronage should be switched at this stage to another administration; to another collection of rather similar Irish men and women who exemplify rather similar attitudes, prejudices and objectives."

A Snowstorm In A Fish Tank

With RTE committed to providing meticulously balanced coverage to the main parties and none at all to some of the smaller ones, candidates were quick to enlist any outside help to boost their profile. The day after the election was called Labour's Conor Cruise O'Brien reportedly phoned Harlech TV in Wales, offering to travel to Bristol for any discussion he might enliven. The offer was made despite the fact that reception of the Welsh station was confined to Ireland's eastern seaboard and most of the time the picture resembled a novelty snowstorm in a fish tank. Jack Lynch opened his campaign with a major interview on the BBC's *Panorama*, followed by another BBC slot from Claremorris. This prompted one commentator to quip: "If he does any more bloody English television interviews he'll end this election as MP for Scunthorpe."

The possible distortions of English television on sheltered Irish minds were raised elsewhere. The TV critic Ken Gray wrote: "Among the latest acquisitions from the BBC is a comedy series called *The Goodies*. This is goon stuff, perpetrated by Tim Brooke Taylor, Bill Oddie and Graeme Gordon (sic) and put over with great ingenuity and originality. But it is a mistake, I think, to plunge RTE viewers into this kind of television comedy without adequate preparation. *The Goodies* is a development of other comedy shows. The techniques employed have got progressively more lunatic with each series and I doubt if it is possible to regard *The Goodies* as anything but sheer nonsense without having some prior acquaintance with the works of Messrs Brooke Taylor, Oddie and Gordon."

Taoiseach Mary Robinson

A total of 14 women stood as candidates in the 1973 election. By way of a vote of encouragement to them, *The Irish Times* nominated an all-female fantasy Cabinet drawn from women notables. The judging panel accepted that many readers would find the exercise either redundant, far-fetched or both. The *Times* said: "An all women Cabinet? What sort of silly election joke is this? What we're offering is a very unlikely coalition that will never take place." It continued: "We decided that the present Cabinet portfolios are outdated and that we could come up with a better division of duties. The first move was to eliminate the Department of Defence, which is not only an anachronism but reflects an undesirable attitude women in general seldom endorse." Selected as the candidate best fitted to be the nation's first woman leader was: "Taoiseach – Mary Robinson. Responsibilities – To lead. In 1970 she led the protest against the Senate's long holidays during a period of national crisis."

The joint FG/Labour manifesto contained a pledge that: "Legislation will be introduced to end all forms of existing discrimination against women." Those forms of legal discrimination were numerous, and even the supportive *Irish Times* had its doubts, reflecting glumly: "This could easily be the most expensive of all the decisions, especially in the field of equal pay for equal work."

For Fianna Fáil's Joe Leneghan, it was self-evident that some women weren't equal to some types of work. The Mayo deputy reasoned: "How could I employ a local secretary? If I got a local lady, the first dance she would go to, out would come your business. You wouldn't want that." As for why Fianna Fáil should be returned on polling day, he told a crowd: "What you got, stick to it. These buckos would tax the farmers."

The same Deputy Leneghan had outlined similar views on women when he told the Dáil that Mayo in the early 1970s was losing its unique character. He argued: "Nobody wants to leave New York and come here to a miniature New York. We are making everything just the same. At the rate we are going, in five or six years' time I will reach Belmullet without knowing I have left Dublin."

With the Troubles raging in the North, tourist numbers in the South had been down. According to Deputy Leneghan, Bord Fáilte wasn't part of the solution, but part of the problem. He told the House: "I remember going into Bord Fáilte one morning with a gentleman who was looking for a grant. We met a lady there with a mini-skirt on her – that is a good few years ago – and that was the only qualification she had. She could not give me any information but after a long time she succeeded in sending me to some fellow. I started to talk to him about Attymass, Ballina and Achill. After a few minutes it occurred to me that, as big a fool as I was, he was a bigger one."

He added that over-fussy planning restrictions were ruining the chance for local people to offer tourists accommodation at more affordable rates than the "super-palatial" hotels. He said: "They are being overcharged in certain places now, especially in Salthill where, I believe, a pint of lager costs five shillings or more." The planning laws were hurting local enterprise. One constituent, for instance, had wanted to build a restaurant onto his house, but was told he would have to keep the size within limits. Lenehen complained: "Nobody could get in except a pygmy if he were to accept this restriction. Is this to be allowed? Because a man wants to build a house between the road and the sea and because an engineer wants to see a lot of mermaids or something, are we to tolerate that type of thing?"

In neighbouring Donegal the hotel lobby flexed their muscle when they took offence at a radio advert for Ranks Porridge Oats. The hoteliers complained that the commercial implied that visitors to Donegal would need to get a warm breakfast inside them because the weather there was so bad. Ranks withdrew the advert.

1977

PROMISES, PROMISES, PROMISES

The Incumbents: FG/Labour coalition led by Liam Cosgrave.
Slogan: A lot done, more to do.
Promise: Less than 100,000 jobless by Christmas.
The Challengers: Fianna Fáil led by Jack Lynch.
Slogan: To make it your kind of country.
Promise: The sun, moon and stars.
The Mood of the Country: 43% said it didn't matter who won.
Prediction: The FG/Labour coalition to be returned.
Result: A shock Fianna Fáil landslide.
Entertainment Value: 9/10.

Who Loves Ya Baby?!
After four years in power, Fine Gael and Labour stood before
the electorate on their record of having tried their best to
grapple with difficult circumstances largely beyond their
control. Within months of their taking office in 1973, the
OPEC oil embargo of the West had floored the Irish
economy resulting in galloping inflation, soaring unemployment and an endless succession of shortages.

The sense of a nation on the brink, but gamely muddling
through, was brought into focus when Limerick car workers
marched through the streets to demand the return of their
kidnapped boss, Dr Tiede Herrema – for the sake of the
economy if nothing else. Addressing the protest, Limerick's
Mayor called on the Republican movement "to find this man
and bring him back, otherwise 1,200 people will be out of
work". One of the Coalition's election promises in 1977 was

to bring the jobless figures down below 100,000 by the end of the year.

The government's response to an overspill of violence and instability from the North had included censorship, curbs on civil liberties, and swearing on their mothers' graves that there was no such thing as a marauding fleet of garda privateers known as the 'Heavy Gang'.

Taoiseach Liam Cosgrave rounded on the disbelievers and the free-thinkers, one of whom was a journalist in possession of a suspect English accent. Cosgrave stormed: "Not for the first time has this party stood between the people of this country and anarchy. And remember, those people who comment so freely – some of them aren't even Irish. No doubt many of you are familiar with an expression in some parts of the country where an outsider is described as a blow-in. Now as far as we're concerned they can blow out or blow up."

Just before the 1969 general election, Fianna Fáil's Kevin Boland had massaged the constituencies in a stroke branded 'The Kevinmander'. Once installed in power in 1973, the coalition gave Local Government Minister Jim Tully the job of performing a reverse massage. In a manoeuvre dubbed 'The Tullymander', he moved the goalposts, the penalty spot and even the half-time oranges, creating new three-seaters where four-seater constituencies had been. The intention was that it would be harder for the dominant party, Fianna Fáil, to hold two seats out of three than it had been to hold two out of four.

The government called the election for the high summer of 1977 confident that it held most of the aces – a view widely backed up by the media. On the eve of the poll, *The Irish Times* assured its readers: "The Coalition will win the general election by a fairly comfortable margin." Few guessed that the government had already sown the seeds of its own unimagined destruction.

A national census had been due in 1976, but the

government had cancelled it. It has entered legend that the survey was scratched to save the State some money during hard times, but this was not strictly true. A proposal did come from Finance to keep a lid on the coffers by nixing the census, but Finance Minister Richie Ryan had shot down his own Department's plan as deeply dippy. Ryan pointed out that the population had recently grown and shifted in mysterious ways and that without an accurate survey, every constituency come the election would be a lucky dip. However, Ryan's well-founded fears were not shared by his cabinet colleagues who were happy to put their trust in the Tullymander, and they ditched the due census while Ryan was abroad. When he learned of the decision, he was furious.

Fianna Fáil entered the contest pitching itself as the natural party of government returning from exile to claim the rightful throne of 'The Real Taoiseach' Jack Lynch. The last time out, the party had conspired successfully to keep 140,000 first time voters sidelined. Four years on, the number of young people who would be voting for the first time numbered around 400,000 and Fianna Fáil had devised a strategy to seduce them with a blast of razzmatazz and a manifesto ready made for a ticker-tape parade. When Lynch was canvassing in Kerry, the party gave out 500 free tickets for a dance in Ballybunion. An hour after midnight, the 60-year-old Taoiseach shimmied on stage and paradiddled with gusto on the drums and cymbals. Taking their cue from Kojak, the hit show of the day, the revellers responded with delighted cries of: "Who loves ya baby?!"

The youth vote was the untapped lode, but Fianna Fáil continued to marshal the valued votes of its elderly supporters, and even of its senile ones. *The Longford News* felt that it was a time for some Irish electoral traditions to be ditched forever. A reporter scolded: "If you look closely you can see the faces of old women peering out into the sunshine from behind the posters and stickers that block their view

from inside the cars. Most of them look bewildered by it all.
We heard the story of one old woman brought to vote in St
Michael's School, who didn't even realise where she was.
The party worker who brought her asked if it was okay to
mark the ballot on behalf of the woman. Nobody objected.
So much for one man, one vote."

Not every older voter was so submissive. At a Fianna Fáil
rally in Kilkenny an elderly woman covered in 'Bring Back
Jack' stickers approached the party stall. She asked for a free
Bring Back Jack tee-shirt "for my little grandson". A report
said: "The Fianna Fáil campaign man was doing his best to
explain that the shirts had run out, and even asked for her
name and address and said he'd send her one. But Granny
wouldn't take any compromise. She ripped off the stickers,
threw them on the ground, and headed home mumbling that
she would never vote for those so-and-so's again."

But Fianna Fáil were not to be stopped. The party
unveiled a political version of *The Greatest Story Ever Told*,
with a manifesto which promised to deliver the sun, moon
and stars with something left over for Christmas. The star
prizes put on offer in the great giveaway included abolishing
domestic rates and doing away with motor tax. Fine Gael's
John Kelly summed up the Fianna Fáil package as "reckless
promises and popdoodle", while his coalition colleague
Conor Cruise O'Brien called it "blatant electoral fraud". The
voters weighed up both sides of the argument and plumped
for the sun, moon and stars.

Getting Amongst Women

Of the 400,000 young voters enfranchised to vote for the first
time, half of them were women. Throughout the history of
Dáil elections women voters had come second best, at best,
on the priority list of the main parties, but 1977 changed
that. Fianna Fáil were quick off the blocks, even if the
stalwarts in some cumainn were determined to drag their

feet. When Party HQ told constituency branches to nominate female candidates, some refused, leading Jack Lynch to impose women on six constituencies.

Making light of its own chauvinist rump, the party littered the press with adverts saying: "The Coalition Discriminates Against Women." The coalition had indeed shown little interest in women at the outset of the campaign, hiving off their concerns under the headings of Children's Allowance and Social Welfare, but now it countered with an appeal: "Promises Or Performance? Women Voters – Nail The Fianna Fáil Propaganda."

Fianna Fáil faulted the Coalition for failing to implement EEC directives guaranteeing equal pay, equal job opportunities, and equal employment rights for married women. 1975 had been International Women's Year and the EEC had ordered Ireland to write equal pay legislation into law by the end of that year. The Coalition complied, and then did nothing to enact the laws which would have entitled a woman to be paid the same as a man for doing the same work. Now, stung into action by the Fianna Fáil attacks, the government announced that female civil servants would be paid equally to men from December 31, and that the Employment Equality Act would become law within weeks of their re-election. They then upped the ante, promising that female school leavers would be allowed to claim the dole just like their male counterparts. Fianna Fáil immediately matched the offer.

As the campaign hotted up, the Women's Political Association (WPA) surveyed the attitudes of TDs and Senators on a range of issues of concern to women, including the touchy subject of artificial contraception. It was so touchy that shortly before polling day, Labour's Frank Cluskey gave a speech to an Irish Family Planning Association seminar without making a single direct mention of family planning. However, in responding to the WPA survey, 100% of Labour's deputies said they favoured the availability of a comprehensive family planning service. That figure plunged to 31% of Fine Gael and 12% of Fianna Fáil representatives. The WPA's vice-president, Gemma Hussey, expressed disappointment that not one of Fianna Fáil's female representatives had bothered to respond to the survey. Neither had Fianna Fáil's spokesman on Women's Affairs, the decidedly unladylike Mister Gene Fitzgerald.

Congolese Call Girls

Fianna Fáil's James Gallagher, standing in Sligo/Leitrim, placed an advert in *The Sligo Champion* promising to work for "the abolition of the Offences Against The State Act which serves to provoke and alienate people from the forces of law and order". Gallagher's statement continued: "Our garda force are preservers of peace and order and should be seen as such, and not as thugs who execute repressive legislation." This objection to the force's thuggish element earned Gallagher a rebuke from his leader Jack Lynch, who was striving to make law and order a main plank of Fianna Fáil's election platform.

A spokesman for Gallagher then came out and said that the advert had contained "mistakes". Where it had said "Offences Against The State" it should have said "Emergency Powers Act". Also, the line referring to the guardians of law and order as "thugs" had come out all wrong. In case anyone was thinking of blaming *The Sligo Champion* for these unfortunate "mistakes" – which had been now identified as typing errors – the Gallagher camp was anxious to point out that it took full responsibility for the litany of botches.

On the eve of polling day, posters went up in Dublin seeking votes for Labour's Conor Cruise O'Brien. They advocated: "Abortion on demand. Private facilities for alcoholic TDs. Suppression of the Irish language. Easy divorce. Legalisation of drugs. Congolese call girls." The outgoing Minister was not amused. He bristled: "This is clearly a black propaganda campaign aimed at damaging the Labour Party. The fact that the printed posters have been widely and quickly distributed shows that there is an organisation behind this scurrilous and despicable campaign. We call on the Fianna Fáil Party, on the eve of this election, to repudiate and condemn this vile propaganda."

If there was no real likelihood of Congolese call girls making an appearance, the prospect of a surprise visitor from next-door Uganda caused great excitement. Days before the election an alert went up that the murderous Ugandan dictator, Idi Amin, was heading for Irish airspace. Reports said that Amin might try to land in Ireland and travel on to England, where he planned to embarrass the hosts by gatecrashing a summit of Commonwealth leaders. An Irish government spokesman said that the Amin alert was from a reliable source, leading to speculation that it came from Britain's air traffic authorities. Irish Army troops, armoured cars, Gardaí and reporters swarmed to Dublin and Cork airports to intercept the so-called 'Flying Pimpernel'. The government's spokesman said the genocidal dictator would be prevented from landing, unless his plane was in urgent need of a closely-guarded refuelling stop.

After several uneventful hours, the reporters at Dublin Airport decided they'd been led on a wild goose chase and began packing their bags. As they prepared to leave, a breathless airport official informed them that a mystery aircraft had been picked up on radar just 15 minutes away. Dramatically, at that very moment, the VHF radios of planespotters on the scene crackled with a broadcast intercepted from the control tower. It said: "Uganda Fight 345. Uganda flight 345. This is Dublin Control. Do you read?" The media scrum regrouped in great excitement.

After 15 minutes elapsed with no sight of the mystery

aircraft, the airport official who had given them the tip-off returned and told the reporters that there had been a mistake. The mystery plane had turned out to be an innocent Aer Lingus training flight, and the calls put out to Uganda Flight 345 had been the regrettable result of a garbled signal.

This failed to satisfy one incensed television cameraman, who mounted a physical force protest and was arrested by airport police for "interfering" with Aer Rianta property.

Music For Buses

In Britain, the summer of punk coincided with Queen Elizabeth's Royal Jubilee, and there were delighted howls of protest from hip young people against the blanket broadcast ban on the Sex Pistols' alternative anthem, *God Save The Queen*. During those same warm weeks in Ireland a home-made song was also banned for its gritty in-yer-face political content, although this time with the wholehearted blessing of the country's young hipsters.

Fianna Fáil invited Ireland's tiny band of music writers to a preview of *Your Kind Of Country*, the party's bid to woo the 400,000 pop kids newly entitled to vote. In a chamber draped with 'Bring Back Jack' tee-shirts and stickers, Senator Eoin Ryan confidently predicted that Fianna Fáil's "very lovely song" would bring out the youth protest vote. Fresh-faced Seamus Brennan said that the young people of Ireland were demoralised and it was Fianna Fáil's mission to boost their spirits. The party had recently set up its youth wing, Ógra Fianna Fáil, and Brennan held up the party's tigerish cubs as the role model for what young people could make of themselves, given a bit of guidance and encouragement. He boasted: "We give them a real say, not just gimmicks."

With the song about to get its first airing, Press Officer Frank Dunlop requested "no dancing". He was given 100% compliance. *Your Kind Of Country* was performed by Colm CT Wilkinson, who had come to prominence playing Judas in the Gaiety production of *Jesus Christ Superstar*. That role, he claimed, had caused a rift with his pious mother. ("Anyone but Judas she'd say.")

The recruiting song identified itself with young voters who knew the pain of going straight from behind the school bicycle shed to the dole queue. With a wounded growl, CT opened up: "*Three years of loneliness, that's what I've been through/When I left school I joined me mates and we all joined the queue.*" Belting along like a runaway milk-float, the Fianna Fáil election vehicle brought to life the demoralising effects of three years of fruitless job-hunting, before steering into a head-on collision with the failed "politics of hardship" perpetrated by a "cruel and heartless" government. Its empowering message was: Don't be a statistic. Go out on election day and vote Fianna Fáil and "show them that you're free".

The music was written by the Rachmananov of the radio jingle, Tommy Ellis, while the lyrics were composed by the advertising agency Des O'Meara & Partners. A handler on the scene confided that the project "cost at least £1,000". One journalist raised the vexed issue of the party's new musical direction. Did this embrace of pop not mean that Fianna Fáil had abandoned its core value of upholding Irish culture against the foreign tide? This line of inquiry was snipped with a dignified silence.

There was no question of RTE playing the party-political *Your Kind Of Country*, but the disc did get heavy rotation on the iPod of the day, the musical bus. In an age well before the first Walkman appeared, CIE's bus passengers could enjoy a selection of MOR pop tunes peppered with adverts, as they languished at some midway point on their commute waiting for their driver to pop back out of the bookies.

It was too good to last. After just a few days, CIE management banned *Your Kind Of Country*. The company wouldn't give a reason, but Fianna Fáil were convinced that the ban had come down directly from the Transport Minister, Tom Fitzpatrick. Fianna Fáil complained that the song had not breached the political neutrality of the on-board playlist – they'd paid fair and square to have it aired as part of the commercial breaks. The party further pointed out that the lyrics made no reference at all to Fianna Fáil. There was, however, a clever subliminal link. There were stickers on the buses bearing the legend *Your Kind Of Country*, which did urge passengers to vote for the party.

CIE insisted that both song and stickers had to go. Fianna Fáil protested that the party had been running sticker campaigns on the buses for 25 years. The company relented and decided it would continue to accept Fianna Fáil's money for stickers. When election day came, *Your Kind Of Country* could be heard blaring from loudspeakers across the nation, apart from Artane in Dublin where the official Fianna Fáil anthem was drowned out by an indie tune called *Charlie's Song*. Originally penned in homage to Bonnie Prince Charlie, the rousing dollop of aural porridge had been adopted to inspire voters to arise and follow Charlie Haughey. One newspaper poll concluded that Haughey's constituency housed the two most unpopular politicians in Ireland – The Boss himself, and Labour's outgoing Post & Telegraphs Minister Conor Cruise O'Brien.

In breach of RTE's carefully balanced time allocations between the various candidates, Radio na Gaeltachta ran an election interview with independent candidates Neil Blaney and Paddy Keaveney. The RTE Authority ordered an investigation, not just because of the time infringement, but because the broadcast was the first in the history of the Irish language station ever to be conducted in English. But even as RTE chastised its Irish language offshoot, one of its spokesmen defended the transgressor, making the ingenious case that Radio na Gaeltachta was a service for the gaeltacht and "people there speak English as well as Irish". Fine Gael jumped in with a demand that Radio na Gaeltachta give it 20 minutes in English to balance the books. When the station refused, the party levelled a charge of "blatant discrimination".

Back in 1969, Fianna Fáil had asked "ordinary citizens" to deplore ESB "autocrats" for hindering the democratic process by removing the party's posters from electricity poles. In 1977 the ESB got its retaliation in first, warning its customers that the electioneers could land them with bigger domestic bills. The supplier took out the following advert: "The Electricity Supply Board would like to bring to the notice of all election workers and the public in general that it is extremely dangerous to climb ESB poles. In addition to presenting a real danger to life, the placing of election posters and literature on ESB poles and other property causes unsightly defacement and can result in damage to the Board's property. ESB staff have been given specific instructions to remove immediately any posters which are erected on its property. This, of course, involves Board staff in additional work and the extra costs incurred are ultimately borne by electricity users."

One candidate counting his pennies was Alderman Kevin Byrne standing in Dublin. When he tried to hand in his nomination papers to City Sheriff Michael Hayes, the official refused to accept a cheque for £100 as a deposit. He said the deposit must be paid in legal tender and a cheque didn't count as such. The next morning Byrne arrived on his bicycle at the Sheriff's Office with 10,000 pennies in legal tender. At this point the Sheriff said he still wouldn't accept the nomination papers because he wasn't satisfied that Byrne had filled them out correctly. When Byrne asked to be shown what needed to be corrected, the Sheriff said he had other priorities. Byrne said that he was going nowhere until his papers were accepted.

At high noon Sheriff Hayes announced that he was going

to lunch and he told Byrne to come back at two. Byrne refused to leave and the Sheriff called the Gardaí. Byrne left under protest, pointing out that the opening hours sign said the civic office didn't close for lunch until 12.45pm. When both men arrived back at 2 o'clock, the Sheriff had with him a set of scales to weigh the 10,000 coins. The stand-off ended with a civil handshake.

1981

WAS YOUR MOTHER A NUN?

The Incumbents: Fianna Fáil led by Charles Haughey.
Slogan: It's a time for strong government, not for experiment.
Promise: To strive for a United Ireland.
The Challengers: Fine Gael led by Garret Fitzgerald.
Slogan: You won't be taking a chance.
Promise: To be Garret The Good.
The Mood of the Country: Mean and Ugly.
Prediction: Too close to call.
Result: A Fine Gael/Labour coalition.
Entertainment value: 9/10

One For Youth And One For Ordinary People

After his government's surprise defeat in 1977, Liam
Cosgrave resigned as leader of Fine Gael. After fully
rehabilitating Charles Haughey with a seat at the Cabinet
table, Jack Lynch found himself ousted and replaced by
Haughey in 1979.

On the day Taoiseach Charles Haughey called the 1981
election, Patsy O'Hara became the fourth Republican
prisoner to die on hunger strike in the North's Maze Prison
where Republicans were demanding political status from
Margaret Thatcher's British Government. Fianna Fáil began
the campaign with a clear lead in the opinion polls, but
support fell away as Fine Gael's first-time leader Garret
Fitzgerald led his party on a charge, and Maze prisoners

standing for election threatened to swipe hard-line Republican votes from the government.

As Haughey travelled the country, hecklers taunted him with yells of: "How many more prisoners are you going to let die?" The Taoiseach's rote response was that entering a conflict with the British over the hunger strikers would benefit no one. He insisted that he was trying to get the European Community to intervene with Britain's Prime Minister, Margaret Thatcher. Maze protesters threw paint at Haughey as he campaigned in Dun Laoghaire, where a statue of Queen Victoria was demolished as a show of love for Ireland. In Donegal, the Taoiseach had an egg slapped on his head. He and his entourage were forced to beat a hasty retreat from Ballyshannon when their garda escort was bulldozed by a mob. In the seaside resort of Bundoran, a hostile crowd threatened to prevent the Haughey helicopter from taking off.

In Castleblaney, Co Monaghan, a gelignite bomb was discovered in the Fianna Fáil election office just hours before the party's leader was due to visit. The Irish National Liberation Army claimed it had planted the device on the grounds that the Taoiseach was a British "collaborator". In Castleblaney, a heckler in a Fine Gael hat shouted "Up Garret!" as Haughey was speaking. It was an ill-advised act. Haughey's solicitor and election agent, Pat O'Connor, was spotted by a reporter "driving his elbow with some vigour into the stomach" of the man in the hat. In Kells, Haughey attempted to stress Fianna Fáil's Republican credentials by telling his audience that the party's top priority was a 32-County united Ireland. To emphasise how serious he was, he made a clenched fist gesture and gave a throaty roar.

Fine Gael played up what became known for the first time in this election as 'The Haughey Factor', stressing the virtue of their leader with slogans such as "Garret Is Good For You". Fitzgerald did not escape the wrath of the hunger strike protesters. In Waterford, one roared at him: "You can well smile on a full stomach." In Arklow, the Fitzgerald tour bus blared out Neil Sedaka as an H-Block mob barracked darkly. One protester yelled that Fitzgerald was as cowardly as Haughey in ducking the hunger strike crisis, and that there was no point in him trying to hide that fact behind his "fancy music". Zipping along on the open road from Cork to Kerry the playlist blaring from the Fitzgerald tour bus included John Lennon and Pink Floyd, but as it pulled into its first Kerry port of call the tape was switched to Philomena Begley. Fine Gael commissioned an election song written and performed by Dennis Allen. The chorus told voters: "*Fine Gael, Fine Gael/A bright new future we hail/Led by Garret the man you know/You won't be taking a chance.*" According to the party's Director of Elections, Séan O'Leary it was: "A real Eurovision sound, I think."

Posters went up telling voters: "You Can Save Irish Lives – Vote H-Block." As the prospect increased that prisoner candidates might steal Dáil seats from the government, Haughey augmented his theme tune, *Charlie's Song*, with a recording of the National Anthem by his occasional back-up band The Morrisseys. *The Soldier's Song* was blasted out at the end of each campaign meeting as a rousing reminder of Fianna Fáil's Republican pedigree. In Britain, BBC bosses had to face the music after the disc jockey Ed Stewart played *The Derry Air* on his Radio 2 requests show. A cruel hoax had been played on Stewart, and the names he'd read out with the request belonged to four British soldiers killed by an IRA landmine days earlier. The corporation apologised for an "unforgivable error". In Ballinamore, Co Leitrim, the tour bus of a party of English anglers was torched, leading to a spate of cancellations from Britain and further afield just as the summer tourist season was getting underway.

The Republican movement's favourite hate-figure, Conor Cruise O'Brien, proposed that the country be repartitioned, with the strongly nationalist southern portions of Armagh, Tyrone, Down and Fermanagh becoming part of the Republic. His own Labour Party rejected the suggestion while Unionists called it "insane". The Taoiseach's mother, Sarah Ann Haughey, gave an interview in which she said she'd dearly like to see a united Ireland. In her 80th year, and with the North's sectarian divide a gaping chasm, she mused with supreme positivism: "I hope to see it in my own lifetime and I'm optimistic about it too." Recalling the Taoiseach as a boy she revealed: "The only fault I had with him is that it wasn't easy to get him to work in the garden. I remember I said to him once would he help me with it and he said that he'd never handle anything heavier than a pen."

Conor Cruise O'Brien arranged for the press to follow him on a canvass in Coolock, in the constituency he shared with Haughey. Despite Haughey's huge popularity in the area, nearly all the householders who answered their doors were sympathetic to the Labour man. When the reporters suggested that this seemed a tad suspicious, O'Brien quipped: "We drugged all the others."

In Kerry, a Fine Gael worker complained that H-Block activists were playing the 'holier-than-Thou' card at after-Mass meetings. He told a reporter: "They're saying that Jesus told them to take care of the prisoners, so it's the Christian duty to vote for Séan McKenna."

Fianna Fáil and Fine Gael both went to the same printer with orders for strikingly similar car windscreen strips bearing the party name. Fianna Fáil organiser Séan O'Connor told the media: "We're running a good no-nonsense, no gimmicks campaign." He went on to explain that the party had two different tee-shirts – "One for youth and one for ordinary people" – plus a range of cardboard hats, stickers, badges and Haughey posters in the style of the Tricolour. Commenting on his party's stickers, a spokesman for Sinn Féin The Workers Party said: "The kids love them. They plaster them all over the mammy's windows and you go out canvassing and think 'Great, here's a supporter' – then they chase you out of the place."

On the Sunday before the Thursday poll, the Health Minister Michael Woods made the surprise announcement that Fianna Fáil back in office would provide free dental and eye care for teens and housewives. The Irish Dental Association protested that it had agreed nothing with the government. Woods rejected claims that his announcement was a cynical gimmick, pointing out that clearly: "It is absurd to say that these schemes are being introduced with the election in mind."

Woods' Junior Minister at Health, Tom Hussey, called on the nation's youth clubs to accept disabled people as members and not corral them away in 'handicapped groups'. The Disabled Persons Action Group parked wheelchairs outside the polling stations attended by the three main party leaders. The organisers hoped – in vain, as it turned out – to get the politicians to sit in the wheelchairs and experience the great difficulties facing disabled voters just to get into the building.

Solicitor Andrew Dillon stood in Dublin as leader of the Young Ireland Party "to answer the needs of the Irish Enthusiast and Idealist". His party promised to provide full employment at a stroke by the simple expedient of taking all the available work in the country and dividing it out amongst the available workers.

As polling day neared, Dillon took the Minister of Post & Telegraphs, Albert Reynolds, to court demanding his constitutional right to have the Post Office mail his election literature free of charge. Following standard procedures he had submitted a draft of his election material to the Department for approval. The Department rejected the application, saying that the material was unfit for free distribution unless Dillon agreed to have it censored first.

One of the passages the Department wanted to cut said: "Today's politicians are dishonest because they are being political and must please the largest number of people."

In the High Court, counsel for Minister Reynolds claimed that this line was "grossly offensive" to politicians, and therefore was in breach of the rules. Mr Justice Ellis agreed that the use of the word dishonest in reference to politicians, especially at election time, was to associate them in the public mind with possible corruption, cheating, deceit, underhand dealing and a host of other forms of wrongdoing which could warrant the attention of the police.

The Judge took the view that the suggestion of dishonesty was a slur on a varied body of outstanding citizens, many of whom had brought great distinction on their country and themselves. The Judge found it difficult to think of a word likely to cause more offense, more displeasure, more annoyance or more insult than the word "dishonest". There would be no free postage for Andrew Dillon, he ruled.

Dillon's barrister, Harry Whelehan, dashed straight off to the Supreme Court which agreed to hear his appeal that same day. The highest court in the land ruled that a candidate could not be denied free postage just because the Minister of Post & Telegraphs didn't like what he had to say. Overturning the High Court verdict, Mr Justice Henchy said that those who practiced what he called "the art of the possible" couldn't reasonably be offended by someone expressing an opinion which rated as no more "than the small coinage of the currency of political controversy".

He continued: "Some of the most revered and successful politicians who have lived have failed, at least in the eyes of reputable historians, to align great political acumen and success with moral or intellectual honesty. A charge of dishonesty is one that rarely penetrates the epidermis of any seasoned politician."

Supporting Justice Henchy's judgement, Mr Justice

Kenny stated that Dillon was not accusing politicians of
being financially bent, but of being intellectually dishonest,
which was "small change" on the trading floor of politics.

The Supreme Court ordered the postal service to mail
Dillon's material for free without further delay.

All Aboard The Pirates

Fianna Fáil published a 16-page newspaper called *Election
Special* for free nationwide distribution. The front page
headline was: FIANNA FÁIL TO WIN. The lead story
began: "Fianna Fáil looks certain to be returned to office with
an overall majority in Thursday's general election." The
inside back page was given over to a game of political snakes
and ladders.

As the governing party responsible for upholding the
broadcasting laws, Fianna Fáil officially took a dim view of
the pirate radio stations which were taking listeners and
advertising revenue from RTE's struggling pop station, Radio
2. However, some Fianna Fáil candidates just couldn't resist
the big audiences and low, low advertising rates. One
deputy's jingle on Big D Radio chimed: "Jim Tunney here,
asking you to support Charlie Haughey and Fianna Fáil."
Minister of State Tunney went on to tell young voters about
his party's policies on education, unemployment and sport.

The heavy rotation plug for Liam Lawlor TD on the same
station offered thanks to the Peace Corps of Ballyfermot for
providing him with a "great day" recently. Meanwhile Gerard
Brady TD, Senator Michael Donnelly and Junior Minister
Seán Moore pooled their funds for a joint advert on Big D
which urged voters: "Let's have three for Charlie!"

The RTE Country'n'Western personality Paschal
Mooney, who was working at Fianna Fáil HQ, told reporters:
"Fianna Fáil has no official contact with the pirate stations –
they're all outside the law. Any inquiries from local
constituencies have been told not to have any contact with

them and, as far as we know, they are going along with this."

Over in Fine Gael HQ, Bill O'Herlihy, also of RTE, said that the main opposition party had no qualms about broadcasting on the pirates. He stated: "We're using them in relation to our youth policy and Dublin plan." Fine Gael candidates could be heard on Radio Dublin, Big D and Southside Radio. Labour were not using the pirates. "We don't have the money," said a spokesman.

Fine Gael were pushing for a mano-a-mano TV debate between Garret Fitzgerald and Haughey, but fearing that the Fine Gael leader was beginning to look far too much like a credible alternative Taoiseach, Haughey backed the claims of Labour leader Frank Cluskey that he should be included in a three-way discussion. RTE turned down Cluskey's demand. With Haughey refusing to go up against Fitzgerald, RTE said it was pulling the plug on the planned programme. Haughey was furious when the *Irish Independent* ran the front page headline HAUGHEY DODGES TRIAL BY TV. In Swinford, Co Mayo, a paint bomb was thrown at the Fine Gael election office, covering it with yellow paint. Fitzgerald told listeners: "The colour of the paint symbolises the attitude of the Taoiseach when it comes to facing me in a television debate."

Having announced that if the TV debate wasn't two-way there would be none at all, RTE did a u-turn and the three leaders were quizzed in studio by a panel of journalists. During the exercise Haughey remained composed, even when statistics were produced that seemed to pull the rug from under his election promises. The day after the TV debate, Fianna Fáil's odds of winning an overall majority shortened from 2/1 to 13/8. The reason was a series of £1,000 bets which Fianna Fáil HQ claimed were evidence that Haughey had won the three-handed TV debate.

A pre-recorded Fianna Fáil party political broadcast spluttered off the air for thirty seconds just at the part where

Minister Albert Reynolds was telling the public how much the country's communications network had improved under his stewardship. One woman phoned RTE to complain that a particular programme had been unfairly biased in favour of Fine Gael. The programme in question was a Fine Gael party political broadcast.

A Typing Blunder

The week before polling day a well-known businessman sent a donation of £500 to Fianna Fáil. The substantial contribution to the election campaign was in the form of a crossed company cheque. The donor was the company's Managing Director. The money was posted to the party's Financial Director, Des Hanafin, at the party's headquarters on Mount Street in Dublin. It ended up instead across the road in Fine Gael HQ where it was photocopied before being redirected to the correct address.

Attached to the cheque was a note. It began: "Dear Des, please find enclosed a cheque for £500 for the general election fund. As in previous times, an invoice for same would be of great benefit." The photocopies were passed on to a newspaper, which ran a front page story pointing out that contributions to political parties are not allowable for tax relief as business expenses. However if a donor was to receive an invoice instead of a receipt, he might be able to claim a tax rebate of up to 45% if the company's auditor wasn't too much of a stickler for detail.

The newspaper phoned the unnamed donor. Why had he asked for an invoice and not a receipt? The businessman said there must have been a "typing blunder". He hung up to check with his secretary and rang back to confirm that the note should indeed have said "receipt" and that only receipts and not invoices had been received from Fianna Fáil in the "previous times" mentioned in his note.

Des Hanafin was contacted on the campaign trail in

Tipperary. He raised the clear impossibility of irregularities taking place, asking: "How could Fianna Fáil send invoices to anybody?" He was asked if he didn't think it a bit strange that the head of a large retail business would confuse a receipt with an invoice. His instinctive answer was the same as that given by the donor: "It must have been a typing error." He added that it was "scurrilous" and "below the belt" for Fine Gael to pass on the misdirected letter to the media.

Fine Gael responded that it was merely serving the public's right to know by publicising the matter. Peter Prendergast argued: "The clear implication of this letter is that companies who contribute to that party's election fund have been given invoices in return so that they can claim these contributions as a tax-deductible expense."

If It's Not Legal, It's Not Legal

Bertie Ahern and Garret Fitzgerald were both quick out of the blocks as soon as the campaign was called. On the day the Dáil was dissolved, Olivia O'Leary of The Irish Times wrote: "Bertie Ahern ran around like a madman gathering constituency ammunition from the photocopying machines."

Garret Fitzgerald arrived at the Sheriff's Office early on a Monday morning with a knot of journalists in tow to witness him lodging his nomination papers. It was to prove a waste of time for all concerned. The official behind the counter refused to accept the documents as it was two days too soon to register. A mortified Fitzgerald aide pointed out that she had phoned in advance to make the appointment. The official replied that they may well have given her an appointment, but they'd never agreed to accept Fitzgerald's nomination forms. "Not until Wednesday," he said. "It's not legal before that." Garret steered his entourage out of the office sighing: "Oh well, if it's not legal, it's not legal."

Fine Gael's Director of Elections, Enda Marron, accused Fianna Fáil of "dirty tricks" after many of the party's posters and hoardings were destroyed in orchestrated blitzes. He charged that Fianna Fáil had paid guerilla gurriers to do substantial damage in Dublin and Wexford, where many large hoardings standing in private fields had been felled with saws and then smashed. Fianna Fáil responded that its election workers hadn't noticed any more vandalism than was usual.

Garret Fitzgerald and his wife each received polling cards to vote at two different polling stations, while a family in Tipperary was registered to vote in three different locations. Fine Gael said that the electoral register was in such a shambles that the party was "extremely worried about massive personation". Labour cited one woman who told a canvasser she wouldn't be around to vote on polling day, and was told that someone would call to collect her card. The party said that it had heard of canvassers going door-to-door collecting 'tickets' and asking householders if they intended to vote.

In Tallaght, Mary Harney of Fianna Fáil called for the legal age of marriage to be raised from the "absurd" age of 14 to 18. Fine Gael tried to woo the nation's married women working in the home by proposing to pay them a weekly State wage of £10. The money would be theirs, and not their husband's. Fianna Fáil responded with the following advert: "Fine Gael Want To Rob Peter To Pay Paula – And They Propose To Make It Lawful! The £500 per annum Fine Gael say they would pay to some housewives would be deducted from their husband's tax relief. Think Paula – would Peter like that? Vote Fianna Fáil on June 11."

The advert provoked a storm of protest from women's groups and was hastily withdrawn.

As polling day approached, the Health Education Bureau sent out a public information pamphlet on the dangers of alcohol. It outlined at length the reasons a person might drink, including anxiety, feelings of inferiority, a lack of self-control, or "to blot out feelings of guilt, shame, depression, meaninglessness or boredom". The last item on the list said: "People may even drink for reasons of thirst."

The academic Maurice Manning stood for Fine Gael in Dublin North East. His election leaflets told voters. "He is the author of several books, including the widely-read *Irish Political Parties*." The pamphlet made no mention of Manning's best known book, *The Blueshirts*.

The Fianna Fáil Minister for State, Jackie Fahy, upset constituency colleagues by running a 'personal canvas' against party rules. He had sent out a circular saying: "You will recall that when you had a problem you came to me for help. I'm sure that you will agree that I did my very best for you and made no small effort to be of assistance. In my turn I now have a problem and you can be of assistance to me … I need to be re-elected to Dáil Eireann in the coming election. Putting it simply, I need your No 1." Fahey agreed to desist.

There were times when the dizzying pace of his whistle-stop touring posed Garret Fitzgerald with problems of his own. Addressing a crowd in Swinford, Co Mayo, he said: "I want to thank the people of (pause) … this town. And I want you to vote one, two, three, in order of your preference for (pause) …" At this point he anxiously scanned his surroundings until his eyes lit upon a Fine Gael placard. Relieved, he continued " … Martin Finn, Jim Higgins and Paddy O'Toole." Canvassing in Gorey, Garret was asked by a nun from the nearby convent: "Was your mother a Loreto nun?"

"What?!"

It wasn't a Fianna Fáil smear. The blushing nun meant to say aunt, not mother. Garret's smile returned and he said that his wife had an aunt in the order.

It was standard Fianna Fáil strategy to belittle the notion of coalition as fundamentally inferior to strong single party government. This time, however, Fine Gael's John Kelly gave Fianna Fáil a helping hand. During a TV debate, Kelly said that the "uncontaminated product" of a Fine Gael majority would be preferable to coalition with Labour. Fianna Fáil leaped on his words, taking out big adverts headlined THE COALITION – A CONTAMINATION. The advert asked: "If you are a Labour Party supporter do you want to join a coalition in which the Labour Party would be regarded as 'a contamination'?" Just for good measure, the ad featured a footnote in the style of a dictionary extract. It said: "Contamination: To defile by touching or mixing with; to pollute; to corrupt; to infect."

Fine Gael's Paddy Harte countered that Fianna Fáil was a pantomime horse, saying: "At the front, Mr Haughey tries to lead one way – at the back Mr Colley and his faction go another." Gerry L'Estrange of Fine Gael likened Charles Haughey to the favourite soap villain of the day, JR Ewing of *Dallas*. L'Estrange remarked: "Both are obsessed with their public images, both behave irresponsibly where other people's money is concerned, and both try to maintain the useless pretence that the houses they rule are not divided."

Only Midgets Need Apply

CIE had ordered a fleet of 300 new buses to be built by Bombardier in Shannon, but the project had been plagued with design faults and delays. In the run up to polling day a demonstration was scheduled to give Dubliners a preview of the shape of things to come in public transport. Two prototype buses were assigned to run up and down the No 8 route from the city centre to Dalkey. The demonstration was scrapped when the National Busmans' Union objected that only "midget" conductors could work the top deck.

Tom Darby of the NBU stated: "They're getting a timely warning from us now. They haven't that many of the yokes built yet and we're not going to have our people crippled up from working in a stoop." Some days later CIE came back with an agreement to raise the roof.

In his role as Minister for Transport, Albert Reynolds had introduced Dublin's first bus lane one year previously, and he now wanted to push through more of them. However, during the campaign the news broke that the Gardaí had tried to block the introduction of bus lanes to Dublin, fighting the Minister tooth and nail on the issue. The Gardaí had even approached the Attorney General, pressing him to advise Reynolds that the lanes were technically illegal. As the traffic enforcers of Dublin, the guards argued that they'd need to provide "massive enforcement" to keep car drivers out of the lanes. They argued that they would be left "holding the baby" when massive enforcement was not resourced and the scheme failed.

It was reported that the Environment Minister, Ray Burke, opposed Reynolds at the Cabinet table over the bus lanes. One of the first planned was for the Swords Road in Burke's constituency and *The Irish Times* speculated that Burke feared "a possible negative reaction from his North Dublin motoring constituents" if their road space was restricted. There was criticism at the time that the Gardaí were misspending too much of their time when they should be out catching the real criminals. The guards' standard defence was that they were overstretched and under-resourced. A body called the Dublin Transportation Task Force offered to free them up for real policing duties by taking over a number of responsibilities including control of the city's traffic wardens. The Gardaí gave a firm 'No'.

It was a time of oil crisis, and a steep hike in the price of petrol was in the pipeline for after the election, no matter who ended up in government. A couple of years earlier as Energy Minister, Fianna Fáil's Des O'Malley had drawn up plans to secure Ireland's power supplies by building a nuclear power plant at Carnsore Point in Wexford. The project generated widespread protests, a Christy Moore dirge and a *Late Late Show* special. Then, with devastating timing, news arrived from the United States of a nuclear leak at Three Mile Island and a sinister attempted cover-up, subsequently dramatised in the movie *The China Syndrome*.

One of O'Malley's Fianna Fáil colleagues gamely attempted to recover the situation by drawing up a 'disaster plan' for Wexford. Disappointingly, instead of boosting enthusiasm for the nuclear plant, the contingency plan to cope with the threat of mass death and destruction had precisely the opposite effect on public confidence, and O'Malley's scheme was abandoned.

As polling day 1981 neared, O'Malley's successor at Energy, George Colley, promised that 2,400 farmhouses in the West would get electricity in the next 18 months. He also predicted that huge reserves of coal below Dublin Bay could be a major source of energy by the mid-1990s. Colley said that the technology would soon be available to mine the estimated 175 million tonnes of coal 2,000 feet down. Colley also proposed investigating harnessing the geothermal energy from the 13 hot underground springs cutting diagonally across the land from Meath to Clare.

1982 Act One

SMALL-FOOTED WOMEN

The Incumbents: FG/Labour Coalition led by Garret Fitzgerald.
Slogan: Fiscal rectude.
Promise: To bite the bullet.
The Challengers: Fianna Fáil led by Charles Haughey.
Promise: Two thousand extra Gardaí.
The Mood of the Country: Not again!
Prediction: Too close to call.
Result: Fianna Fáil and some independent friends.
Entertainment value: 9/10.

Two Thousand Extra Gardaí

When Garret Fitzgerald's Fine Gael/Labour government
came into office following the June 1981 election, they
quickly asserted that the previous administration of Charles
Haughey had cooked the books and that the nation's
finances were in a far worse state than had been supposed.
Pledging himself to a policy of hardline fiscal rectitude,
Fitzgerald implemented a range of spending cutbacks that
didn't go down well with those who had to suffer them.

The resentment at the new regime started in Leinster
House itself, with the elected representatives of the hard-
pressed public. TDs and Senators were (and still are) able to
claim generous expenses for travel, accommodation and
other costs associated with their attendance at Leinster
House. These expenses were (and are) unvouched and paid

on trust, leaving the way open for members to claim for costs never actually incurred.

In order to set a good example for the rest of the country, the new Taoiseach set out to tackle the culture of abuse. Fitzgerald had a roll book placed at the entrance of Leinster House where he expected Oireachtas members to sign in as proof that they'd actually dropped in on their workplace. The TDs and Senators treated this affront with the contempt they felt it deserved, and the offending article contained only two signatures when it was quietly removed.

A more serious misjudgement of in-House affairs was the undoing of Fitzgerald's minority government in January 1982 when he unveiled a savage debut budget. He had failed to heed the warnings of Independent Socialist Jim Kemmy, who'd threatened that he would resist the removal of subsidies on food and the imposition of VAT on clothing. Fitzgerald patiently explained that if you exempted children's shoes from VAT, selfish small-footed women might be tempted to diddle the State of its rightful revenue. True to his word, Kemmy withdrew his support and the coalition collapsed in numbed shock after just seven months in office.

With all the parties still in debt from the campaign of the previous summer, and with the winter biting hard, it was an election that nobody wanted, especially Defence Minister Jim Tully. Pronouncing the country "very nearly ungovernable", Tully said he was retiring from politics after "seven months of Hell". By stepping down, Tully saved himself several weeks of Hell on the doorsteps, as government candidates got a tongue-lashing from the voters. It was put to Fine Gael's golden boy Michael Keating that his reception in Cabra had been extremely hostile. "Quite right too," he replied. "I'd have been worried if we hadn't got it."

The Labour leader Michael O'Leary was rebuked by one woman for preaching belt-tightening for the general populace while he himself dined at the Mirabeau Restaurant.

The Mirabeau was so fabulously expensive that the printed menus didn't display any prices. The constituent told O'Leary: "You shouldn't be eating in the Mirabeau, a socialist like you. I didn't see you myself – I couldn't afford the prices – but a friend saw you there last summer." Elsewhere, O'Leary availed of a photo-opportunity at St Agatha's Church in Dublin for the annual Blessing Of The Throat. He was photographed with a priest holding two candlesticks up to his windpipe like a pair of shears.

Even though the outgoing Fitzgerald government managed to move the public finances to the epicentre of the campaign, other issues were raised on the doorsteps, with rising crime a concern of many. Heroin had taken a grip in central Dublin over the past two years, with the result that drug-related crime had soared. Charles Haughey promised that Fianna Fáil, if returned to power, would recruit 2,000 extra Gardaí.

The Haughey Factor

Having taken a pratfall over a botched budget, the Coalition parties did their best to make that Dáil defeat look like a point of principle, pitching themselves as the true upholders of moral and economic virtue. Their remedy to the nation's financial woes wouldn't be easy, they said, but the alternative was rack and ruin for everyone. They challenged Fianna Fáil to come up with something better. When their rivals did produce a solution supposedly less painful, Fine Gael's John Bruton accused Haughey of trying to con the electorate with "funny money".

The Fitzgerald government's cause was helped when a Department of Finance source leaked information to *Magill*, which ran a damaging cover story headlined: HOW HAUGHEY COOKED THE BOOKS IN '81. The story asserted that the then Taoiseach had massaged the figures to disguise promiscuous levels of borrowing. Haughey responded that he hadn't read, would not read and would not comment "on articles in the gutter journals of this country". He slated Vincent Browne's *Magill* as "a rubbish magazine".

The calculated attempts by the Fitzgerald government to raise doubts about Haughey's character had their effect and, as Haughey's satisfaction ratings in the polls slipped, his photo was dropped from a range of Fianna Fáil election material.

Fianna Fáil fought back by accusing the government of waging a diabolical whispering campaign against Haughey instead of focusing on the real issues. Fingering one of those real issues, Padraig Flynn maintained: "There's one thing we have that they [Fine Gael] can never have, and that's a love of the four green fields of Ireland."

Former Minister for Posts & Telegraphs and tee-totaller, Albert Reynolds, targeted the country's public houses as the transmission points for the nefarious whispering campaign against his leader. Reynolds – who maintained that the Coalition themselves were guilty of cooking the books – said that pub talk was the most effective bush-telegraph in Ireland and the government smear campaign against Haughey had been systematic from the outset. However, he insisted that the Irish people could be trusted to swallow their beers without the smears.

Reynolds was asked to spell out how exactly this whispering campaign was being orchestrated? His answer was that anyone who took the trouble to send pub spies into the nation's watering holes would quickly find that out for themselves.

Nine years later in 1991, after openly challenging Haughey's leadership, Reynolds would complain of a whispering campaign directed against himself, adding that a white Hiace van seemed to be keeping his Dublin home under surveillance.

The Haughey Factor was not just an issue of division between the parties, but a divisive issue within Fianna Fáil itself, where some had deep qualms about his fitness to lead the party. Senior figures Des O'Malley and George Colley insisted that Haughey liaise with the party's economics guru Martin O'Donoghue, whom Haughey had dropped from the cabinet two years earlier. Haughey reluctantly agreed, but there was no disguising the rift between the chief and his trio of would-be watchdogs.

One of Haughey's party pieces was to have just one microphone at press conferences, and to keep a tight rein on it, in an effort to control the contributions of party colleagues. At one Q&A session the vexed question of Knock Airport came up. As Taoiseach, Haughey had given the project the go-ahead, but the Fitzgerald administration had deemed it an extravagance and had cocked the white elephant gun. At the press conference, Haughey was asked if he would allow work to resume on Knock. "Yes," he said. He aimed the microphone at Des O'Malley, who said he might not have started it in the first place, but he believed the work begun should be completed.

Next Martin O'Donoghue was asked if he was of the same mind as his leader. Over the open microphone, Haughey could be clearly heard hissing at him: "Say yes." O'Donoghue's response was: "No." Then, after a pregnant pause, he added: "I don't think government commitments should be dropped."

There were other prickly patches. Haughey joined Bobby Molloy on the canvas in Eyre Square to provide a leader's endorsement of the Galway Deputy. The pair didn't get on, but business was business. At a press conference, Haughey was asked why he'd dropped Molloy from the front bench during the last Fianna Fáil government.

He objected: "I did *not* drop Mr Molloy from the front bench."

Molloy sulkily made the Jesuitical distinction: "I was dropped from the *Cabinet*."

Why did you drop Bobby Molloy from the Cabinet?

"I did not drop him from the Cabinet. There was a new government of which Mr Molloy was not a member."

Vote Early And Vote Often

On the morning of polling day, Charles Haughey's close friend and solicitor, Pat O'Connor, was sensationally charged with attempting to vote at two polling stations in the extremely tight constituency of Dublin North. O'Connor had been allocated ballot papers at two polling stations and had opted to use his full allocation. By lunchtime the damaging news was splashed across the front of *The Evening Herald.* Fianna Fáil activists mobilised, and drove around the district's newsagents trying to snap up every copy in bulk. After the polling booths shut that night, a car pulled up outside the Fine Gael headquarters in Malahide and one of the occupants hurled a bundle of *Heralds* through the front door.

Just as RTE's six o'clock news was about to go on air, the constituency suffered a widespread power blackout. Locals said that someone had thrown a bicycle into an ESB transformer. If the cause was a flung bicycle, the fling was for nothing because RTE decided not to mention the hottest news story in yonks. Accused of craven cowardice, and worse, the national broadcaster maintained it was "normal practice" to delay coverage of an alleged offence until the accused person had been charged in court. O'Connor's wife claimed that the whole furore was a Fine Gael-inspired "malicious smear campaign".

The case took longer to come to court than most other personation cases from the same day, and election workers who gave statements concerning the incident were revisited by a senior police officer and given the chance to double-check the accounts they had sworn and signed on the day it happened. After the garda's intervention, two witnesses

opted to change their statements. One had been "too tired
and hungry from work" to be fully reliable at the first time of
asking. The other had been "tired and weary after a 14-hour
day without a decent meal". In court, the judge cleared
O'Connor on the grounds that the method of secret ballot
used at Irish elections makes it impossible to tell if someone
has voted once, never mind twice. Leaving the court, Pat
O'Connor Pat O'Connor, as he had now been redubbed by
the public, praised the judge's verdict as "excellent".

Off Message

The Fine Gael Press Office sent out a press release headed:
FORMER COMMISSIONER RICHARD BURKE
SPEAKING IN CLONDALKIN. According to the
statement, Burke had made a speech in the Dublin suburb of
Clondalkin attacking Charles Haughey for opposing food
subsidies. To *The Irish Times*, the news that the populist
Charles Haughey would have a go at food subsidies for the
less-well-off sounded entirely out of character. The
newspaper phoned Burke to ask when Haughey had
launched his tirade against the relief on food prices. The Fine
Gael deputy said he had no idea Haughey had attacked food
subsidies, and he'd certainly never said that Haughey had
said anything of the sort. Burke added that he hadn't made
any campaign speeches to date, and he wouldn't be making
any in Clondalkin because Clondalkin wasn't in his
constituency.

Not to be outdone in the "Earth Calling ..." stakes,
Labour leader Michael O'Leary gave a radio interview to
John Bowman on RTE. In order to underline the gravity of
the financial crisis facing the country, the outgoing
government had offered Fianna Fáil the use of the
Department of Finance's number crunchers to cost the
opposition's budget proposals. O'Leary told Bowman: "Now
the electorate are beginning to put questions to the

opposition party and the answers are not forthcoming, and it's very interesting to see they have refused to take up Garret Fitzgerald's invitation that they should come in and look at the books."

Bowman: "No – they have accepted that invitation."

O'Leary: "Have they accepted that? When?"

Bowman: "About two days ago."

There followed the hush of dead air.

The face-to-face TV debate between Fitzgerald and Haughey was billed as the main event of the entire campaign. When it was all over, there was widespread agreement that the clear winner was RTE's moderator, Brian Farrell.

1982 Act Two

CAR CRASH GOVERNMENT

The Incumbents: Fianna Fáil led by Charles Haughey.
Slogan: It's the economy, stupid, not all the other stuff.
Promise: You name it, we'll do it.
The Challengers: Fine Gael led by Garret Fitzgerald.
Promise: To be decent, honest and trustworthy.
Slogan: To restore sane government.
The Mood of the Country: Dazed and Confused.
Prediction: Win for the FG/Labour Coalition.
Result: A Coalition win.
Entertainment value: 9/10.

A Campaign Of National Sabotage

At the start of 1982 Charles Haughey had won his first general election as the leader of Fianna Fáil by a slender margin. Before the year was out his minority government was wobbling and his own position at the head of the party was under open attack from within. Just weeks before the administration collapsed, there were ructions within Fianna Fáil when a little known TD from Kildare, Charlie McCreevy, launched a heave against The Boss. In McCreevy's memorable words, it was time for the anti-Haughey faction to "shit or get off the pot".

The McCreevy-led 'Club of 22' lost the parliamentary party vote to ditch Haughey. After the conclave broke up, the conspirators were roughed up by Haughey supporters in the corridors of Leinster House as they left the building. One anti-Haughey deputy, Jim Gibbons, was struck on the head in the Dáil car park while another, Mary Harney, was jostled and subjected to a torrent of verbal abuse. Gardaí urged McCreevy to leave by a side exit, but he insisted on walking tall. He left under heavy protection, with howls of "Judas!" and "Blueshirt!" ringing in his ears.

As the second general election campaign of 1982 began weeks later, Dublin Corporation pointed out that some posters from the contest of the previous February had still not been taken down. In Fianna Fáil's few months in power the jobless figures had shot up by 30,000 to 171,000, but what really had the public's attention was a spectacular Grand Prix of car-crash government which had already been characterised as GUBU (Grotesque, Unbelievable, Bizarre and Unprecedented).

The GUBU acronym had been coined by Labour's Conor Cruise O'Brien after a deranged double murderer, Malcolm MacArthur, had been tracked down to the home of Haughey's Attorney General, Patrick Connolly. Earlier, Haughey had perpetrated a political grotesquerie when he deprived one of his own tribe of a top European post, by giving it to the Fine Gael TD Dick Burke. The cunning plan was to win the subsequent by-election, trading the prized Euro perk for a badly needed extra Dáil seat. It all came horribly unstuck when Haughey's man bombed in the by-election.

Throughout the campaign, allegations were rife that Haughey's Justice Minister Séan Doherty had placed illegal phone taps and had generally been throwing his weight around like a latter-day Wyatt Earp, riding roughshod over the niceties of the law. Two months before the election, a garda car on protection detail with Doherty crashed in mysterious circumstances. The car, which contained a pistol and Uzi sub-machine gun, was abandoned for a time.

When Fine Gael tabled a Dáil motion of no confidence in

the government, Fianna Fáil's Chief Whip Bertie Ahern worked to cobble together a deal which would prevent the administration's fall, but the writing was on the wall. Within two hours of the government's collapse, voters in Ahern's Drumcondra constituency received a letter reminding them of how hard he'd worked for them since the election of the previous February.

In the Dáil no confidence debate, Fianna Fáil went down kicking and screaming. Taoiseach Charles Haughey accused the opposition of "undemocratic haste" in rushing to fell the government. The Minister for Industry & Commerce, Gene Fitzgerald, accused Fine Gael of waging a campaign of "personal vilification and accusations". Addressing his Fine Gael namesake Garret, he raged: "It is not going too far to accuse him and his party of a campaign of national sabotage that reflects no concern for the people we all represent or for the economy, but is directed solely to the attainment of political advantage. It is hypocritical in the extreme." He continued: "Smears, insinuations, allegations and charges have been made at each and every member of the government and our leader. To take an example, we had this great story about telephone tapping, and we all know now the true story there. We know now that that was concocted and arranged by the leader of the main opposition party and some of his colleagues prior to the election last year but it was not proceeded with then. Why? Because it did not suit their purposes at the time."

The man under most pressure, Séan Doherty, bullishly accused the opposition of vandalising the office of the Minister for Justice, the reputation of the Irish State, and much more. He declared: "I have been vilified. I have been pursued by certain elements in the media, by politicians in the Fine Gael party, in this House and outside it. I do not wish to say more than that I will not allow my character, my integrity, nor indeed that of my wife or children to be impugned and vilified in the way it has been attempted." He continued: "It seriously damages Parliament and in many ways affects the capacity of the Minister for Justice, whether the office be held by me or by somebody else, to pursue his function in the way which is so essential at this difficult time."

He went on to complain about the "scurrilous" media coverage of his involvement with the crashed patrol car. Then, under parliamentary privilege, he named four opposition deputies and said he thought it strange that "there has been no mention of the accidents involving" them. At this point, Fine Gael's Enda Kenny asked the Justice Minister why he hadn't included on his list a separate accident involving a certain Fianna Fáil TD.

And so the tit-for-tat continued. Doherty said of the previous Justice Minister Jim Mitchell: "It is a pity Deputy Mitchell is not present. I ask him to tell us if his State car was involved in an accident, if there was a passenger in it, if that passenger was a lady, if anybody was injured, and if his driver had the full visual capacity to hold that position? I invite Deputy Mitchell to come into the House and answer those questions."

He further accused Mitchell of "direct interference with members of the Garda Síochana in the course of their duty", and he raised the issue of a relative of Mitchell's who he claimed had been stopped behind the wheel and found to be over the limit. Mitchell was Justice Minister at the time that the medical report, which was necessary to bringing a prosecution, had mysteriously gone missing. The Gardaí said that they'd never received the report, despite the fact it had been sent to them by registered post.

The reputation of the force was further tarnished during the campaign when the socialist deputy Jim Kemmy told reporters that there was a special cupboard in the interview room of the Bridewell Prison which was designed to allow detectives illegally eavesdrop on private conversations between prisoners and their solicitors. Kemmy showed reporters photos of a door with 20 spy holes drilled in it, which he described as "a form of dirty tricks by Gardaí in Detective Branch". He claimed that the photograph had been sent to him by a disenchanted officer, explaining: "Some Gardaí are afraid of what is going on in the force now." The photo showed that the cupboard door had a second highly unusual feature apart from the spy holes. This was a bolt which allowed it to be locked from the inside. Kemmy questioned why anyone would want to lock themselves into an ordinary cupboard. The hidey-hole was positioned convenient to where a consulting solicitor would sit facing his client.

The garda Press Office issued a statement saying: "It does not exist. There is no such cubbyhole in the Bridewell." A follow-up statement admitted that the cupboard in the photo did exist, but for the sole purpose of storing books, not spooks. A spokesman then said that a senior officer would investigate to establish the truth of the matter. And that was the end of that.

Glass Houses Throwing Stones

Garret Fitzgerald started the campaign as 1/2 favourite for the post of Taoiseach, and quickly improved to 1/3. In response, Haughey snorted: "This is not a beauty contest." The toppling of Haughey's government had begun with the loss of the voting power of two TDs. Deputy Bill Loughnane had died, while Jim Gibbons lay in hospital recovering from a double heart attack which had struck shortly after he'd been struck by a Fianna Fáil colleague in Leinster House. Ray Burke told a radio audience that Fine Gael, driven by "power lust", had "walked across the new grave of Bill Loughnane" and then dashed off to Kilkenny to go "crowding through" the intensive care unit where Gibbons lay weak as a kitten.

When Labour's Barry Desmond released a statement based on a government finance memo, Haughey claimed the document was stolen property. He charged: "Both Labour and Fine Gael seem to be engaging in a tactic of stealing documents from the Department of Finance and publishing them out of context to create a false impression." Desmond revealed that Bertie Ahern had freely handed the document to Labour's Mervyn Taylor as a matter of Dáil protocol. Haughey responded that no one had a right to hand over Department of Finance documents, and muttered darkly about the consequences for anyone committing "grave breaches" of the Official Secrets Act.

Having made the conversion to Fine Gael-style fiscal rectitude, Fianna Fáil wanted to fight the election on economic policy, but the public was more interested in filling its nostrils with the unmistakable whiff of sulphur. Brian Lenihan deplored the fact that: "The sort of rumours going around in recent times, like those about the Minister for Justice, are lies, absolute lies, lies."

At times, the Minister of Justice himself was literally incoherent with rage. At one point Doherty said: "I hate to see glass houses throwing stones when the panes in those houses are smashed, and the panes in Deputy Fitzgerald's are smashed." Another time, he warned Fine Gael: "You are a can of worms and I've taken the lid off you, and you'll be used as bait by the people of Ireland when they play with you in the next three weeks."

In a TV debate with Fine Gael's Jim Mitchell, Séan Doherty promised that if he was returned to Justice he would set up a judicial inquiry into himself to get to the bottom of allegations that he'd interfered with the Gardaí.

During the Falklands War earlier in the year, Haughey had infuriated Britain's Prime Minister Margaret Thatcher by voting against EEC sanctions on Argentina for invading the British possessions. At election time, with Fitzgerald getting favourable coverage in the British media, Haughey delivered the message: "Britain, stay out of our election. The Irish people are perfectly capable of deciding which government they want. They can choose for themselves." He added: "We arranged their departure from our country 60 years ago and we don't want them coming back in 1982."

Haughey told the voters of Waterford that he was arranging the decentralisation of 400 Posts & Telegraphs jobs to the town, which was an employment black spot. The jobs were ready to go "full steam ahead", along with thousands of other public service posts to be decentralised all over the country. "This is not an election gimmick," he stressed.

Albert Reynolds claimed that he had tapes which "proved" Fine Gael canvassers in the previous campaign had tried to smear his party leader. However, he would neither play nor display them. He commented: "I have the tapes locked away in my own safe. I will not be giving them to anybody. They were just used for my own information during the last general election."

With the character assassins stalking Haughey, his wife, Maureen made a rare public intervention to confirm that the opposition and their media lackeys were not playing cricket. She remarked: "He is always Garret The Good. Garret has a halo and Haughey has horns." The born-again Christians of U2 admired Garret's halo, and in the run up to polling day Fitzgerald dropped in to Windmill Lane Studios for a photo opportunity with the band as they completed their breakthrough album *War*.

Just before the election was called, Labour's Michael O'Leary dramatically quit the party, saying: "I would not stay on as a scarecrow leader." Within days he had joined Fine Gael. After O'Leary jumped ship, Labour's Barry Desmond told the viewers of the current affairs show *Today Tonight*: "We have cleared the decks for an election." "Yes," replied the host Brian Farrell, "and you've a man overboard too."

Checking The Death Notices

An anonymous civil servant wrote a letter to the papers accusing his Fianna Fáil Minister of using state employees to run his constituency clinic at the taxpayers' expense. The secret correspondent further charged that another civil servant in the same Department had been given the job of scanning the death notices every day and sending telegrams of condolence to any bereaved family that lived in the Minister's constituency. The writer complained: "This corruption goes on while the rest of the Department suffers vacancies, embargos on recruitment and promotion, a clampdown on official travel and exhortation to limit the use of phones and telex machines."

The civil servants of RTE were so concerned with the waste of scant resources that their unions said they would oppose the broadcast of any party political messages during the campaign, because the expenditure on these at a time of savage cutbacks would be "unfair". Montrose management told its workers that the station would stay within budget by cutting back on-location reports in favour of cheaper studio coverage.

With the pirates and super-pirates making serious inroads into RTE's radio advertising revenue, especially in Dublin, RTE's civil servants announced that they would 'black' any politician appearing on an illegal rival. RTE's chapel of the National Union of Journalists slammed the politicians for failing to sink the pirates, and said that it would also black all coverage from any party event where pirate reporters were allowed to attend.

The RTE workers proved as good as their word and nixed coverage of a Workers Party conference because a pirate reporter, Jenny McIvor of Radio Nova, had managed to gain entry. The 'father' of the RTE newsroom chapel, Charlie Bird, said the news blackout of the event was "an unfortunate case" but "a ban is a ban and we are sticking to it".

Crisis, What Crisis?

In the aftermath of the election, with Haughey defeated, there was a widespread belief that he would be heaved overboard by his party. Bookies installed Des O'Malley as 6/4 favourite to take over, and *The Irish Press* ran a full-blown political obituary, featuring a big photo-spread of key moments in Haughey's life and career. Employing the past tense, the *Press* said that Haughey had alienated many of "the traditional acceptable politicians of his own persuasion. It was this weakness above all else that led to his political demise."

In the event, the *Bangkok Post* had its finger nearer the pulse. Albert Reynolds arrived back from Thailand on the day the *Press* obituary was published. He had a copy of the *Bangkok Post* with him. Under the headline IRISH WATERGATE, the Thai paper carried a much more positive prognosis for Haughey's future. It said: "Former Prime Minister Charles Haughey appeared determined yesterday to flush out dissidents in his Fianna Fáil Party."

The new Dáil met on the day *The Irish Press* pronounced Haughey a dead duck. One newspaper report said that as the deputies arrived at Leinster House in the morning, Haughey's room to manoeuvre was on a par with rearranging the deckchairs on the Titanic. By the end of the day, with Haughey having pulled off yet another Houdini act, some TDs were wondering with awed admiration whether the Titanic would have gone down if The Boss had been on the bridge.

1987

A 32-COUNTY BRITISH IRELAND

The Incumbents: FG & Labour led by Garret Fitzgerald.
Slogan: Fine Gael did not invent unemployment.
Promise: More of the same hairshirt policies.
The Challengers: Fianna Fáil led by Charles Haughey.
Promise: Things can only get better.
Slogan: Health cuts hurt the sick and elderly.
The Mood of the Country: Deep depression.
Prediction: Fianna Fáil to shade it.
Result: Fianna Fáil shade it with no overall majority.
Entertainment value: 8/10

I Wouldn't Give Him The Itch

The backdrop slogan of the 1987 election didn't come from any of the declared runners. Instead it came from the broadcaster Gay Byrne whose stock response to his listeners' endless gripes was: "The country is banjaxed." The Society of the Irish Motor Industry held a mock funeral procession through the centre of Dublin to mark the death of the car trade. A float made up as a coffin and a lone piper were followed by a cortege of black cars. The banners said: 'Axe The Tax'. They called on the government to stop taxing cars as a luxury item when they were an everyday necessity. At a time when the rest of Europe was choking with traffic, the number of cars on Irish roads had plunged by 20,000 in the previous six years.

The Independent in London remarked sympathetically: "Elections without hope are sad businesses indeed." Looking on from that corner which will always be Little England, *The Sunday Telegraph* said of its destitute neighbour: "If the country were an individual it would have been arrested." *The Economist* would have denied Ireland even the small comfort of protective custody. It lashed the "domestic extravagance" of increased spending on State help-outs over the previous six years.

The commentator Brendan O hEithir picked a Polish parable to illustrate the state of the nation as polling day approached. A man under Poland's communist yoke spends all morning queuing for food, but when he finally reaches the shop counter he is told that every last scrap is gone. He then spends the afternoon in line for soap, only to find there's no soap left. Dirty, hungry and frustrated, he mutters aloud: "This country has gone to the dogs!" A passer-by taps him on the shoulder and says: "In the old days that remark would have got you put up against a wall and shot, but times have changed and these days we're all free to speak our minds." The man goes home empty handed and tells his wife: "Things are even worse than either of us imagined – now they've even run out of bullets!"

A journalist on the campaign trail picked up a young man home on holiday from Libya, where he considered himself fortunate to have found work rebuilding Tripoli, even as more bombs flattened it. The situation in Ireland was so grave that there were calls, led by *Magill* publisher Vincent Browne, for the voluntary formation of an all-party national government before one was forced on the nation by impending calamity.

After five years waiting to reclaim power, Charles Haughey was having none of it. He argued: "National governments are, in a way, a denial of democracy. There would be no opposition. National governments are only appropriate in a war situation."

Even without actual war, the doom and gloom was stultifying. Browne's *Magill* magazine convened a panel of experts in 1987 to predict the state of Ireland in 1997. The panel concluded that the country would have "a smaller, older population", "continuing high unemployment", a "steady loss of young people through emigration" and "no end to violence in the North". After four years of cutbacks, Taoiseach Garret Fitzgerald sounded beaten before the campaign began. He reflected: "If people evaluate the programmes, in logic they will come to us – if logic means anything in politics, which I tend to doubt." His shaky grip on power was unwittingly underlined shortly before the campaign by a BBC commentator who announced: "The future of Dr Fitzgerald's government depends on two DTs."

Bob Geldof said it would be "scandalous" if Charles Haughey was elected Taoiseach, but admirers of Haughey argued that he should be given the chance to succeed where four years of coalition policies had failed. After all, he had transformed himself from a pauper into a prince. If he could work the magic for himself, why not for the country? The difference in approach between the alternative Taoisigh formed the basis of a lame joke.

Q: Would you buy a used car from Charlie Haughey?

A: No, but Garret probably would.

Themes of poverty and hardship dominated the campaign. For their party political broadcast, the Workers Party did a spoof of the Mastermind quiz entitled *Fastermind*. It went: "What is Fine Gael's economic policy?"

"To attack the poor before the election."

"Correct."

"What is Fianna Fáil's economic policy?"

"To attack the poor *after* the election."

"Correct."

Charles Haughey was doing a radio phone-in with host John Bowman when a caller rang to say that the free coal for the poor from the Mayor of Limerick's Christmas Fund had arrived too late to fend off a recent cold snap. He was livid that when the coal did belatedly arrive, the vouchers that accompanied the deliveries were printed with a message from the Mayor, Jack Burke, to vote Fianna Fáil. Describing the stunt as "disgraceful", Haughey said: "I don't think the poor should be exploited at all in this way." Burke's blunt response was: "I could see nothing wrong with this. We are not in a boy scouts rally."

Things were so bad that even alleged attempts to buy the election were done on the cheap. *The Cork Examiner* reported that Gardaí were investigating the involvement of an unnamed politician in Kerry South, in a scam to forge P60 forms for farmer constituents to claim headage payments. Fifteen farmers had already been convicted and more prosecutions were on the way. All of the sitting TDs in the area denied any involvement.

One candidate complained that he was being victimised by the system because he had no job. John McGrath, 25, from Ballyfermot, went to collect his weekly unemployment assistance payment of £33.05 to find he'd been cut off. He was told that because he was standing as an Independent candidate in Dublin West, he was unavailable for work. He argued to the contrary: "I was actually attending an interview with the 78,000 people of Ballyfermot and asking them to give me a job at £18,000 a year." He withdrew from the contest, having been told by other candidates that with only his dole to fund him he had no chance of election.

But while the dole queues were long, and the economy was officially in dire straits, hints and rumours would occasionally emerge of a parallel black economy that was doing much better. Fianna Fáil's finance spokesman Ray MacSharry was asked whether his party would give the Revenue Commissioners the power to access private bank accounts in pursuit of tax dodgers. His response wasn't all that clear. It was left to his leader, CJ Haughey, during a dull TV debate with Garret Fitzgerald, to say that as far as he could make out the current tax collection system was working superbly in the national interest, and that the Revenue Commissioners could get a court order if they wanted to investigate any suspect individual. Haughey underlined that maintaining the confidentiality of the banking system was of paramount importance.

Host Brian Farrell slid in a tackle, asking: "Even if someone has seven bank accounts and two building society ones?" Haughey told Farrell that it was not for politicians to do the jobs of the Revenue Commissioners for them. Des O'Malley called the debate "a nil-all draw".

On the subject of finance, Garret Fitzgerald dismissed Fianna Fáil's manifesto as "a grotesque mishmash of economic buzzwords, blind faith, pulled punches and invented employment targets". Joe Rae of the Irish Farmers Association concurred, calling it "something like Spot The Ball and hope to win". Fianna Fáil's Brian Lenihan defended his party's economic policies in a rambling oration which was utterly devoid of hard figures. He closed with the assurance: "We're not in the business of playing games with the Irish public."

RTE's Fergal Keane: "Why don't you tell them where you're going to cut if you're not in the business of playing games?"

Lenihan: "Because we're not playing games."

An RTE crew was on hand to capture the excitement as Charlie Haughey went walkabout in Cork. The reporter asked a woman would she be giving her vote to the Haughey cause. She replied: "I wouldn't give him the itch if I thought he'd get warm on a cold day scratching himself. He's a megalomaniac. I wouldn't put the reins of an ass and cart in his hands." At this point she was jostled away from the RTE microphone by a Fianna Fáiler who told her: "Get out you Thatcher lover."

After the votes had been counted, Haughey was Taoiseach once more. His friend Dr John O'Connell had lost his Dáil seat. Asked how he felt, O'Connell responded: "Maybe it's a good idea. I was worrying unnecessarily about the problems of the country."

Jaysus, There's Confidence For You!

Going into the 1987 election a new party promised to break the mould and forge a third way in Irish politics. Liberal on social issues and Thatcherite on money matters, the Progressive Democrats had been founded in 1985 – sprouted from the spare rib of anti-Haughey Fianna Fáil. As they approached their first electoral test, Fianna Fáil candidate Mary McAleese dismissed them as "stale bread in a new wrapping" and, sticking with the same recipe, as "very stale leftovers disguised in a spicy new sauce". Labour's Barry Desmond called them: "The Plastic Democrats – with all due respect." With a bamboozling dribble, Fine Gael's Alan Dukes ventured: "The PDs are like a substitute coming onto the pitch with five minutes to go and saying 'Hey look! It's because I'm here that the ball is round'."

However, the most memorable quip of the entire election belonged to Labour's Frank Cluskey. On learning that Fianna Fáil had appointed Paddy Lawlor as the party's Director of Elections, Clusky remarked: "Jaysus, there's confidence for you." However, one PD newcomer could see where Fianna Fáil would have grounds for confidence in the workrate of its foot soldiers. He observed: "They can't think and they can't speak but, by God, those fellows go out in the rain."

One of the seats the new party contested was in Limerick West where Fianna Fáil and Fine Gael had previously had no rivals in the three-seater. One farmer in Abbeyfeale declared with absolute certainty: "Having an election here is like taking the temperature of a man in the whole of his health. It's a pure waste of time and money and can only produce one result. If

Fianna Fáil lost one of its seats here the older people would take to the hills thinking it was the end of the world." John McCoy sent the old-timers scurrying for the hills, winning election in Limerick West for the PDs as the new party swept up 14 seats nationwide to become the Dáil's third biggest party.

Led by Des O'Malley, the Progressive Democrats styled themselves as a party of young go-getters, leading Labour's Michael D Higgins to brand them "a yuppie party". This rankled with the PDs, who took pains in Sligo-Leitrim to tell prospective voters that they numbered members of the unemployed in their ranks. For all that, they couldn't find a single suitable candidate from the locality and had to bring in Dr Frank Dobbs from Mayo.

The Progressive Democrats argued that the two rivals for Taoiseach, Haughey and Fitzgerald, were both past it, and the party presented the 51-year-old Des O'Malley as a tigerish young alternative. However, O'Malley's image was not young and alternative enough for some. In Dublin South East, his colleague Michael McDowell was getting grief on the doorsteps over his leader's enthusiasm for blood sports. At the launch of the PD manifesto, O'Malley announced: "The party has decided that enclosed hare coursing should be phased out, and I submit to that."

Targeting Fitzgerald and Haughey, O'Malley said: "I think the mood of the country is for someone to take over who has never been Taoiseach before." Haughey countered that his old Fianna Fáil nemesis was no spring chicken himself and remarked: "It would be no harm to point out that Deputy Desmond O'Malley was one of the prime architects of the infamous 1977 election manifesto which has caused so much opprobrium these days." As for the reasons behind his split with O'Malley, Haughey said that it was unfair to suggest that previous Fianna Fáil governments had acted above the law. He added that past allegations of wrong-doing were simply not relevant to an election in 1987.

The Progressive Democrats' one-and-only allotted TV party political broadcast was nearly scuppered after the tapes were stolen from a film-maker's van on Dublin's Baggot Street. General Secretary Pat Cox said that while he had no proof of "dirty tricks", it was "very curious" that of all the items in the van, the only ones taken were two tapes of the PDs' broadcast. An emergency replacement was edited together in the nick of time from the original footage.

Sinn Féin, fielding 27 candidates, were banned from presenting their case on the airwaves under Section 31 of the Broadcasting Act. Des O'Malley was canvassing in the Coombe district of Dublin when a group of men rushed at him shouting "no more Section 31". The initial reaction of his minders was to get out of the way, leaving O'Malley face to face with the mob. His supporters regained the initiative and dragged him into a youth training workshop where they locked the door. After some time, members of his entourage suggested continuing the walkabout. The PD leader resisted, saying: "They'll start again and tear the suit off me. My suit is torn." Gardaí arrived and provided a bodyguard for the rest of the canvass, however some shopkeepers denied him entry and some women mocked him with laughter. Sinn Féin issued a statement which denied orchestrating the hot reception, while claiming, with gallant disregard of their own situation, that O'Malley's support for Section 31 "borders on fascism".

In the closing days of the campaign, Sinn Féin set up its own pirate station broadcasting to a radius of eight miles from the centre of Dublin. A recurring theme of Sinn Féin's campaign was that the party was suffering the same injustice as South Africa's blacks under the repressive apartheid regime. In Dublin, a woman told a man canvassing for Sinn Féin's Christy Burke that the leaflets he was handing out were rubbish. He replied: "You're right too missus – just remember the name."

Fine Gael in Mayo East accused Fianna Fáil of showing a "blatant disregard for democracy" in its campaign there. Fine Gael's director of elections in the county, Pat O'Connor, said: "Election material, including posters and canvassing literature of the Fine Gael party, have been consistently sabotaged, interfered with, removed and destroyed by certain individuals whose identity is known."

Fine Gael in Dublin Central said that unknown forces in the constituency were recycling the election leaflets of one of its candidates, Dr Pat Lee, by cutting out the photos of his head and attaching them to defamatory leaflets. The new makey-uppy pamphlets accused Lee of chasing the seats of his party's sitting TDs in the area. It charged: "This greedy doctor wants Michael Keating's and Alice Glenn's jobs." Glenn, from Fine Gael's arch-conservative rump, had recently fallen out with the party leadership after she produced a newsletter which contained a list entitled Enemies Of The People. The enemies named by Glenn included several prominent Protestant church leaders.

The Protestant faith provided the most optimistically ambitious candidate of the election in Michael Brooks from Dundonald, in Northern Ireland. Brooks stood in Donegal on an Ulster Protestant ticket campaigning for a 32-County British Ireland. Sizing up his chances, he remarked: "I don't know much about miracles but I reckon I'll need about two of them." Asked where he might find a support base, he reasoned: "The people in Dublin are equally as British as the English, if not more so. They are always watching the Queen on television and their relations all live in London, Birmingham and Bristol and get nice pictures of the Queen on their pound notes." Brooks said he had nothing against Catholics. "I just don't agree with their religion – if I did I would join it." He admitted he was a supporter of the British National Front but insisted he was against "skinheads with Union Jacks".

Stan Gebler Davis stood in Cork as a Conservative & Unionist hoping to win acceptance for a pooled UK and Irish citizenship to reunite the peoples of the British Isles. He said: "I don't expect they'll throw any dead cats at me." However a Skibbereen man commented: "All he'll get down here is a black eye." No such threats were made to Ronald Peter Smyth who stood in the North East as a God In Louth candidate on a platform that there should be Bible readings in the Dáil chamber.

Neither Brooks, Davis nor Smyth were elected.

The Trouble With Childsex

The 1980s was a decade of bitter struggle between modernisers and traditionalists for control of the nation's moral compass. Labour's Barry Desmond announced he was seeking legal advice about a "scurrilous" document which was being dropped through letterboxes in brown envelopes addressed to the Registered Elector of the household. On the eve of polling day he was granted an injunction against a body calling itself the Children's Protection Society. The envelopes contained a circular entitled "Mr Barry Desmond And Sexual Exploitation". The document alleged that Desmond, the outgoing Health Minister, favoured making contraceptives available with no age limit, which would encourage promiscuity amongst the very young. A man called John Clerkin confirmed to the Labour Party that he was the author of the letter.

The Children's Protection Society later made the same accusation at Fine Gael, saying the party was promoting "childsex" by dint of favouring condom sales with no age limits. The CPS said specifically that children aged ten would be encouraged to pollute their bodies and souls through childsex.

Clerkin was asked how the CPS had settled precisely on the age ten. He explained: "Well, you wouldn't favour age two. And you wouldn't favour age 15 or 16. So it would have to be somewhere in between, and we've plotted it on the graph at age ten."

Interviewer: "But why age ten? Why not nine or 11?"

Clerkin: "Well, age ten is generally accepted in this business."

The Censorship of Publications Board was also pre-occupied with protecting young people from having sex. Days before the poll the Board banned Dr Alex Comfort's bestselling manual The Joy of Sex. The book had originally been banned shortly after its publication in 1974 but that 12 year ban had lapsed. Unaware that the book was banned in the first place, many bookshops had been stocking it and the Irish Family Planning Association had sold over 1,000 copies. Dr Maura Woods of the Rotunda Hospital said she was "surprised" at the ban, remarking: "It is not one of those crazy sex books. It is a perfectly ordinary sex book which couples can use."

Responding to criticism of the ban, the Board's Chairman, Judge Diarmuid Sheridan, pointed out that The Joy of Sex had been prohibited to protect adolescents. He said: "You put this book on an ordinary bookshelf. Imagine the effect it would have on a 13-year-old." He added that if any citizen wanted to import a copy they could apply to the Minister for Justice. The ban was merely on the sale and supply of the manual, not on its possession. Any medic who wanted a copy could get it on licence.

The public health scare of the day was AIDS, and the coalition had recently made it legal for over-18s to buy condoms without a prescription. There were calls for this liberalisation to be reversed. Fine Gael's Alan Shatter was campaigning in Dublin's Clonskeagh, when a constituent shouted at him: "Shatter! Shatter! Shatter! You're the fella that's going around pushing condoms down everyone's throats."

At the launch of Fianna Fáil's *Programme For Young People*, Charles Haughey said that his party in government would have no problem with condoning the use of condoms in a preventative campaign against AIDS.

Days later the Department of Health confirmed that a public health campaign against AIDS had been postponed until after the election. The thrust of the health campaign was that the best defence against AIDS was to abstain from sex. The slogan was: 'Casual Sex Spreads AIDS'. The Prison Officers Association attacked the delay in the scheme as "a cynical abdication of responsibility" and warned that people could die as a result. There were leaks that the government had decided to water down the campaign's endorsement of condoms. Health Minister John Boland refused to say if this was the case.

Meanwhile, Fianna Fáil's Albert Reynolds came up with a publicity campaign of his own. The pet food magnate announced he would sponsor the feeding of Heidi, the Army's new mascot dog, at Connelly Barracks in Limerick for the next year. He remarked that everybody knew the coalition had made a dog's dinner of running the country, but dogs, like everyone else, were entitled to expect that their lot would improve at election time.

In Galway West, Eamon O Cuiv dropped the 'O' from his name in an attempt to move alphabetically towards the top of the ballot papers. The stunt worked for the list of candidates on the joint Fianna Fáil posters, but it was ruled out of order for the general election itself.

1989

A HOSPITAL TROLLEY IS JUST A BED WITH WHEELS

The Incumbents: Fianna Fáil led by Charles Haughey.
Slogan: Coalitions equal multi-party chaos.
Promise: Painful fiscal rectitude.
The Challengers: Fine Gael led by Alan Dukes.
Slogan: Put us in power with the PDs.
Promise: Painful fiscal rectitude also.
The Mood of the Country: In no mood for an election.
Prediction: The electors to punish Fianna Fáil.
Result: FF ditches 'core value' and beds in with the PDs.
Entertainment value: 4/10.

The Opposition Is A Box Of Smarties

More than once in the run-up to polling day on June 15, it was put to Taoiseach Charles Haughey by interviewers that he had made an awful blunder in calling a snap election just two years into his term of office. The move was no mistake, he insisted, even as it was becoming abundantly clear with each slip in the polls that he'd made a grievous misjudgment.

Haughey called the election after his minority administration lost a Dáil vote on compensation to haemophiliacs infected by the State's health services. The defeat needn't have brought about the dissolution of the Dáil. Fine Gael and the Progressive Democrats had set out their stall as Haughey's loyal opposition as long as Fianna Fáil stuck to a programme of severe belt-tightening. However, when Haughey called the surprise poll in the hope of picking up extra seats, the rival parties were ready for a contest, unlike Fianna Fáil which didn't even have a manifesto prepared. The government finally got its policy document, entitled *The Next Phase*, back from the printers with just nine days to go.

Fine Gael jilted the Labour Party and agreed a pact with the Progressive Democrats which, in the event of victory, would result in Alan Dukes being installed as Taoiseach and Des O'Malley as Tánaiste. The Labour leader Dick Spring dismissed the pairing as "the politics of Zig and Zag". Fianna Fáil's Padraig Flynn claimed enigmatically: "The opposition is a box of Smarties. The PDs were essentially a phase in Ireland's political development and Fine Gael have repositioned themselves as fast buck merchants handing out goodies they don't own and haven't counted accurately."

Identifying hospital waiting lists and health cuts as a live issue, Fine Gael dug out Fianna Fáil's posters from the 1987 campaign which featured a frail, elderly woman together with the copy-line: "Must the old and the sick suffer more vicious cuts?" In government, Fianna Fáil had imposed vicious cuts of their own. Highlighting this, Fine Gael doctored the old Fianna Fáil poster with the line: "Some u-turns are enough to make you sick."

Fianna Fáil's initial response to this line of attack was one of flat denial. Health Minister Rory O'Hanlon informed the nation that: "Waiting lists are a very unreliable measure of the availability of hospital services." His party colleague, Dr John O'Connell pointed out that just because patients found themselves on trolleys didn't mean that there was a shortage of beds. A trolley, he patiently explained, was simply a bed with wheels.

Now, well into the campaign, the Taoiseach conceded that shortcomings in the health services were of serious concern to the people forced to endure them. Interviewer

Pat Kenny asked if it wasn't very late in the day to be discovering this issue. Haughey responded: "I accept that. But, after all, that's what democracy is all about. We have found a situation where there is considerable public disquiet and hardship over these waiting lists and we're tackling it."

Kenny asked if it had really taken a hostile response on the doorsteps to alert the government to those hardships.

He replied: "I have to admit that's true. We were not aware – I personally wasn't aware of the full extent of the problems and difficulties and hardships it was causing." Asked if he would disown O'Connell's remarks about trolleys, he said he didn't want to disown anybody, and that all the doctor meant was that "just because a person is on a trolley doesn't mean they are being neglected".

The opposition had a field day with Haughey's remarks. Tomas MacGiolla of the Workers Party accused the Taoiseach of "a pathetic attempt to evade responsibility". He added: "If he didn't know it's because he was not listening". Alan Dukes said that the leader of the country had demonstrated himself to be hopelessly out of touch with his people.

Fianna Fáil's Seamus Brennan saw it very differently, arguing: "His remarks displayed a compassionate commitment to resolve the waiting lists and other problems in the health services, and it is regrettable that the opposition leaders have no response except to continue with these unworthy personal attacks on the Taoiseach."

When Des O'Malley was on the campaign trail in Limerick, a paper seller outside a church pulled up his trouser leg to display a festering lump on his leg. He told the PD leader: "That has been there for two months and I cannot get into hospital. What can you do about it?" The answer was to agree with a Fine Gael proposal to raid the National Lottery funds for £60 million to pump into the groaning health service. Fianna Fáil's Mark Killilea lashed this plan as a "slush fund" to try to buy the election.

The Taoiseach's own health became an issue in the campaign, with Fine Gael making repeated references to the fact that Haughey was using an inhaler for respiratory problems. Haughey refused a TV debate with Alan Dukes, claiming that the format was "outdated". The Fine Gael spin on his refusal was that Fianna Fáil's strategists did not want the public to see their sick and tired man up against a young and vigorous one. Haughey insisted: "There is absolutely nothing wrong with my health." He said it was "a degrading form of political debate" for Fine Gael to question his well-being.

Saddam Is An Honourable Man

The Progressive Democrats leader Des O'Malley repeatedly attacked the government for promoting "low standards in high places". He said that Fianna Fáil was working to a "hidden agenda" which included helping out a cluster of close businessmen and suppressing the truth about irregularities in the beef trade until the election was safely out of the way. Sticking with the theme that the Taoiseach was up to more than met the eye, Labour's Dick Spring said: "His idea of being accountable to the people appears to consist of being photographed with celebrities. Oddly enough, he's never managed to be photographed with some of the very rich people to whom he's particularly close."

The allegations that the impoverished Irish taxpayer might lose untold millions in an unsound deal involving Fianna Fáil, beef-baron Larry Goodman and mass murderer Saddam Hussein were broached at a Haughey press conference. At first, the Taoiseach maintained that his government's position on beef exports to Iraq was unchanged from that of the previous FG/Labour coalition. Choosing his words carefully, he said that the previous government had taken a position on Goodman exports to Iraq, and his administration had simply "followed through with that".

It was put to him that in May 1986 the previous government had, in fact, stopped insuring Goodman shipments to Baghdad because it feared there was every chance the Iraqis would stiff the Irish taxpayer. Faced with this statement of fact, Haughey agreed that one of Fianna Fáil's first acts after returning to office in 1987 had been to switch back on the Goodman insurance. They'd done this because the coalition had been "wrong" to switch it off. He added that he had no business relationship with Larry Goodman and had not received any financial assistance from him. He told the media that his private financial affairs were nobody's business but his own, and that nothing in those affairs interfered with his capacity to carry out his public duties.

He was asked if O'Malley had any grounds for claiming that the Irish taxpayer might stand to lose countless millions in the three-way arrangement between Fianna Fáil, Goodman International and Saddam Hussein. Not in the slightest, he replied, assuring all present that the Iraqi despot and his henchmen were "honourable people".

It's A Change From Making Beds

Emigration had reached such levels by 1989 that Labour claimed the recently compiled electoral register was already badly out of date. The crisis was so bad that there were repeated calls for emigrants to be given the vote in general elections. Haughey rejected these calls out of hand, saying the process would pose a logistical nightmare. It was the first general election of the mobile phone age, and at the bigger count centres there was a scramble to secure power points where the portable bricks could be recharged. At the Dublin Central count centre, Fianna Fáil and Fine Gael set up personal computers to crunch the numbers. They taunted that the Workers Party had only an abacus.

Even having a job was no guarantee of earning a comfortable living. The newspapers reported that Irish Army soldiers were being forced to take second jobs to make ends meet. Three Army wives stood in protest at their husbands' poor pay. Labour's Dick Spring claimed that moves were afoot at the highest levels of government to pressurise the women to withdraw. Spring said senior Army personnel were "instructed to convey the impression to the people concerned that any such candidacy would be in breach of regulations and would have a negative impact on the standing of their spouses". The Taoiseach dismissed the allegation as "absolute rubbish". The three women stood, with one, June Kiernan, reflecting: "It's a change from making beds and making dinners."

Get Married Again!

Elsewhere, women candidates were thin on the ground, making up just ten of Fianna Fáil's 115 hopefuls. Nor were women candidates welcome everywhere. A poster in the window of a house on Dublin's Grand Canal Street said: "Electioneering women are requested not to call here. They are recommended to go home, to look after their children, cook their husbands' dinners, empty the slops and generally attend to the domestic affairs for which Nature intended them." On the campaign trail, an elderly woman asked Charles Haughey to: "Put a five percent rise on the widow's pension." He jested in response: "Get married again."

Canvassing in Dublin Central, Fine Gael's Dr Pat Lee asked a young woman for her vote. She told him straight out that she'd give him her 14th preference out of 14. He remarked: "I prefer that – it stops me wasting my time."

1992

THE WINCE FACTOR

The Incumbents: FF/PD coalition led by Albert Reynolds.
Slogan: We didn't end this temporary little arrangement.
Promise: A Fianna Fáil giveaway manifesto.
The Challengers: Fine Gael led by John Bruton.
Slogan: We're ready to govern again.
Promise: A Rainbow coalition.
The Mood of the Country: Down on Albert Reynolds.
Prediction: A resurgent Labour Party to be kingmakers.
Result: Labour hop into bed with Fianna Fáil.
Entertainment value: 5/10.

All We Want To Do Is Run The Country
Ever since first attaining power in 1932, it had been an article of faith with Fianna Fáil's strategists that 'coalition' was a collective noun for instability, ineptitude, compromise and weakness. After calling a misguided snap election in 1989, Charles Haughey had sacrificed his party's core value of single party government for the greater imperative of holding on to power, entering into coalition with the despised Progressive Democrats. In February 1992, after his former Justice Minister Séan Doherty shopped him on national TV for tapping the phones of journalists, Haughey made way for Albert Reynolds. Two years earlier, while Minister of Finance, Reynolds had called Fianna Fáil's first ever coalition, with the Progressive Democrats, "a temporary little arrangement" which "won't be there all that

long". Just months after becoming Taoiseach, he proved himself right.

In October 1992, giving evidence at the Beef Tribunal, Reynolds disputed the sworn testimony of his coalition counterpart, Desmond O'Malley. Reynolds insisted that O'Malley had exaggerated the financial risk to the Irish taxpayer of a deal between Goodman International and Saddam Hussein's Iraq which had received Reynolds' blessing as Minister. The Taoiseach said of O'Malley: "He puffed up Goodman's claim for what I regard as cheap political gain. He was reckless, irresponsible and dishonest to do that here in the Tribunal." In cross-examination he declined the opportunity to substitute "incorrect" or "inaccurate" for the word dishonest.

Reynolds' attack signalled the kick-off of a blame game between the two coalition partners, as each tried to shove responsibility for the unexpected and unwanted election onto the other. An anonymous Fianna Fáil Minister was quoted as saying: "Someone has got to be blamed for causing the election and we are going to try to put ourselves in the position that it's not us." As the countdown to polling day ticked on, it became increasingly apparent that Fianna Fáil was in a lamentable state of disarray. When this was pointed out to him, Bertie Ahern's despairing response was: "The unreadiness shows that we didn't want an election." He pleaded: "All we want to do is run the country."

As Fianna Fáil slumped in the polls, Albert Reynolds tried to look on the bright side, insisting: "In the past our strategy has been to start high and finish low. This time we will start low and finish high." This provoked only cruel ridicule. Since the party's foundation, Fianna Fáil's greatest strength was its well-oiled, expertly-tuned electoral machine. This fact sat uneasily with Reynolds' contention that: "Fianna Fáil is a very large, complex organisation and it takes a while to get it into gear."

As the campaign wore on, the sense grew within Fianna Fáil that perhaps the golden days of single party government had gone forever. Brian Lenihan said that Fianna Fáil could only form a coalition with a "properly structured" junior partner. He explained: "We cannot have a repeat of the last government performance where the minority party exercised blackmail at regular and irregular intervals."

Fine Gael's leader John Bruton went on a solo run and suggested forming a Rainbow Coalition with the Progressive Democrats and the Labour Party. The label "Rainbow Coalition" caught the public imagination and in the days before the election it was invoked to cover a multitude of possible permutations involving a mix of Fianna Fáil, Fine Gael, the Progressive Democrats, Democratic Left, the Workers Party, Labour and a number of independents. Tomas Mac Giolla of the Workers Party drolly observed: "We may be the only opposition party in the next Dáil."

The Labour Party under Dick Spring entered the contest full of beans, and Spring refused to agree any coalition pact before the big day. Such was the level of confidence within the Labour Party that Spring said he would like to see Fianna Fáil and Fine Gael coalesce in order to set Irish politics on a Right-Left axis. Asked to describe his relationship with Fine Gael leader John Bruton when the pair had shared cabinet office during the coalition of 1982-87, Spring replied: "That is a Cabinet secret – otherwise I would say truculent and difficult." There is a saying in Irish politics that Deputies appointed as Junior Ministers had won themselves the "half-car". Spring's insistence that there might be a rotating Taoiseach after the election prompted jibes that he was after the "half-jet".

There were murmurs from inside both the Progressive Democrats and the Labour Party that coalition with Fine Gael would be a more pleasant experience for all involved if that party's leader, John Bruton, would stand aside in favour of someone perceived as softer and more flexible, such as his colleague Peter Barry. The precedent cited was that of John A Costello, who had headed up two Inter-Party governments in the 1940s and 1950s despite the fact that he wasn't the leader of his Fine Gael party. Costello had been a compromise Taoiseach acceptable across the rainbow of the day. Bruton was not going to follow in the footsteps of the stand-aside party leader John Mulcahy whatever the national interest. He made it crystal clear: "The only way there will be a change of government is if it is led by myself."

In order to capitalise fully on what would become known as 'The Spring Tide', the Labour Party steered itself steadily from the hard shoulder of the Left to the middle of the road. At the previous election in 1989, its anti-Progressive Democrat manifesto had stated that "radical changes in tax structures inevitably create winners and losers". As one commentator pointed out in 1992, Labour's manifesto three years on made no mention of losers – the party was going all out to market itself as positive and unthreatening to the middle classes. Delivering what some saw as a dig in the ribs to Fianna Fáil, the Labour manifesto warned voters that "highly sophisticated white collar crime is on the increase". To counter this, Labour promised 2,000 extra Gardaí.

Fianna Fáil's manifesto had a section called *Five Years of National Achievement*. In it, the Taoiseach Albert Reynolds credited his party in government with "causing the arts and sport to flourish". Also collected within its pages were "notable achievements such as the winning of the Tour de France by Stephen Roche, the performance of the Irish soccer team, and the winning of Olympic medals by Michael Carruth and Wayne McCullough".

Years later, in a TV documentary entitled *Jack Charlton: The Irish Years* the former Republic striker Niall Quinn told a yarn about events in the dressing room minutes after Ireland had exited Italia '90 as the moral victors of the World Cup.

Charles Haughey entered and London born-and-raised Tony Cascarino wondered aloud: "Who the fuck is that?" Quinn hushed him, telling him: "Shut up, it's the Taoiseach." Next, another Anglo, Andy Townsend, asked Cascarino who the guy in the suit was, getting the reply: "Dunno, but he owns a tea-shop."

During the run-in to polling day, the Republic played Spain in Seville in a qualifier for the 1994 World Cup Finals in the United States. Days before kick off it was reported that the Blackburn Rovers manager, Kenny Dalglish, was preparing to buy Ireland's Roy Keane from Nottingham Forest for £3.5 million. Forest manager Brian Clough told the press: "If Kenny wants to buy him he'll have to pay a lot of money and still throw in the Thames, the Trent and whatever river runs through Blackburn."

Ireland drew 0-0 in Seville after having a perfectly good John Aldridge goal disallowed in a game which was dominated by the 21-year-old Keane. The game's main point of controversy wasn't the disallowed goal, but the fact that at either end of the pitch there were huge hoardings bearing the message: 'FIANNA FÁIL CAN MAKE IT HAPPEN.' Under the 1960 Broadcasting Act, RTE was prohibited from running party political adverts, but the governing party had cleverly bent the rules. The Fianna Fáil Press Office booted the allegations of foul play into Row Z. A spokesman gloated: "We had a good result in Spain, and there will no doubt be the usual bunch who'll tell you it had nothing to do with the 'FIANNA FÁIL CAN MAKE IT HAPPEN' banners at each end of the pitch in Seville. But we know better."

Crap, Pure Crap

When Albert Reynolds ousted Charles Haughey as leader of Fianna Fáil, many in the party had breathed a sigh of relief that the so-called 'Haughey Factor' would no longer dog their prospects at election time. They were dismayed to discover that the outcome of the first post-Haughey contest might be decided by an 'Albert Factor'. In an interview, the Taoiseach was asked if it was true that he had been playing happy families in public with his Progressive Democrat counterparts ever since he became Taoiseach, only to give them the cold shoulder in private. He dismissed the suggestion as: "Crap, pure crap!"

Some of Reynolds' political enemies claimed rather outlandishly that the very use of the word "crap" was grounds for impeachment, but one commentator felt that the Taoiseach had done himself more damage when he had rid himself of the Progressive Democrats with his Tribunal charges that Des O'Malley had made comments that were "reckless, irresponsible and dishonest".

With each passing day of the campaign, the public seemed to take a new turn against Albert Reynolds. During a radio interview he rejected two newspaper reports which claimed he'd incited a crowd in Listowel, Co Kerry, to roar out "a bad word". Miriam Lord of the *Irish Independent* had written: "He rounded off a triumphant end to what had been a pretty dismal day by rubbishing the opinion polls. 'I don't believe in polls and you know what they are?' he told his rapturous audience, 'a load of …' '*Crap!*' roared the delirious grassroots." On the airwaves, the Taoiseach disputed the accuracy of the report. Lord stood over her words. Tom McGuire of Radio Kerry, who'd been on the scene, said that he didn't think that Reynolds' intention had been to provoke the crowd, but the essence of Lord's report was true.

With the Taoiseach's personal popularity in meltdown, and his party predicted to lose five or more seats, Reynolds went on the RTE programme *This Week* to give an interview which his handlers hoped would rescue the situation. The interviewer, Joe Little, asked a question on the withdrawal of maternity benefits from unemployed women.

Reynolds told him: "Charlie McCreevy is looking at

the whole system to make it, to dehumanise it, to make it more ..."

Little: "To humanise it, surely?"

Reynolds: "To dehumanise it, yes."

In the same interview, a flustered Reynolds referred to his rival, John Bruton, as "John Unionist." An unnamed former Minister who'd lost his cabinet seat when Reynolds became leader was quoted as calling the Taoiseach's radio performance "a whinge" that exposed him as a political "lightweight".

As polling day neared, it was reported that many Fianna Fáil deputies had begun fighting personalised campaigns because the party brand name conferred no advantage anymore and might even be a turn-off.

The Sligo Champion refined the 'Albert Factor' to the 'Wince Factor'. It editorialised about "the newly discovered 'Wince Factor' which has arrived on the political landscape in relation to Mr Reynolds' personally. After only a relatively short time in the Taoiseach's job, it would appear he may prove a negative ingredient in perhaps a more damaging way than Mr Haughey ever did – and that is saying a lot considering that the so-called 'Haughey Factor' assumed almost mythical proportions in every recent election."

Opinion polls showed that most people chose to believe Des O'Malley's account to the Beef Tribunal over that provided by the Taoiseach. Reynolds' credibility increasingly became an issue in the campaign. In a move which was derided by critics as a desperate rehash of the wish-list manifesto of 1977, Fianna Fáil produced a £750 million job creation fund. At a press conference, the Taoiseach was asked how many jobs the initiative would actually create. He replied that he couldn't exactly say "because if I did, no one would believe me". Michael McDowell of the Progressive Democrats rubbished Fianna Fáil's jobs package, saying: "On November 26 the magic wands being wielded with such abandon during the election will be put away and Albert Reynolds' brief brush with Tommy Cooper economics will be over."

As it became clear that Labour stood to make big gains in the capital, Fianna Fáil switched its focus to Dublin, and on to Finance Minister Bertie Ahern. The authentic face of Real Dubbalin became the front man for a package of new projects promised for the city. Fintan O'Toole in *The Irish Times* found significance in the switch of emphasis, writing: "His chummy image, his lack of abrasiveness, were what Fianna Fáil needed to counter the harshness that has been their keynote since the break-up of the coalition government."

When Reynolds went head-to-head with the Fine Gael leader in a televised debate, the Taoiseach who'd misfired on the radio asked to be allowed the use of an autocue. The broadcast itself was criticised as stilted and outdated, but Fine Gael scored points by accusing RTE of "fundamental unfairness" and of showing "a craven attitude to Fianna Fáil" in accommodating Reynolds.

Elsewhere, Fianna Fáil's former Minister for Justice had now been demoted to the rank of Senator Séan Doherty, but he was hoping to win back his Dáil seat. On Shannonside FM he warned: "I don't know what the future is if we get a Rainbow Coalition with the Five Headed Taoiseach and Proinsias de Rossa as the Minister of Finance." His interviewer, Ciaran Mullolly, put it to him bluntly that: "A lot of people see you as a wart on the face of the party." Doherty replied: "In some countries the culture of such would be considered a beauty."

Turkeys Want Christmas
An abortion referendum was held on the day of the general election. Two weeks before that poll – known as 'The Big A' to activists of all parties – 48% of voters sampled said that

they would vote 'Yes' to a proposition that would outlaw women from seeking an abortion on the grounds that they were feeling suicidal. When it came down to the wire, the people voted in the opposite direction and the number approving abortion in certain circumstances shot up from 30% to 65%. As voting day neared, An Post issued a public warning that anyone mailing literature featuring photos of scrambled foetuses would be prosecuted for sending "objectionable material". The warning came following complaints from householders that a bogus 'Ann Maguire' was posting upsetting photographs from the United States.

An Post upset the Green Party when its labelling branch misfired. The postal service was supposed to send out one Green pamphlet to every household, but instead sent one to every voter. John Gormley apologised, saying: "I very much regret the excessive use of paper and I very much hope that Green voters will understand our dilemma."

As the complexities and contradictions of the abortion issue came to the fore, the *Nationalist & Leinster Times* left no reader in doubt as to where it stood. It ran a fiercely entertaining Pro-Life editorial which proclaimed: "Ireland will finally lose its virginity next Wednesday if the opinion polls are correct. No matter how mean, no matter how shoddy Ireland's enemies within and without have portrayed its virginity to be, it stood for something in a sordid world of the quick fix and the easy solution. But no more." It continued: "Women's organisations want abortion. Turkeys want Christmas."

For the Minister for Social Welfare, Charlie McCreevy Christmas couldn't come soon enough, and he was in the happy position to help it along. Ten years earlier, McCreevy had rebelled against the prevailing culture of his Fianna Fáil gene pool, insisting "the days of political strokes, deals and convolution politics must end". Days before the coalition fell apart in 1992, McCreevy had made the routine announcement that the annual Social Welfare bonus would be paid in the first week of December. However, the date set for the next election had now been dramatically brought forward to the last week of November.

Within 24 hours of the dissolution of the Dáil, the Department of Social Welfare sent out a press release entitled 'Minister Clarifies Christmas Bonus Arrangements'. McCreevy delivered the glad tidings that: "The Dáil yesterday passed a supplementary estimate of £102 million for the Department of Social Welfare well ahead of the normal time. Consequently, it will be possible to have the payment orders in place at collection points from the week ending November 20."

Social Welfare payments were still the sort of thing that could swing an election. During the campaign, the British chat show host Robert Kilroy-Silk denounced Ireland's Euro-Commissioner Ray MacSharry as "a redundant second-rate politician from a country peopled by peasants, priests and pixies". Accused of making racist remarks, Kilroy apologised for his comments in the *Daily Express*. Not only did he apologise, but to ensure that everyone understood that his regrets were true and sincere, he added: "I fully associate myself with this apology."

So People Could See They Were Normal

A new contender in the 1992 election was the Natural Law group, which didn't seem entirely sure if it wanted to be a fully functioning party or a more laid-back collective. One of its candidates was Mary Daly. She pointed out the flaws in the existing political system, saying: "If governments want to know how to be successful they should look at how nature functions ... The sun rises, seasons change, the planets move in the sky ... Nature governs itself easily, effortlessly, without debate. This is the model for all administrations."

The Natural Law group formed as soon as the election was

called. They didn't favour either the lapsed coalition or a Rainbow of any particular speckle. A spokesperson handed down the verdict under Natural Law that: "The politicians are tired, stressed, not properly nourished and their education is week."

The Natural Law grouping fielded nine candidates, all of whom expressed an enthusiasm for Transcendental Meditation. Asked how the electorate viewed them, the group's founder, John Burns, ventured: "To what degree they feel we can run the country we are not sure. We feel we can make as good a shot of it as anybody else – and probably even better." The newspaper report of the group's first press conference ended with the line: "He asked if a photograph could be included of yesterday's group so that people could see that they were normal."

There was no photograph with the article.

1997

SOME SORT OF HANDSHAKING MARATHON

The Incumbents: Rainbow coalition led by FG's John Bruton.
Slogan: Don't swallow Bertie & Mary's lethal cocktail.
Promise: Stability and prosperity.
The Challengers: FF/PD coalition led by FF's Bertie Ahern.
Slogan: Look – No Anorak!
Promise: Not to mess with single mothers.
The Mood of the Country: Unusually upbeat.
Prediction: Bertie Ahern's coalition to win.
Result: Bertie Ahern's coalition win.
Entertainment value: 4/10.

This Is A Cow

After the previous election in 1992, Labour had dismayed some of its supporters by climbing into bed with Fianna Fáil. When those two squabbling partners broke up acrimoniously in late 1994, Fine Gael and Democratic Left caught Labour on the rebound and the *ménage à trois* formed a Rainbow coalition without running it by the electorate. The Rainbow presented itself for re-election in 1997 as a safe pair of hands which had piloted the unprecedented boom already dubbed The Celtic Tiger. Across a score of previous campaigns, Fianna Fáil had cast coalition-ready Fine Gael as a promiscuous agent of impure and unprincipled government. This time, with Fianna Fáil and the Progressive Democrats cosying up to each other, the roles were reversed. Fine Gael spent a big slice of its campaign budget on press adverts featuring a lit Progressive Democrat match poised to ignite a can of Fianna Fáil petrol. The attached slogan warned of a "Lethal Cocktail".

The Irish public wasn't swallowing it. Starting with a clear lead in the polls, Fianna Fáil and the PDs pitched themselves as a trustworthy alternative coalition. The larger party slashed its spend on newspaper adverts in favour of a poster campaign featuring a brooding and statesmanlike Bertie Ahern. The pensive expression was to convey the message that the mumbling bumpkin of old had hung up the anorak and acquired the gravitas to run the country. The billboard format was chosen on the advice of strategists who decided that posters would appeal to voters on an emotional level, whereas policy issues risked confusing and/or boring them.

Fine Gael's Alan Shatter acknowledged that there was an emotional charge in the Bertie posters when he remarked that: "Ghost-like Godfather apparitions peering out of a heart of darkness on lampposts in Dublin South are frightening the dogs." In keeping with the image-driven rather than policy-driven approach, Bertie Ahern kept his speeches to a bare minimum until the end days of the campaign. The Taoiseach John Bruton followed suit. One of the new breed of spin-doctors was asked why his party leader wasn't saying much. He replied: "Because I tell him not to."

With Bertie Ahern zipping around the country like a Duracell Bunny, pressing the flesh, Fine Gael tried to lure him into a pit-stop by challenging him to a television debate with the Taoiseach. Ahern's refusal prompted Bruton to sourly gibe: "He sees politics as some sort of handshaking marathon, not a serious matter that affects the real lives of real people."

Fianna Fáil pulled off an A-list publicity coup when Ahern was granted a photo opportunity to rub biceps with movie tough guy Sylvester Stallone. A large crowd gathered in St Stephen's Green to see Stallone announce the imminent opening of Ireland's first Planet Hollywood eating emporium. Ahern reportedly received the honour over other politicians because his campaign manager, PJ Mara, was a buddy of U2 accountant Ossie Kilkenny who was a partner in the soon-to-be-short-lived burger venture. The Labour Party made a lame attempt to gatecrash the scene on the Green when a light aircraft chugged overhead as the crowds drifted home, trailing a banner saying "Vote Labour".

A gap opened up between putative partners Fianna Fáil and the Progressive Democrats after the PD leader, Mary Harney, launched her party's manifesto with a proposal to cut State payments to single mothers. The PD manifesto stated: "Anomalies in the social welfare system encourage people not to get involved in stable relationships." Harney's intent was to move single mothers back into the enabling environment of their parents' home. She insisted that her plan was not "going back to the bad old days" of "stigmatising illegitimacy", but her enemies had a field day framing it just that way.

The proposal wasn't just manna to Harney's rivals. It went down like a lead balloon with the Progressive Democrats' would-be partners in government, and Fianna Fáil moved decisively to swat it off the bargaining board. Sounding more than a little hurt, Harney indignantly protested that the proposal had been made in the interests of better social engineering rather than any intended penny-pinching. The Rainbow parties elbowed in on the first sign of a rift and ridiculed the Progressive Democrats as callous Thatcherites. Labour's Ruairí Quinn charged that Fianna Fáil in coalition would "have to dance to Mary Harney's tune".

The government parties' line of attack switched to Fianna Fáil after Bertie Ahern took time out to make it clear that he would be calling the shots in any FF/PD government. The Taoiseach John Bruton retorted that: "Like any would-be bully, he [Ahern] was telling Mary Harney what the house rules would be from the time she gets up early in the morning to the time she goes to bed." Employing a metaphor from the ugly world of wife-beating, he likened the FF/PD pact to: "The marriage arrangement dictated by Charlo in Roddy Doyle's drama. Mary Harney is cast as the woman who walks into doors."

Fianna Fáil countered Fine Gael's "Lethal Cocktail" campaign with posters featuring a photo of a cow and a point of information for Democratic Left's Proinsias De Rossa and Labour's Dick Spring. The copy line told the city-slicker party leaders: "This Is A Cow." Labour came back with the riposte that the creature in the advert was not a cow, but a calf, and that the party led by dyed-in-the-wool Dubliner Bertie Ahern clearly didn't appreciate the difference.

Fianna Fáil and the Progressive Democrats persisted with their targeting of Democratic Left as farmer-hating communists. Bobby Molloy of the PDs called on the Taoiseach, John Bruton, to state the blindingly obvious by giving an assurance that De Rossa would not be made Minister of Agriculture if the Rainbow was re-elected. According to Molloy: "The hostile attitude of Democratic Left towards the farming sector is a source of real concern." Fianna Fáil posters went up in Offaly and Wexford cattle marts featuring a quote from De Rossa saying: "They are rolling in it." The tagline was: "There is nothing at the end of the Rainbow for farmers."

When the posters were removed in a hurry, a solicitor's letter was fired off to the management of the marts demanding that the paid-up adverts be reinstated. Fianna Fáil's Agriculture spokesman, Joe Walsh, charged that the Minister for Agriculture, Ivan Yates, had used his clout to have the posters taken down. Fine Gael replied that the management of the venues had decided for themselves that the partisan posters were unsuitable for public display during an election campaign. Walsh defended the use of the De Rossa quote, pointing out: "It's on the record, it's the truth and it's very embarrassing for Fine Gael. They know the farming community is very upset and they want to cover it up. We are just reminding them of it."

When RTE excluded Democratic Left from a party leaders TV special on *Question & Answers*, the party, a breakaway from the Workers Party, kicked up a fuss. Fianna Fáil jumped on the protest as evidence that the Democratic Lefties had changed their name but not their spots, and were trying to intimidate Montrose with the sort of "bullyboy tactics" they'd learned from discredited Eastern Bloc regimes.

Annoyingly Insistent On His Rights

On walkabout in a supermarket, the alternative Taoiseach Bertie Ahern was handed a free sample of fruit juice. "Is that the best Dunnes Stores can offer?" he joked. Midway through the campaign, investigators from the McCracken Tribunal arrived back from the Cayman Islands where they had followed the money trail left by the holders of secret Ansbacher offshore accounts. The investigators had stumbled across the swag while investigating suspiciously tax-efficient payments by the multi-millionaire grocer Ben Dunne to former Taoiseach Charles Haughey and to Fine Gael Minister Michael Lowry. Going into the 1997 election, the pair were the only politicians outed as the recipients of bungs from publicity-shy supporters of the democratic process.

Haughey The Elder had retired from politics having modestly eulogized his own service to the State, but his son Séan was canvassing to retain the family beat. Observers pointed out that the name SÉAN was writ large on his posters, while the word HAUGHEY was left to dwindle in the small print. Séan's campaign team insisted that his father's under-the-counter relationship with the supermarket boss had not merited a single solitary mention on the doorsteps. This claim was somewhat undermined when one constituent loudly declared in the presence of journalists that Séan would not be getting his vote on the grounds that "one of those fuckers is enough".

Fine Gael's lavishly gifted fundraiser Michael Lowry had been sacked as a Minister the previous year after it emerged that Ben Dunne was a behind-the-scenes benefactor of his. Although the disgraced Lowry was standing this time as an independent, Fianna Fáil made great play of their contention that he and John Bruton were "the same political entity". Fianna Fáil's Noel Dempsey said that Lowry "really is John Bruton's forever friend", adding that the pair were "umbilically linked".

Lowry stirred it for the party which had banished him by declaring that he would readily support John Bruton for Taoiseach. Fine Gael impotently protested that the opposition's attempt to strike an umbilical chord between the two was "totally phoney" since no party was in any position to stop even its worst enemy from lending it support. When Lowry defiantly canvassed the Mid-Tipp Co-Op he brandished a cattle-prod and remarked: "I can tell you, I have no shortage of people I could give a slap to."

Bruton toured Lowry's home turf with Tom Berkery, the man Fine Gael hoped would take Lowry's seat. Berkery's (doomed) argument was that Lowry had no right to keep a seat that rightfully belonged to Fine Gael, for his own selfish purposes. Berkery told his audience: "I can represent the people of every part of Tipperary. I don't think any person has sexual ... eh ... sexual rights to represent any part of this constituency." A bewildered hush fell on the listeners which was only broken when someone gave the speaker a much needed prompt. "Sectional – I meant sectional", he corrected himself to the relief of just about all those present.

Standing for the Socialist Workers Party in Dublin, Doctor Peadar O'Grady attempted to make political corruption a key issue in the campaign. Despite the odd exchange of potshots between Dáil deputies, the SWP felt that there existed a sneaky gentleman's agreement between the opposing coalitions not to smear each other with the muck surrounding Fianna Fáil and Fine Gael. Early in the campaign, when he climbed up on a Dublin soapbox to decry the relationship between big business and politics, O'Grady was arrested for "offensive behaviour" under the Public Order Act. He was further charged with conducting himself violently in a garda station.

The good doctor protested that the Act in question was being used to suppress freedom of speech in a way that blatantly interfered with the electoral process. As he awaited trial, he argued: "Bertie Ahern held a street meeting in Ennis on the same day. The difference was who we were and what we were talking about." A cross-section of politicians, medics, lawyers, academics and other notables found his case persuasive and many signed a petition to that effect. A street demonstration in his cause was attended by publisher Vincent Browne and Green TD John Gormley amongst others. The Irish Council of Civil Liberties objected that the legislation had been introduced supposedly to tackle the problem of nasty behaviour by drunken gangs, but had instead been misappropriated to smother legitimate democratic protest. By the time his trial date arrived, O'Grady's Socialist Workers Party colleagues had a martyr in the shape of "the only person to be prosecuted in connection with the Payment To Politicians tribunal".

In court, the child psychiatrist was found guilty as charged of violent behaviour in a garda station. The judge then said that he would make the stain on O'Grady's character vanish by striking out the charge, on condition that the defendant paid £200 into the poor box. Justice Desmond Hogan added: "If the accused does not learn to control his temper there might be another day in another court."

The judge criticised the defendant for being truculent, for engaging in conduct unbecoming a gentleman and for being annoyingly insistent on his rights. He said that the doctor's conduct as he made his campaign speech against corruption had bordered on vulgar abuse. Vulgar abuse is not an offence. The judge dismissed charges of offensive conduct, of failing to leave a place when directed to do so by a Garda, and of assaulting a policeman and breaching the peace at Rathmines garda station.

The court heard that the doctor had shouted at officers in the garda station "tíochfaidh ar fucking la" (an embellishment on an old Republican saying) and "fucking bastards" (a popular saying). A guard gave evidence that he'd been called to the Swan Shopping Centre after a member of the public took exception to O'Grady's views on political corruption, and in particular to his yells of "Jail Haughey!" and "Jail Lowry!" The policeman told the judge: "It was as if he was insane. He was harassing people, roaring and shouting in a frantic manner. He was extremely loud and interfering with the free passage of people going about their business."

A young lady working in a nearby pharmacy said that she couldn't hear what her customers were asking because of the doctor's loud exclamations on the topics of Ben Dunne and on the need for a minimum wage. The court heard that O'Grady's response to police instructions to lower his voice was: "Get out of my face." He had appealed to the gathered crowd to witness the "police harassment" he was suffering.

The arresting officer flatly denied the suggestion by O'Grady's lawyer that it was the contentious content of the defendant's speech that had landed him in trouble. The guard also denied that he told O'Grady in the patrol car: "You can't say those things about corruption in the State."

The court further heard that the doctor had been "awkward and contrary" in the station, and had pushed officers and even punched one of them. Apologising for his behaviour, Dr O'Grady explained that he'd never before been up for election or in custody and that "things" had "got out of hand" because he found himself in unfamiliar circumstances.

Another individual convinced he'd been victimised for exercising his right to free speech was anti-pothole campaigner Martin Hannigan. The Cavan man had been deeply unhappy with the state of the local roads for some time, and he'd mounted a vigorous campaign to encourage Cavan County Council to improve the public highway. What Hannigan didn't have in mind was that the Council would erect a big road sign right outside his front door. As polling day neared, he went on hunger strike in protest against the protruding erection. The local Fianna Fáil TD, Dr Rory O'Hanlon, offered his services as a conciliator and was soon able to bring Hannigan the good news that he could resume eating. Council workmen moved the sign 20 metres down the road, while senior officials denied that there had been any intent to punish the pothole protester for having a bee in his bonnet.

With Charles Haughey and Michael Lowry recently exposed as the lapdogs of big business, there was a great deal of public interest as to who might next be rumbled for crooked behaviour. Concerns were raised that wealthy wrongdoers would successfully hide behind the State's money-hugging libel laws. At the launch of Labour's manifesto, Dick Spring was asked if it was his party's policy to reform the defamation code. He replied with a firm "No".

At this, his handler Fergus Findlay approached the conference table and passed a note to the party leader. After some hurried consultations and a brief perusal of the manifesto document, Spring reappraised his audience: "I want to go back to the question of reform of the defamation laws ..."

Get The Nignogs Out And I'll Vote For You
Democratic Left attacked the popular and profitable culture of double-jobbing within the garda force, asserting that some

commonplace extra-curricular earners amongst police
officers were damaging the public's respect for the police.
The party pointed out that moonlighting as a surly bouncer
was not the best way to win over the young people of any
community, while the occupation of landlord was held in
even lower esteem by some than that of a policeman. The
garda Federation responded that officers were so badly paid
that they often needed to make a bit on the side, and cited
the members of the Oireachtas as world leaders in the field of
income-multiplication.

Respect for the force was damaged close to polling day
when it was reported that a guard was being investigated for
fraud after putting in a compensation claim for injuries in a
car crash while on duty. The officer said he'd been hurt when
a stolen vehicle slammed into the back of his patrol car, but
the damage to the car didn't tally with his claim. Pressurised
to come clean, the driver's partner withdrew a statement
backing up the crash story and confessed that the officer had
deliberately reversed the patrol car into a wall.

The Progressive Democrats were asked repeatedly if they
would curb garda double-jobbery, but the party's standard
response was that being a policeman is "a full-time position".
One of the buzzwords of the election campaign was "zero-
tolerance" and the Progressive Democrats expressed the view
that this policy should be directed towards rampaging
wrongdoers rather than at workaholic guardians of the law.
The Progressive Democrats proposed employing 1,000 extra
Gardaí and opening 1,500 new prison places to contain their
improved catch of criminals.

Fianna Fáil were even more committed to the zero-
tolerance approach, and Justice spokesman John
O'Donoghue pledged 500 more prison places and 200 more
Gardaí than his prospective coalition partners. When Fianna
Fáil launched their crime policy with a special press
conference, keen observers noted that it was the fourth

time in two months that the same proposals had been unveiled.

Fine Gael were not to be outdone. The self-proclaimed party of law and order took out adverts stating that in the previous thirty months the FG-led Rainbow government had "created 800 more prison spaces" and "provided 1,500 more Gardaí". A sceptical Bertie Ahern responded with the hard facts at his disposal that the outgoing administration had created less than 200 new prison spaces, while the number of serving Gardaí had actually fallen. A Fine Gael spokesperson sorted the seeming confusion, explaining: "We have created the spaces in that they *will be* there. The actual spaces aren't there, in terms of walls and bars around them." Fine Gael further clarified that the advert was intended to highlight the party's *intent* to eventually add 800 places to the penal system. That appeared to be that, until Fine Gael followed up with a yet another clarification which superseded its earlier clarification, stating that: "Every fact contained in our recent advertisements is accurate."

Fianna Fáil also found itself needing to issue a clarification after Fine Gael claimed that Fianna Fáil had "sold a pup" to the voters of west Dublin. The constituents had been circulated with quotes from a Dáil statement by Bertie Ahern attacking proposals to build a controversial casino in the Phoenix Park. Fine Gael's Austin Currie highlighted the fact that Ahern had made no such speech in the House. The Fianna Fáil handlers indignantly responded that their leader had *intended* to make a speech to that effect.

For possibly the first time ever, the supposed criminal tendencies of immigrants surfaced as an election issue. Shopkeepers on Dublin's Camden Street had barred "Romanians" AKA "Bosnians" AKA "refugees" from entering their premises for fear that the shelves would be stripped bare. Fine Gael's Gay Mitchell was taken aback with the levels of hostility to foreigners he encountered on the doorsteps of central Dublin. He reported "One man said get the nignogs out and I'll vote for you."

Standing as an independent candidate in Cork, schoolteacher Aine Ní Chonaill pressed for an urgent curb on the number of non-nationals arriving in Ireland. Miss Ní Chonaill objected to the number of British "hippies" moving into her neck of the woods. She maintained that, in addition to the influx of British and German nationals diluting the national stock, there were far too many asylum seekers being allowed into the country, many of whom were here on false pretences.

In the neighbouring county of Limerick, the unfortunately-anagrammed Nora Bennis ("born insane") expressed confidence that her National Party could equal or better the share of the vote which had put the despised Democratic Left in government. The National Party's platform included preventing "the killing of pre-born children", overturning "the liberal agenda" and showing the city of Limerick in a more flattering light. To combat the growing pressure on mothers to work outside the home, Bennis pledged to pay them £100 each week to keep house and raise their children. This platform was not a vote-getter with one woman Bennis encountered on the campaign trail, who told her: "If you're going to give £100 to every stay-at-home mother, I'll be out of a job. I run a crèche."

Payback Time

A caller to Radio 1's *Liveline* show lamented that: "This is a poor country. We've no structures, no roads, no railways, no bridges, no rivers ..." (Perhaps not coincidentally, the contributor went on to call for more funding for the State's mental health services). What rural Ireland did have in abundance was illegal television deflector schemes. These pirate operations allowed communities to receive a range of TV channels for free instead of buying them from licenced providers. The billionaire media mogul Tony O'Reilly had invested some £75 million into transmission rights and he was deeply unhappy with the Rainbow's failure to shut down the pirate schemes which were extremely popular with large swathes of the voting public.

In the run-up to election day, members of the Rainbow parties became convinced that the coverage in O'Reilly's Independent Group Newspapers was less than supportive of the government. On the day before the country went to the polls the *Irish Independent* led with the headline FF, PDs SURGE TO BRINK OF VICTORY. Strapping belt to braces, the newspaper ran a front page meditation headed FOR YEARS WE HAVE BEEN BLED WHITE – NOW IT'S PAYBACK TIME.

The editorial told readers: "John Bruton has a record of commitment to fiscal rectitude. But his Fine Gael party are in thrall to Labour and Democratic Left ... This is bad for the economy. It is also undemocratic." Ireland's best-selling daily concluded that Fine Gael's "surrender to its partners" had "jeopardised our future". It ended: "On any objective analysis, it is a vote for Fianna Fáil and the Progressive Democrats tomorrow which offers the better chance of securing our future."

Years later, at the Moriarty Tribunal, a former advisor to the Rainbow coalition said that in 1996 he had represented the government at a meeting with Independent News And Media where there were heated exchanges over TV deflectors. Séan Donlon said that he was left in "no doubt" as to the "hostility" of the Independent group towards the Rainbow. Tony O'Reilly told the same inquiry that his foreign business partners in the TV operation were "seething with us as well as the government in relation to the amount of money they were losing in Ireland".

At the same time, O'Reilly insisted, as he had consistently done in the past, that he'd had no input into the

PAYBACK TIME editorial, or into any of the content of his newspapers. He had no role in the matter and didn't know what was going on the front page. When it was put to him that the editorial was "interventionist", he answered that such a description could be put on it by "enemies".

For better or for worse, the day after the PAYBACK TIME editorial appeared, the Rainbow government was swept from office.

2002

YOU HAVE A GREAT CHANCE OF GETTING A VOTE IF A DOG BITES YOU

The Incumbents: FF/PD coalition led by Bertie Ahern.
Slogan: Much done, more to do.
Promise: To end hospital waiting lists by 2004.
The Challengers: Fine Gael led by Michael Noonan.
Slogan: Vision With Purpose.
Promise: Coalition with the Labour Party.
The Mood of the Country: Football crazy.
Prediction: Fianna Fáil to get an overall majority.
Result: Fianna Fáil fall just short of an overall majority.
Entertainment value: 4/10.

Nobody Should Be Above Or Beneath The Law
In the closing days of a dull campaign, one newspaper ran the emphatic headline SHORT OF FALLING UNDER A BUS, BERTIE AHERN WILL LEAD THE NEXT GOVERN-MENT. The Republic of Ireland football team led by Roy Keane were about to fly off to the World Cup finals in Japan and South Korea, and the outgoing Fianna Fáil/PD coalition had the fair wind of a massive feelgood factor behind them. The former Fine Gael Minister Ivan Yates had swapped politics for the life of a bookie, and two weeks into the campaign he stopped taking bets on Bertie Ahern being returned as Taoiseach, having slashed the odds from 5-1 to 1-25.

After five years in office together, Fianna Fáil and the Progressive Democrats set out separate stalls. The two men steering the Fianna Fáil election effort, PJ Mara and Martin Mackin, had held their first re-election summit almost four years earlier in the autumn of 1998. Fianna Fáil strategists travelled to Millbank in England for a grind on the art of media micro-management as practiced by Tony Blair's spintastic New Labour. Long before Ahern called the election, his party had drawn up the floor-plans for a "message management" centre closely modelled on the New Labour operation.

The Fianna Fáil election command included a press team to funnel a steady flow of what Mackin called "pre-buttal and rebuttal" to the media. Rebuttal time usually began in the early afternoon, when Fianna Fáil spokespeople would be sent out to trash the tidings of the other parties. Another media-monitoring crew kept a close watch on television, radio and internet developments. Every hour, 15 minutes off the top of the hour, the monitoring group would input a summary of the latest headlines from the nation's news bulletins.

The Fianna Fáil figure best briefed on but least engaged in the game of pre-buttal and rebuttal was the party leader, Bertie Ahern. The Taoiseach spent the campaign zipping up and down the highways and byways in a cavalcade of fast cars. His walkabouts were also notable for their terrific tempo as he speed-dated the voters. When journalists commented on what a dash he cut, Ahern revealed that he had built up his stamina throughout the previous winter with a regime of early morning jogging. In Ferbane, Co Offaly, the Taoiseach managed to squeeze several photo opportunities and a walkabout into 25 action-packed minutes. The fleeting nature of this personal appearance appeared to upset one man wearing an I'm Backing Bertie badge. A journalistic inquiry yielded the instruction: "Fuck off!"

The Taoiseach's tempo in motor traffic did not attract the same widespread admiration as his walking pace. Some hacks tried to raise serious safety concerns about the breakneck speed of Ahern's bandwagon, which cynics suggested was flouting speed limits not in any identifiable service of the State, but in the interests of getting himself and his party back into power. Previously, launching a safety initiative which had since run out of gas, Ahern had decried speeding on the roads as "an unacceptable social problem". Now, he was timed covering the 22 miles from New Ross to Wexford town in a hair-raising 17 minutes, breaking the speed limit almost all the way. At one point, journalists clocked the blur of his convoy at 95 mph.

In Wexford town, it was put to the Taoiseach that he had violated the speed limit for most of the 22 miles. Was he not concerned about the dangers to himself and other road users? With blustery levity, he countered: "Ah no, we were going slow today. When we are in the car we try to keep to the speed limit." At another point he joshed: "The only speed limit we break is when we're walking." Asked to get serious for a moment, he blamed the "travelling press" for slowing his all-eyes-to-the-stopwatch schedule.

Eddie Shaw of the National Safety Council said that the Taoiseach's cannonball runabout was "unacceptable". This encouraged the media to tackle the Taoiseach again on his flippancy in the face of danger. Would he bow to the evidence of witnesses and admit to breaking the speed limit even once on his travels? "I haven't been monitoring," he replied, "but I don't think so."

On national radio, the Taoiseach was lectured by an irate caller that as "the chief legislator of this country" he was setting an appalling example. Ahern slipped smoothly into neutral and, sounding like an uninvolved third-party in the matter, gave her the soothing assurance: "Nobody should be above or beneath the law and neither am I."

(In October 2006, during the marathon run-in to the 2007 general election, complaints were made that Bertie Ahern's cavalcade had again smashed the speed limits, this time on a busy Westmeath road. Just minutes before the alleged incident, which came at the end of a week of carnage on the roads, the Taoiseach had made a solemn appeal to drivers to slow down. Addressing the nation's motorists, he'd said: "I ask you to join with me in preventing deaths and serious injuries." Pressed that no one should join with him on his past and current form, Ahern patiently explained that his entourage wasn't "going that fast". The Taoiseach's Department refused to say more, arguing that because the driver of his Mercedes was a police officer, all inquiries should be directed to the Garda Press Office. The response from Garda HQ was: "We are not going to be responding.")

Eight months before the 2002 row over the ton-up Taoiseach, the State car of Justice Minister John O'Donoghue had been caught doing speeds of 90-115 mph on the public highway. The Minister was not in the vehicle himself at the time, having loaned it to family members for the pressing matter of attending the All-Ireland Hurling Final. With the issue once again live during the 2002 campaign, O'Donoghue was asked how many State cars had been monitored outstripping the speed limit during the government's five years in power. He replied that he hadn't the foggiest, adding: "The cars concerned are driven by garda drivers, and as such are garda cars. It is not desirable, but they *are* garda cars."

The First Time The Opposition Has Been Voted Out Of Office
On walkabout in Galway, the Taoiseach magnanimously paused for a friendly chat with a protester who was handing out leaflets bearing the message: "Indict Bertie – No Irish Airport For Bush's Criminal War." The war referred to was the post-9/11 invasion of Afghanistan, promoted by the

United States as Operation Enduring Freedom. With Labour running to stand still in the polls, a peevish Pat Rabbitte ventured that: "The Taoiseach's face has been more in evidence this last month than Kylie Minogue's backside." A reporter on the Newstalk 106 radio station raised the bar dauntingly high for Rabbitte's party, with the announcement: "Labour will unveil plans to end poverty and deprivation later today."

If it all appeared to being going flat for Labour, for Fine Gael there was a real threat of electoral meltdown. Over a year earlier, Fine Gael had shot itself in the foot with a woefully misbegotten and very costly anti-government campaign featuring a Celtic Snail. The intent was to ridicule the Fianna Fáil/Progressive Democrat coalition for squandering the rewards of the Celtic Tiger, but it was Fine Gael that ended up looking gooey and gormless. Within three months, John Bruton was made walk the plank and Michael Noonan easily saw off the challenge of Enda Kenny for the party's leadership.

With Bertie Ahern, the most popular politician in Ireland, at their helm, Fianna Fáil felt confident that Fine Gael's new leader would fare no better than its old one, or the one before that. Shortly before the election, at the Fianna Fáil Ard Féis, Brian Cowen suggested that Noonan's best chance of winning anything was at the Winter Olympics "because he can go downhill faster than any skier". As for Noonan's putative No 2 in an alternative coalition, Cowen remarked of the Labour leader Ruairí Quinn: "Now there's a breath of hot air."

Pressing the flesh in the Roscommon town of Boyle, Michael Noonan was pushed in the mush with a custard pie. Later, he put a game face on the incident, saying: "We were expecting it. That's why I had a spare set of clothes on the bus." The assailant, Jessamine O'Connor, was apprehended by a Fine Gael minder but let go when she revealed that she was five months pregnant. During her 15 nanoseconds of fame that followed, she told a newspaper that she'd splattered the leader of the opposition in a protest against the government's refusal to accommodate women who wanted to give birth at home.

In the final week of the campaign, the Irish edition of the *Sunday People* flung a custard pie of its own, running a front page mock-up of the Fine Gael leader as a red-nosed Bozo. Beside the photo, the organ asked in a spirit of deep patriotism: "Would YOU trust a useless clown like this to run Ireland?" In the event, Fine Gael did suffer the meltdown some had predicted, with 22 deputies declared utterly redundant to the needs of the nation. Applauding the wipeout, Fianna Fáil's Charlie McCreevy crowed: "This is the first time the opposition has been voted out of office."

We Are Nobody's Moral Mudguard

As Bertie Ahern's high-speed circuit of Ireland entered the closing stages, the prospect grew that he would become the first Fianna Fáil leader to win an overall majority since Jack Lynch in 1977. The more the pundits speculated that this might happen, the more Ahern insisted it couldn't and wouldn't, and that it was the moral duty of every Fianna Fáil supporter to turn out and vote on the day. "We have difficulties," explained the Taoiseach.

The Progressive Democrats were having difficulties of another sort. Although left with only four seats after the previous election in 1997, the party had helped steer the ship of State for five heady years. They rammed home their message that the country had never had it so good, by taking a crew of journalists on a magical mystery tour from their cushy Dublin dens to Prosperous, Co Kildare.

But now, with Fianna Fáil seemingly coasting solo towards the comfort zone, the Progressive Democrats faced redundancy and the outside chance of slipping over the horizon forever. Boldly seizing the initiative, the PDs turned fiercely on their ex-partners, printing up posters which said: "Single Party Government? No Thanks." When Michael McDowell mounted a lamp-post in Dublin's Ranelagh to proclaim that message, Fianna Fáil's Seamus Brennan delivered the schoolmasterish riposte: "He's a bit like a screaming child at the moment trying to name-call and hope to get a bit of attention."

Invoking the name of a murderous Communist despot, McDowell denounced Bertie Ahern's plans to build a stadium and sports campus in north Dublin as "a Ceausescu-era Olympic project". Having initially gone sheepishly along with the scheme, the Progressive Democrats now savaged it as a waste of money which, according to Mary Harney, would fudge together "the party interest and the national interest". Facing shrill charges that the Abbotstown development was a vanity basket-case that would squander €1 billion, Fianna Fáil sounded the retreat. It was left to the PD-friendly Finance Minister Charlie McCreevy to break the news that the project would be slashed back to just the bare stadium. Asked how he felt about the severe damage done to his pet project, Bertie Ahern said he had "no problem" with the downsizing.

The tribunals were trudging along, and the opposition parties nursed faint hopes that the steady ooze of sleaze might yet leave Fianna Fáil on a sticky wicket with the voters. Deputy Liam Lawlor's life had turned into one long pantomime victim-impact statement, but his scenery-chewing performances as a wronged choirboy didn't save him from a stay in the least life-threatening wing of Mountjoy Jail. As Lawlor was imprisoned in January 2001, the political commentator Gene McKenna noted: "Fianna Fáil have been distancing themselves from Fianna Fáil on this."

Around the same time, a totally baseless story was published claiming that Bertie Ahern had received a discrete donation of £50,000 from an ardent supporter of the democratic process. The Taoiseach later sued and had his good name vindicated. Instructively, however, while the unfounded story of the £50,000 was still doing the rounds, an opinion poll showed that 46% of those surveyed said they didn't believe Bertie's plea of total innocence, but they still rated him as the best person to run the country.

With sleaze lapping around Fianna Fáil, the self-styled party of probity, the Progressive Democrats, found their enemies trying to smear them as the dog that didn't bark. Mary Harney made a fine distinction, saying: "I don't see ourselves as moral watchdogs but as *economic* watchdogs." Her colleague Liz O'Donnell added: "We are nobody's moral mudguard. We are not plaster saints." Rejecting any watchdog duties as futile when it came to his coalition partners of five years, Michael McDowell said: "If Cúchalainn's dog was there watching the gates making sure Fianna Fáil didn't get up to mischief, they would still get up to mischief." Mary Harney stressed that the Progressive Democrats were not in the business of making an election issue of any mud slung at Fianna Fáil. During the very same press conference, the very same Mary Harney made sleaze an issue by making it clear that if it wasn't for the PDs' firm moral guidance in government, Fianna Fáil on their own would have buried a bundle of dirty laundry in the concrete foundations of a new motorway.

As polling day drew close, Harney went to the High Court to defend her own reputation after *Magill* magazine splashed her photo on the cover along with the headline: TROUBLE SEEMS TO FOLLOW ME EVERYWHERE. The story, which had been doing the media rounds for yonks with no takers, claimed that the Planning Tribunal had instructed her to open up her financial records for inspection. Harney told the High Court that the story was malicious nonsense and that it would damage her prospects, and those of her party, in the looming election. The Progressive Democrats staged a photo shoot where a copy of the magazine was dumped with dramatised disdain in a rubbish bin.

The *Magill* camp countered that their sources were impeccable and that there would be no backing down. The Tribunal then stepped in decisively on Harney's side, declaring that the *Magill* story was hogwash. *Magill* capitulated, apologised and handed over €25,000 to a charity of Harney's choosing.

At one point in the campaign, vandals doctored posters which featured a statesmanlike Bertie Ahern conveying the message: "A LOT DONE, MORE TO DO." The hoodlums amended the posters to say: "A LOT DONE FOR THE BOYS." Fine Gael accused the Taoiseach of arrogantly abusing his power by hosting a private party for his girlfriend, Celia Larkin, at Farmleigh, the official State guesthouse which had been bought and lavishly restored at the taxpayers' expense. Fine Gael's Nora Owen pointed out that charities had been refused access to Farmleigh for fundraising bashes, and she charged that the private gathering the previous Christmas might have had a "promotional aspect" for Celia Larkin's beauty business.

Ahern responded that the get-together had been arranged through "the proper channels" with the Office of Public Works, and that everyone present had been a personal friend of either Celia or himself. He said that Fine Gael had saved up the six-month-old story in an attempt to smear him at election time. When asked who had paid for the function, he set it straight that there had been no "function". This was the reason that press inquiries to the OPW concerning the event had drawn a blank. The Taoiseach explained: "The OPW were asked if there was a major reception." Not for the first time in contemporary Irish politics, the wrong question had been asked.

Ahern faced hostile questioning at the close of the campaign when it emerged that one of his best friends, Joe Burke, had been made Chairman of the Dublin Port Authority the day after the Taoiseach had called the election. Fine Gael and Labour denounced Burke's installation as "croneyism", with FGs' Jim Higgins calling it "a sneaky, secret appointment of the Taoiseach's closest associate". Dismissing the fuss, a spokesman for Ahern said that as a matter of routine courtesy, the Taoiseach had been informed of his friend's advancement by Marine Minister Frank Fahey shortly before it was announced. The Progressive Democrats said that they would be saying nothing.

Joe Burke ran a successful business gutting authentic Irish pubs and refurbishing them into traditional Irish pubs, but in so far as he was known to the public it was as a figure in the deeply perplexing Sheedy Affair, which began with a fatal car crash and ended with the resignation of two judges. Speeding along a Dublin road with drink taken, architect Philip Sheedy left a woman driver dead in an horrific collision. Joe Burke visited Sheedy in prison while Bertie Ahern made representations to have Sheedy granted regular day release, but the two friends were adamant that the topic of the jailed architect at no point ever entered any conversation between them.

The day after Ahern's statement that he had been "routinely informed" of his friend's appointment by the relevant Minister, it emerged that Burke had been given the position of Chairman after asking Ahern for a place on the Authority. However, Ahern clarified that Burke's request and his appointment were not connected. The Taoiseach explained: "He made me aware that he would possibly like to be on the board. I certainly did not lobby for him to be Chairman." As for the charges of cronyism levelled against him by political rivals, the Taoiseach said regretfully: "I must say that I am very disappointed that that would be said about Joe Burke." He added that Burke "was always a great protector of people in the port" and that there was no "ulterior motive" behind the failure to inform the Progressive Democrats of the builder's richly deserved advancement.

An outraged Fintan O'Toole wrote that Burke's elevation was a "startling" case of Fianna Fáil "rubbing our noses in it", which betrayed "a special kind of arrogance" on the Taoiseach's part. Having taken a few hard swipes at Fianna Fáil in the previous ten days, the Progressive Democrats pulled on their kid gloves and boxed clever over the Bertie & Joe show. After all, the plan was to make-up the next government with Fianna Fáil, not provoke a rancorous break-up. Putting the national interest before her party's yearning for the high moral ground, Mary Harney said: "This is not the biggest issue around. The biggest issue for me is to ensure that we have a coalition government."

Joe Burke's Chairmanship of the Dublin Port Authority was not the only appointment made by Frank Fahey which attracted harsh partisan comment. Labour criticised Fahey for placing Tom Welby, a Fianna Fáil stalwart from his own Galway constituency, to the board of the Dún Laoghaire Harbour Company. In order to attend each meeting, Welby would have to make a 360 mile coast-to-coast trip. Labour estimated that the Galway garage-owner would be entitled to claim €324 in travelling expenses for each epic two-way trek. For his own part, Welby said: "I haven't looked into the details."

Another new Fahey appointee faced with attending meetings on the opposite side of the country was Pat McHugh, a Fianna Fáil councillor from Mayo who was nominated to the board of Dundalk's Harbour Company. Yet another was Tom Hussey, a former Fianna Fáil TD from Galway whom Minister Fahey spotted would be a valuable asset to the Dublin Port Authority under its new Chairman.

The Battle Of The Biscuit Boxes

The preamble to the May 2002 campaign was Finance Minister Charlie McCreevy's budget of December 2001. By then, all of the parties were firmly in pre-election mode. Shortly after McCreevy outlined his housekeeping measures, Fine Gael produced a leaflet for members of the public entitled *Know Where You Stand?* The content was distributed to all of the party's candidates, to be customised with their mugshots and parish notes.

In no time at all, the Independent TD Michael Lowry – who had been booted out of Fine Gael for being a bought man – began distributing a leaflet also called *Know Where You Stand?* Lowry's publication featured remarkably similar content to the Fine Gael document of the same name. When these striking coincidences of composition were pointed out to Lowry, he remarked: "Maybe Fine Gael are copying me."

The fluky coincidences didn't end there. Fine Gael's deputy Paul McGrath brought out *Know Where You Stand?* in his constituency of Westmeath. The order of contents was: 2002 Is The First Jan-Dec Tax Year And The Tax Credit System Will Fully Operate; Calculating Tax Credits; Standard Rate Cuts In Tabular Form; Social Welfare; Health; Housing.

At around the same time, McGrath's Fianna Fáil constituency rival, Donie Cassidy, also distributed a leaflet spelling out the implications for citizens of the recent budget. Its order of contents was: 2002 Is The First Jan-Dec Tax Year And The Tax Credit System Will Fully Operate; Calculating Tax Credits; Standard Rate Cuts In Tabular Form; Social Welfare; Health; Housing. When he saw Cassidy's pamphlet, Paul McGrath expressed "outrage" and insisted that there was more to the similarities than mere chance. In support of his argument, he pointed out that his leaflet contained three spelling errors, including 'domicillary' which should have been spelled 'domiciliary'. What were the chances, he asked, of Cassidy's completely original document containing the exact same spelling errors?

A hurt Donie Cassidy strenuously rejected any suggestion of plagiarism, clarifying that: "Anything I have used has been based on Fianna Fáil Bills and Fianna Fáil Acts." He added: "I cannot understand what these people are crying about all the time. These people have spent years in opposition, achieving nothing for most of the time." He expressed confidence that, on polling day, the voters of Westmeath would bear him out. And they did, electing him to the Dáil after a 20 year apprenticeship in the Séanad.

In Mayo, another Fianna Fáil TD was banking on the voting public to silence a gallery of detractors. Beverly Cooper-Flynn had recently been found guilty in court of encouraging tax evasion during her previous life as a bank official. As polling day approached, she reached out to voters through their local press to remind them of the national media's "very personal" reporting of the trial which had deliberately and systematically cast her in a bad light. She said that the coverage was "a terrible shame" and had upset her supporters to whom she offered her sympathy.

Those same supporters were visibly upset again when they attempted to take up a church-gate collection for Beverly, but found themselves fighting a turf-war against fund-raisers for her party colleague, Deputy Tom Moffatt. Gardaí were called to break up the argy-bargy. Describing the belligerent parties as like "spoiled children", one observer remarked: "The laughable thing is that there wouldn't be €50 to be got from the entire collection." Reflecting on the so-called 'Battle Of The Biscuit Tins', a police officer said Fianna Fáil's four candidates had agreed a pre-election roster, but that one side had "reneged" on the pact.

In neighbouring Roscommon, the battle between rival Fianna Fáil factions had ended up in court, with the result that one party veteran stood in the 2002 general election on an independent ticket. Publican and businessman Tom Crosby had been a Fianna Fáil activist and councillor of long standing, but the relationship between the two fell apart when he caught his constituency colleague Séan Doherty seeing people behind his back.

In late 1998 a District Court judge ordered Crosby to pay £500 to the former Minister for Justice after the court heard that the councillor had trespassed into a private home, shouted abuse at the Cathaorleach of the Séanad, Brian Mullooly, and assaulted Doherty. The judge commented: "It was an outrageous assault exacerbated by an equally outrageous trespass." Crosby had gate-crashed a private meeting at the home of Fergal McGuinness, a local shopkeeper and Fianna Fáil hopeful. McGuinness said that in order to further his business plans, he'd been lobbying Doherty. The ex-Minister had arranged to meet several interested parties in the McGuinness homestead, but had stipulated that Crosby was not to be invited. It emerged that there had been bad blood between Doherty and Crosby for years, despite the fact they were both playing for the same Fianna Fáil team.

During the gathering, there was a ring on the doorbell. It was Crosby who demanded to be let in. McGuinness told the court that when Crosby was told it was a private meeting: "He said, 'I want to know what's going on in my village', and barged past me and into my house and down the hall, and went into the kitchen where he started abusing people."

According to McGuinness, the first target of Crosby's abuse was Senator Brian Mullooly, who was ensconced in an armchair in the kitchen. The witness said: "He abused Mr Mullooly quite severely and used words like bastard and fucker. At this point Séan Doherty stood up and said 'I'm leaving'. Tom Crosby then jumped up and lunged at him, hit him in the back with his right forearm and struck him with his left fist in the back of the head."

Doherty said that he ducked the first swipe, "but I got hit with the second one. It was very frenzied, he was very violent. It was impossible to understand what he was saying." McGuinness testified that after assaulting Doherty, Crosby was restrained on the kitchen floor "practically incoherent and literally foaming at the mouth with rage".

Crosby told the court that on the night in question he'd received a phone call from his wife while on his way to a business meeting: "She said come back home, that there was a meeting of the Development Association and that it was being held in such a manner that I would be excluded." Crosby had been a founder of the Development Association and felt entitled to be privy to its activities. He dashed back to the village of Termonbarry and went about searching the public houses for a meeting, with no success. But when he spotted Senator Mullooly's chauffeur-driven Merc with the driver inside, he knew something was definitely up and entered the McGuinness home.

Crosby's solicitor said that his client felt strongly about development issues in the locality and "may have misinterpreted" a meeting that was going on without him. He said that Crosby was galled because he felt Mullooly and Doherty were intent on trying to ruin him politically by driving a wedge between him and the local community. Unimpressed, the judge replied: "The charge is one of assault and not an investigation into the machinations of local politics." The former Justice Minister and member of the Garda Special Branch denied that he had leaned into Crosby as he left, promising: "I'll nail you for this."

Back in court some weeks later before a different judge, Crosby's response to the £500 penalty was that he'd pay it into the court poor-box, but: "I'll rot in prison before I pay Doherty. I wouldn't trust him with 5p." He then suggested that the former Justice Minister had been involved in the judge's appointment, leading the judge to threaten him with a week behind bars for contempt.

Doherty's solicitor said that the former Minister would be happy to accept the £500 and then redirect it to the Roscommon-Mayo Hospice. The judge opted to cut out the middle man and Crosby was allowed to pay the hospice directly. Crosby then claimed that he'd suffered a "very serious injustice", adding: "He was Minister for Justice and he was bragging about appointments to the judiciary. It's about time it came to light."

As he turned to leave the courtroom, Crosby told the judge: "I respect your decision to withdraw from hearing the case the last day, because he was involved in your appointment." At this, the judge called him back, saying: "I want an apology. I'm not going to put up with any of your nonsense."

Crosby apologised, and the judge said: "That's fair enough."

After years representing Fianna Fáil on the council, Crosby contested the 2002 general election as an independent, failing to land a seat.

Mary Harney's Vanishing Vegetation

One of Fianna Fáil's election promises was to set up a Department of Transport, having abolished it after the previous election. Another pledge made by Bertie Ahern was to end hospital waiting lists permanently by 2004 – something which Fine Gael's Michael Noonan predicted would turn out to be "blatant lies". Fianna Fáil, Fine Gael, Labour and the Progressive Democrats backed each other into a tight corner but then co-operated to get out of their awkward huddle. All four had agreed to submit their economic manifestos to a panel of experts who would tell the voters which five-year projection was most grounded in reality. Affording each other wriggle room, the four arrived at a cross-party agreement that the experts should be left undisturbed and the electorate given their democratic right to do the hard sums for themselves.

Labour's Senator Joe Costello went to the High Court to stop An Post stamping the mail with the slogan 'Fianna Fáil, The Republican Party – A Lot Done, More To Do'. In court, lawyers for Fianna Fáil argued that Costello was trying to curb freedom of expression, and that he had no right to tell An Post how to run their business. Lawyers for the Labour Party argued that An Post had no right to print messages on envelopes, which were the private property of either the sender or the addressee. Labour maintained that by stamping the Fianna Fáil message, An Post was guilty of mail "tampering". Costello lost the case, but the judge ordered An Post to provide him with a franking machine so that he could be sure there was no Fianna Fáil slogan on his election mail.

An election poster put up by Fianna Fáil's Tom Kitt came loose from a lamppost in Dublin and struck a motorcyclist, causing him to fall off his motorbike. His injuries meant he had to stay off work for three weeks. At the time, Kitt was the Junior Minister for Health and Safety.

The election posters of Sinn Féin were also destined to cause grief, although the bother came at the end of a long fuse. Five months after polling day 2002, Gardaí swooped on five men who were acting suspiciously in Bray, Co Wicklow. The men were found to be in possession of a stun-gun, a CS gas canister, car number plates, a flashing blue light similar to those of the emergency services, and a large number of Sinn Féin posters, including ones saying 'Sinn Féin No 1 Aengus O Snodaigh'.

O Snodaigh, who had been elected to the Dáil the previous May, had "absolutely no idea" what his posters were doing in the possession of the five, who were subsequently jailed for IRA activities. He had known one of the men when they were growing up as neighbours, but had fallen out of touch with him. The owner of the van containing the posters said that on October 10, 2002 someone had called to his home, indicated they were from Sinn Féin and asked could he have a loan of the van for election purposes. Clearly unaware that there was no election on at the time, he handed over the keys. However, the next morning when it was time to go to work, the van hadn't been returned. Asked if he felt aggrieved that his vehicle had been "used in this fashion", he answered: "Sort of."

Back to May 2002, and the Labour Party complained that in some marginal constituencies their posters were being torn down as fast as they were going up. Putting a positive spin on the vandalism, a spokesperson said: "To an extent that's a sign that our campaign is going well and others are getting worried." A caller to Today FM suggested that Labour and Sinn Féin could strike up a coalition of the Left-ish and pitch themselves at the voters as Guns 'n' Roses. Sinn Féin's Dessie Ellis failed to land a seat in Dublin North West, despite having earlier taken out an advert in the *Northside People* which said: "Dessie Ellis is available to provide practical assistance with housing, social welfare, rent, industrial relations, anti-social behaviour …".

Fine Gael's luminescent Mayo TD, Michael Ring, was canvassing in Carrowholly near Westport when he encountered some anti-social behaviour of his own. He explained: "I was doing mighty on the canvass with John O'Malley when we called to this house where I knew them all well. Before I knew what happened, this little hoor of a dog had his teeth in me. He brought blood. My trouser was torn and I had to go home and change into another suit." The dogged Deputy continued: "I was bit before in the County Council election in 1999. There was no one at home at the house I was canvassing and I was writing a note to say I called when another big bitch came around and bit me. I was a bit frightened that time alright. These dangers go with the territory. I reckon you have a great chance of getting the vote in a house if a dog bites you. No matter what side they are on, they have fierce sympathy for you and won't let you down on polling day."

In the west Dublin district of Quarryvale, a stand of tall trees was planted just hours before the Tánaiste, Mary Harney, arrived to open a resource centre. Immediately after the Tánaiste left the trees were uprooted. For some, this brought to mind a by-election in June 1982 when Fianna Fáil Environment Minister Ray Burke had conjured up a forest of trees in the Dublin suburb of Clonsilla the night before the poll. No sooner had the votes been cast than the trees were uprooted by their rightful owners. Asked what had happened to Mary Harney's vanishing vegetation, Dublin County Council explained that the trees had been planted "on a temporary basis". A spokesman said: "They were brought in specially for the occasion, to make the place look nice." A spokesperson for the Tánaiste said that she would be highly disappointed if plants had been placed for the sake of optics, saying: "Anyone who knows Mary Harney knows she doesn't stand on ceremony, so that trappings aren't important."

2003

FROM TIME TO TIME I SMOKE IT MYSELF
THE UPS AND DOWNS OF A REZONING WINDFALL

If the members of the planning watchdog An Táisce ever had a collective nightmare, it might be that the Bogeyman would bear a strong resemblance to Donal Kinsella, a colourful Fianna Fáil activist from Dunleer in Co Louth.

In 2003 Kinsella saw the potential value of his land jump twentyfold when it was included in a rezoning move which was decried as "perverse" and "a travesty", and which raised a clamour for the Environment Minister Martin Cullen to reverse the decision.

The rezoning paved the way to turn sleepy Dunleer into a Dublin dormitory town, quadrupling the population. Meanwhile, Kinsella unveiled a parallel scheme to build a "tourist retail outlet village" on the site of his home there. Opponents were up in arms because the new Dunleer blueprint flew in the face of the National Spatial Strategy which sought to stop the overspill of Greater Dublin into south Louth by locating new developments further north in the 'gateway' town of Dundalk.

The controversial reshaping of Dunleer came at the end of a long and winding road with 180 degree bends. Initially, Louth County Council engaged a firm of Dublin urban designers to propose developments for the area. Then, five councillors commissioned a rival plan of their own, which featured extensive rezoning. 'Plan B', as it became known, was voted through in May of 2002 on the casting ballot of one of the councilors who'd commissioned it.

However, shortly afterwards, one of the five, Councillor Tommy Clare of Fianna Fáil, turned against the newly-adopted plan he himself had proposed. Clare, the only Louth councilor resident in Dunleer, went so far as to condemn Plan B as "a complete sham" because the local community had not been consulted.

The next twist came in the summer of 2003 when Plan B was dumped by Louth County Council by a margin of 16 votes to five. This decision to revert to 'Plan A' seemed to reflect public opinion in the Dunleer area. Of the 67 submissions received, over four-fifths favoured the original scheme devised by the Dublin firm. Then, weeks later, Plan B was tabled again and the rezonings were passed by a vote of 18 to one.

This author met up with Donal Kinsella in his Drogheda office where he was basking in the afterglow of a job well done. It had taken him years of lobbying to get his agricultural land rezoned for industrial and commercial use. Soon, he hoped, it would house 80 "high brand label shops" stocking "Adidas, Puma, Calvin Klein" and other designer desirables. Kinsella dismissed the squall surrounding his windfall as the bleating of NIMBYs, begrudgers and political enemies. He exuded an air of absolute entitlement, breathing fire against the planners and politicians who had stood between him and his dream retail park for so long.

Other landowners benefited from the Dunleer rezoning, but Kinsella felt that most of the begrudgery had flown his way because at the time he held the Chair of the South Louth Comhairle Ceanntair of Fianna Fáil. He cited one headline "referring to me as some sort of Fianna Fáil bag-carrier, or hack, or 'Yes' Man. Using the term 'Fianna Fáil' was probably much more important than describing the sort of individual I am. The attachment there is of Fianna Fáil to making a lot of money, but there isn't a lot of money made. If I, or someone else, can't put something of commercial value on this land it isn't worth two squirts of goat's piss." He insisted, "I'm not a developer and never have been", adding that he purchased the land 13 years earlier purely "to live on". He continued: "I resented the motorway coming through the farm. I was very upset."

Kinsella was born into a staunch Fianna Fáil family. Once very active in the party, he drifted away for some years before returning to the local fold in the 1990s. By his own account, he galvanised the party in south Louth to stand up against a situation where the north county was getting the bulk of new jobs and development. "Why did I come back? Because I felt I could contribute quite a bit to the town and community of Drogheda and south Louth by getting hold of the party and giving it a good shaking, and teaching it that it had enough confidence to be itself, rather than be a tail of the Dundalk dog which we can't wag."

The aims of the National Spatial Plan were of secondary concern to him. He expressed the view that his re-energised south Louth Fianna Fáil had brought about "some seriously good investments" and that the Plan B rezoning of Dunleer represented more of the same. Those behind the breached Spatial Plan would not have shared that view, but Donal Kinsella insisted that he was also on the side of "sustainability". It's just that the side he was on was the opposite side of the county to Dundalk.

He explained: "Why not take a full look at the urban sprawl of Dublin and say, okay, this is where we're gonna run it. We're gonna put an extra 5,000 or 10,000 acres into the greater Dublin area and we're gonna reduce the price of those houses ... What we have done is we have created a shortage. It's like selling skunk or selling any sort of drugs." [Skunk is a super-potent form of cannabis, an herb about which Kinsella's party colleague, Charlie McCreevy, once said: "I never did drugs. That's the only thing I missed out on. I never even smoked – what do you call that oul thing? – shit."]

Kinsella elaborated: "I know (young people) buy the fucking thing and they smoke it, and from time to time I smoke it myself, though the last time I smoked it I swore I'd never do it again ... But they go off and they pay ten times as much for it as they should be paying for it, because the legal statutory body says it's not allowed, in the same way as developing land is not allowed."

Everywhere he looked in the world of planning and development, Donal Kinsella could detect naked self-interest wrapped up as concern for the common good, together with mean streaks of pure begrudgery. He pointed out on the local map one "grand envelope" of land where "some entrepreneur could come and build some fucking thing or other" if it was rezoned. The upshot would be new jobs in the locality. However: "What's wrong with us, and it's a natural thing, is that we're fuckin' jealous and begrudging and feel that if we do (rezone) we're going to make some fucker money. But we forget that we're gonna *have to* make money if we're gonna create jobs!"

According to Donal Kinsella, the Plan B rezoning of Dunleer wasn't just going to mean affordable housing for young couples, it was also one-in-the-eye for the NIMBYs of south Louth who "get on to their friends in Ranelagh and Dublin 4 and say there's no way you can let this go on – we're giving scavengers money, we're making very rich men out of these fellas. It's not that at all. The real problem here, as Ross O'Carroll Kelly says, is we're going to put in 'skangers'."

2005

FUCK IT, WE'LL SAY NO MORE
FREEDOM OF SPEECH IN THE DÁIL CHAMBER

In theory, the Dáil chamber is the first and last sanctuary of free speech in the State. Under parliamentary privilege, members have the freedom to say things which – in the outside world where the law has fangs – would get the speaker gagged and sued under the tyrannical libel laws. In practice, a body of club rules has grown-up over the years which make plain speaking an increasing rarity in the Dáil.

In 2005 the Ceann Comhairle, Rory O'Hanlon, apologised for uttering the faint curse "for frig's sake" while trying to quell a squall in the Dáil. It was a mild but unfortunate slip, given that O'Hanlon, as the Dáil's referee, had not so long before issued a written warning to all deputies that they should mind their language in the House.

However, some mystery benefactor moved quickly to save the Ceann Comhairle's blushes, and his use of the word frig never ended up on the official transcript. The result is that the annals of posterity will show O'Hanlon apologising to the House for something he never said in the first place, even though a lot of people heard him say it.

There was nothing new in this piece of sleight of hand. The independent Irish State lifted the trappings of its parliamentary democracy wholesale from Westminster, including the convention that the keepers of the official parliamentary record are entitled – obliged even – to 'touch up' the imperfect verbals of the speechmakers. The Westminster record, *The Hansard*, was never designed to be a verbatim account of proceedings, and the earliest compilers gave themselves the task of joining the dots and eliminating "repetitions and redundancies".

A Westminster euphemism imported directly into the Oireachtas is that the term "interruptions" can be used to cover a multitude of sins. In 2004, former Defence Minister Michael Smith was caught on a Dáil microphone clearly saying: "Fuck it, we'll say no more." On the official record this became "interruptions".

In one infamous case, the "interruptions" on the record were indeed the loud, unruly and garbled interruptions of a general clamour in the House, but not of a spontaneous one. Instead they were part of a well-planned set piece to ensure that three prepared speeches would never be allowed sully the official record of the Oireachtas.

It was 1984 and US President Ronald Reagan was on a state visit to Ireland. At the time the hawkish Reagan was menacing the Soviet Union with his pie-in-the-sky Star Wars nuclear strike system. Back in the real world, the covert and not so covert operations of US forces in the Philippines, El Salvador, Nicaragua and Chile had won Reagan few fans amongst the brutalised local populations, or amongst Irish humanitarians.

As the climax of his visit, Reagan was scheduled to address the joint Houses of the Oireachtas. A score of TDs and Senators opted to boycott the event, including Mary Robinson, Michael D Higgins and Brendan Howlin. Weeks earlier, Taoiseach Garret Fitzgerald had warned US officials to prepare the President for a protest, going so far as to describe the layout of the Dáil and where the protestors would be positioned.

Three Deputies decided they wanted their protest to be chiselled forever onto the official record of the Oireachtas. As Reagan began his address, Tomas MacGiolla stood and said: "Ceann Comhairle, on a point of order ..." He was shouted down by angry colleagues. Proinsias de Rossa rose to his feet and his words too were obliterated by howls of abuse. Tony Gregory was drowned out by the same wall of noise.

As the three Deputies walked out, Reagan jeered them with the smug quip: "There are countries in the world today where representatives would not have been able to speak as they have been here." The point that the three had been denied the right to speak freely on the record was lost in the enraptured applause of the Oireachtas members. As an extra precaution to keep that record clean, all the microphones had been shut off bar one for the President and one for the Ceann Comhairle.

Fast-forwarding back to the future of 2005, Labour leader Pat Rabbitte expressed concern for Rory O'Hanlon's abducted "frig", remarking: "I have wondered about the spoken word, as spoken in the Dáil, and what appears in the Official Report." Rabbitte himself had once benefited from the Dáil practice of improving the truth when he referred to "Peter O'Toole in *The Field*" during a Dáil debate. When the official transcript emerged, his error had been corrected to "Richard Harris in *The Field*".

Sometimes the blemishes on the record are cleaned up for motives which need no explanation. In the 1980s the *Sunday Tribune* carried the following report: "Mr Haughey's Minister of State (the speaker was named in that less litigious time), made a curt contribution saying: 'Cluskey, you're a fucking cunt.' But that will hardly appear on the official record."

Occasionally, the "corrections" in the record are genuine fix-ups of innocent errors. During a 1967 Oireachtas committee debate on censorship, Deputy Owen Lancelot Sheehy-Skeffington said: "In general, in this assembly, I find the official reporting very accurate, but I did notice the other day, when I made the point that other things besides literature can arouse sexual passions – that when I said 'the mini-skirt, for instance', in the first version of the transcript this read 'the Minister, for instance'."

Senator John Benignus O'Quigley chipped in: "The Minister will be flattered."

"I am," said Minister Brian Lenihan.

Sheehy-Skeffington responded: "I don't know whether the Minister will be disappointed to learn that a later hand had crossed out 'Minister' and re-established 'mini-skirt'."

Some months before the Ceann Comhairle's 2005 slip of the tongue, Pat Rabbitte's Labour colleague, Emmet Stagg, had been ejected from the House for barracking Taoiseach Bertie Ahern during a heated debate. Stagg had accused the Taoiseach of being "miserable" in failing to provide for elderly Irish emigrants, and Ceann Comhairle O'Hanlon felt that Stagg's behaviour warranted a red card. There was a bit of previous history between the two. Two days earlier Stagg had attacked moves by O'Hanlon to tone down the flinging about of emotive language in the House. The Ceann Comhairle had sent a letter to all TDs warning them against using terms like "deliberately misled". Stagg complained: "[Before], you couldn't accuse anyone of lying. Now you can't use the word 'lie'."

The conventions of Parliamentary oration are collected in a publication entitled *Salient Rulings Of The Chair*. In his letter to deputies, Ceann Comhairle O'Hanlon made this constantly evolving document required reading. Drawing on precedent, *Salient Rulings* sets out the ground rules for the behaviour of Deputies within the Dáil chamber. While the House is in session, deputies must not read the newspaper. They may not ask a question while in a seated position (wheelchairs presumably excluded), and they must not propose that the Dáil takes a break to have a bite to eat or to watch a sporting event on the telly.

The most intriguing rules concern the behaviour of TDs towards each other. Deputies are specifically forbidden from calling each other a cookoo, brat, buffoon, chancer, communist, corner-boy, gurrier, guttersnipe, hypocrite, scumbag or yahoo. It's okay to call a policy or motion "fascist", but not to call an individual "a fascist". Calling someone a rat is expressly forbidden, but calling them a "dirty rat" is not. Even though "dirty rat" was bandied loudly in a 1934 debate it's not on the banned list because the Ceann Comhairle apparently didn't hear it.

Deputies should not refer to the business dealings of other Deputies or to members of their family. They must not engage in personal criticism or threaten other members. During a 1952 debate one TD was warned to stop threatening the legendary Oliver J Flanagan, while during a 1982 debate Labour's Barry Desmond accused a Minister in Charles Haughey's GUBU cabinet of threatening him in a Dáil corridor.

The *Salient Rules* say that the Ceann Comhairle must protect TDs from any "innuendo, insinuation and allegation" made in the chamber. This instruction refers to a 1980 tirade by the Fine Gael leader Garret FitzGerald against Taoiseach CJ Haughey. FitzGerald was cautioned for using Dáil privilege to accuse Haughey of breaking almost every rule in the book, including wielding "political influence ... to keep law enforcement away from areas where it might embarrass party supporters [and lead to] prosecutions being quashed by political intervention ... the Garda being interfered with ... and of this coming from Government level and not just from party supporters. Moreover, when we in this House have sought to raise these allegations of grave abuses, every effort has been made to intimidate us into not doing our duty by hints that files exist in relation to members of the Opposition."

While it may not be always in the public interest, the *Salient Rules* explicitly forbid TDs from accusing each other of committing murder, blackmail, corruption, perjury, physical or moral cowardice, graft, embezzlement, robbery, seditious libel, fraud, deception, dishonesty, being a black-marketeer, a smuggler, a rogue or a scoundrel. It is out of order to accuse an elected representative of giving or taking bribes, or making criminally irresponsible decisions, of doctoring an official report, of being steaming drunk in the House or just a wee bit tipsy.

The bans on accusations of cowardice, hypocrisy and even murder have their precedent in many offside rulings against them by the Ceann Comhairle. Other rules are strikingly case-specific. A TD must not be accused of "interfering in the distribution of land while a Minister of State at the Department of Agriculture", or "of trying to deliberately sabotage the Dublin Light Rail Project". Deputies are also forbidden to accuse a judge of giving a prejudiced summing up and of being a disgrace to his profession.

The biggest no-no of all under the club rules is to accuse a fellow member of lying, even when he or she is brazenly doing just that. According to the rulebook, this courtesy is "essential if orderliness of the House is to be maintained".

2007

SOMEWHERE, IT HAD ALL GONE HORRIBLY RIGHT

The Incumbents: FF/PD coalition led by Bertie Ahern.
Slogan: The boom times are getting even more boomer!
The Challengers: A FG/Labour coalition led by Enda Kenny.
Slogan: Government driven by your dreams (E Kenny).

PS I Owe You

Having come tantalisingly close to realizing the dream of an overall majority in the 2002 general election, Fianna Fáil had a rude awakening on the way to the 2007 contest, taking a pasting in the local and European polls of June 2004. At an ill-tempered post-mortem that dragged on for four hours, backbenchers bellyached to their superiors that the plain people of Ireland had punished the party for living it up, lurching Right, and losing touch. The blame was dumped squarely on the Progressive Democrats, who were a bad influence at the Cabinet table and who weren't even needed by Fianna Fáil to make up the numbers for government.

One month earlier, the PD Justice Minister Michael McDowell had needled the nation's bleeding heart liberals with a mission statement proposing that a dynamic "economy like ours demands flexibility and inequality". Charitable bodies and opposition deputies denounced this insight as "warped logic", "utterly disgraceful", and evidence of a view from the top table "that the economy is more important than the people".

At the inquest into Fianna Fáil's worst electoral performance since 1927, McDowell was the pin-up boy on the dartboard. "They roasted him," said one TD present. There were also muted mutters that Fianna Fáil's penny-wise Finance Minister, 'Champagne' Charlie McCreevy, was scaring off traditional FF voters infected with a queasy gut feeling that he was a screaming closet PD. Bertie Ahern rejected demands for an urgent Cabinet reshuffle to give the optics more of a soft-focus.

Conveying the mutinous mood on the backbenches to the wider nation, the Cork deputy Noel O'Flynn said that Fianna Fáil should ditch its PD partners, take the next turn to the Left and rule as a minority administration. He fretted: "We will not be in government after the next election unless there is change, and change at Cabinet level is essential. The public face of Fianna Fáil is the Cabinet and the present grouping does not reflect the views of the people."

Following Fianna Fáil's frank exchange of views behind closed doors, the rumour mill had it that Charlie McCreevy would be invited to give his Taoiseach a dig out by accepting a plum job offer to become Ireland's European Commissioner. McCreevy knocked that one firmly on the head by reassuring his admirers: "I think my best role is in Irish politics. I've enjoyed being Minister for Finance." Three weeks later he walked the red-carpeted plank of advancement. Asked what brought about his dramatic change of heart, he quoted the British Prime Minister Harold Macmillan, sighing wistfully: "Events, dear boy, events."

With McCreevy removed to a higher calling, the time was ripe for Fianna Fáil to reveal its true-blue red colours as Ireland's leading Socialist party. Mikey Graham of the dreamy crooners Boyzone had earlier observed that: "A socialite is someone who thrives on constant Socialism." Just weeks after McCreevy's departure from Finance, Bertie Ahern revealed that Ireland had been thriving on a new, improved, Fianna Fáil model of Socialism which had floated the boats of all socialites, rich and poor. The Taoiseach explained: "Socialism, as it is historically understood, is dead. All of the people who carried that ideology in Great Britain and in Europe, they're gone. When I meet the great leaders of former Socialist countries in Europe now, half of them would be to the right of Margaret Thatcher. My brand of Socialism is the one that people now want to follow."

But not everyone. One person who wavered gravely when it came to following the Taoiseach's path of Socialism was the lone representative of the Socialist Party in the Dáil, Joe Higgins. Higgins grumbled that under Ahern's new Socialist regime, the cost of buying a cardboard-and-superglue semi-d had flown beyond the means of most working folk. He suggested that Fianna Fáil had turned its back on the ordinary decent citizens of Ireland, to slavishly turn tricks for the primped pimps of the building game.

The Taoiseach told Higgins that he was very much mistaken. Setting forth the reality of the situation with ringing clarity, he explained: "You have a failed ideology. You have the most hopeless policy that I ever heard pursued by any nitwit. You are a failed person. You were rejected and your political philosophy has been rejected and you're not going to pull people back into the failed old policies that you dreamt up in south Kerry when you were a young fella. Now go away."

In late 2006 there was a premature ejaculation of election fever after a heartwarming story emerged involving the Taoiseach himself. It was a tale which emphatically illustrated his point that no single brand of Socialism has exclusive bragging rights on the impulse to care and share. In the early 1990s, when he was Minister for Finance, Ahern had been given "dig-outs" to the tune of tens of thousands of pounds – at a time when tens of thousands of pounds were worth something – by an assortment of friends and strangers who wouldn't see a friend, or a stranger, stuck for a large amount of money. After Bertie said a few token words at one dinner in Manchester, a group of wealthy businessmen had a whip-around and surprised him with £8,000 as a token of their appreciation. More than a decade after receiving that sum, and others, he was unable to say who precisely had dug-out what. There was a cruel jibe that if only the Taoiseach could scribble down a total recall of his benefactors, he could follow his daughter Celia onto the bestseller lists with a book of his own called *PS I Owe You*.

Enemies of the government clamoured for clarifications. There were invasive and impertinent questions about a large sum which Ahern had saved up over a six-year period when, despite being Minister for Finance for some of that time, he had no bank account. The Taoiseach did his level best to maintain a dignified silence, divulging fragments of information to the prying ill-wishers on a strictly need-to-know basis. For two weeks rival parties tried to drive a wedge between the coalition partners over the issue. On one occasion, as the Taoiseach batted away yet more questions in the Dáil, Michael McDowell and Mary Harney of the Progressive Democrats were conspicuous by their absence. Harney was spotted that same day at a conference entitled 'Planning for Disaster'. But whatever the PD's recently-stepped-down leader was planning, it was her replacement McDowell who had to decide: should I stay or should I go? If the boss of the self-professed party of probity had to wrestle hard with his conscience, he eventually emerged the clear winner. The Taoiseach and Tánaiste renewed their vows at a brief ceremony for the cameras. As they departed to get back to running the country, McDowell was heard to whisper to Ahern: "We survived it."

Bertie Ahern survived the toxic fallout from an English

dinner engagement to lead his party into the 2007 general election. For Ahern's protégé, Royston Brady – a man once touted as a potential future leader of Fianna Fáil – a rich London lunch kept repeating on him to the embarrassing extent that old party pals publicly disowned him.

At the tender age of eleven, Royston Brady was Bertie's Boy Friday at Ahern's constituency HQ, Saint Luke's, delivering pamphlets and generally helping with the smooth roll-out of the democratic process. Twenty years later he became an overnight sensation when Fianna Fáil installed him in Dublin's Mansion House as the capital's first citizen. To the clink of the Lord Mayor's chain, Royston set about troubleshooting the city's blues with the swagger of a gun slinging sheriff.

In no time at all he'd branded his less gifted fellow city councilors "clowns"; talked up a showdown with the "arrogant" Justice Minister Michael McDowell; come out against his own party's plans to fast-track a smoking ban; sounded off in support of the lap-dancing industry; sounded off *against* the lap-dancing industry; and inaugurated a gala Lord Mayor's Parade to be held every New Year's Day.

Royston tried to move seamlessly from the Mansion House to the European Parliament in the summer of 2004. Shortly before polling day he regaled an interviewer with a gripping story, claiming that in May 1974 his taxi-driver father had been hijacked and his vehicle used as a getaway car by the perpetrators of the Dublin-Monaghan bombings which killed 33 people. He said: "I was only two at the time but what happened had a devastating effect on my dad. He was a taxi driver and his car was abducted in Dublin, then he was taken up the mountains at gunpoint and had to beg for his life. So in the end they tied him up and left him there. But he did think he was going to be shot and his car was used as one of the getaway cars the next day."

After starting the European campaign as a hot favourite

to become an MEP, Brady found himself branded a bigmouth fantasist and his nosedive only stopped when the polling booths shut. A week after the votes were cast, front page newspaper reports from 1974 turned up proving that his father had indeed been abducted on the eve of the bombings.

Where Bertie Ahern had once managed to raise generous funding at an English dinner without even trying, Royston managed to preside over a lavish London lunch held in his honour, without collecting a single penny towards his cause. The Michelin-starred celebrity chef Richard Corrigan laid on a three-course meal for 40 well-heeled members of the London-Irish business community in his swish Soho restaurant, Lindsay House. A year later, in 2005, Brady's exasperated campaign manager revealed that Fianna Fáil had banked on the event raising some €50,000 towards the Euro election expenses, but the money had "never materialised". For Royston's wealthy guests, there really had been such a thing as a free lunch.

Richard Corrigan, who absorbed the hefty cost of the opulent lobster and beef spread, said that Royston's failure to cash in on "a golden opportunity" had left him "perplexed".

Their Tubes Inflated With Nitrogen

In December 2003, Finance Minister Charlie McCreevy revived an old Fianna Fáil party favourite and announced that 10,000 civil service jobs were to be decentralised from Dublin to the regions. Three years on, towards the close of 2006, his successor at Finance, Brian Cowen, told the Fianna Fáil Ard Féis that the process was going full speed ahead, although he neglected to mention that the number of people who'd moved so far was short of 600. The State development agency, Enterprise Ireland, which was relocating to Shannon under the scheme, had just taken out a 25-year lease on offices in Dublin designed to house 600 staff.

In December 2005 the radio station Midlands 103 ran a

text poll to find out what the public thought of the
government's plan to lift and separate 10,000 dug-in Dublin
civil servants. Following an on-air debate between the
Progressive Democrats' Minister for Decentralisation, Tom
Parlon, and Labour's Joan Burton, the poll brought
unbelievably good news for the government, with those
supporting its strategy prevailing by a resounding 94% to 6%.

The news was unbelievable in the literal sense. Taken
aback by the landslide of texts in the government's favour,
staff at Midlands 103 did a spot of detective work. After
running traces, the station's head of news deduced that there
had been a heavy discharge of opinions from "persons
working for, or associated with, the Progressive Democrats".
The phone numbers identified included those of Tom
Parlon's special adviser and of his constituency secretary, plus
a PD Senator, a PD councilor and a senior PD officer. One
person had texted five times in quick succession, each time
giving the thumbs-up to the government's plan.

Parlon made it clear that neither he nor anybody
associated with him, or his party, had attempted to
orchestrate the outcome of the text poll. At the same time,
the Junior Minister pointed out: "In a competition like *You're
A Star*, if someone had €1,000 to spend on texts, then it's
about winning the competition." Parlon thought it "a bit
silly" that the radio station would try to make an issue of the
average PD member's zeal for text voting. Asked whether the
taxpayer should have to foot the bill for the texts apparently
sent by two of his office staff, and for the loss of working time
paid for by the taxpayer, Parlon said that it was common for
workers in the public and private sector to sent texts during
working-hours. He added: "If you decide to have a text
competition, then you should say if someone is not entitled
to vote."

The appliance of science to a more weighty poll was a
topic of hot debate in the long run-up to the 2007 general

election. The government had spent €52 million to purchase electronic machines which – the Taoiseach finally confirmed late in 2006 – would spend polling day 2007 idling in high-rent storage. Having initially entrusted the safe-keeping of the computers to dozens of well-imbursed landlords, the government had decided to centralise the storage of the machines in order to reduce the high rental costs which had attracted a lot of flak. However, Labour's Pat Rabbitte pointed out that the belated move to store all the voting machines in one place would now oblige the taxpayer to buy out the long-term storage leases signed just a couple of years before with the favoured bevy of landlords. Rabbitte noted that in Co Monaghan, the State had entered into a storage lease for 25 years, at €25,685 a year, "although the lifetime of the machines is 20 years".

Brushing off the nit-pickers, naysayers and nitwits, the Taoiseach gave his solemn word that the controversial voting machines would prove their worth at some unspecified point in the future before their 20-year lifespan was up. "Otherwise," he said, "we go into the 21st Century in this country being the laughing stock with our stupid aul' pencils." On the same vexed issue of electronic voting, RTE's *News At One* issued the anatomically-dubious statement that: "The Comptroller And Auditor General John Purcell said that the issue of costing was the Achilles tendon of the project."

In his last annual report to be published before the 2007 general election, the Comptroller And Auditor General spied squandermania on an heroic scale across a range of government departments and State bodies. Purcell estimated that Justice Minister Michael McDowell had signed off on a price tag of €29.9 million for a prison site in north Dublin which could have been bought for just €15 million if he'd gone about his shopping in a different way. The Comptroller found that a scheme to introduce integrated ticketing for

Dublin's public transport had over-run from its initial budget of €29.6 million to €42 million with just more tunnel at the end of the tunnel. Not only had the Rail Procurement Agency spent €1 million on one project to solve the problem, which had failed to solve anything – the only tangible return for the million doled out was to set-back the whole integrated ticketing scheme by at least one year.

In the same report Purcell noted that the maintenance of garda cars had still not been put out to competitive tendering, and that taxpayers' money "in the range €200,000 to €420,000" was being paid to garages around the country at the discretion of local garda teams. This was in direct defiance of a 2002 report stating that the police force should "outsource the entire maintenance activity including maintenance of the fleet, the contracts and costs, quality and performance management and compliance, to a national service-provider or consortium".

There was good reason for taking the maintenance arrangements out of the clutches of the Gardaí and entrusting it to a specialist body. The 2002 report had found the custodians of law and order badly wanting when it came to getting value for taxpayers' money from their contacts in the motor trade. The recommendation for an autonomous body to be entrusted with the task came on the back of an investigation which found that one patrol car had been fitted with 30 new tyres in the course of clocking up a mere 75,000 miles. There were other striking extravagances. Instead of having their tyres filled with free air, Gardaí would regularly pay €1.50 a blast from the public purse to have their tubes inflated with nitrogen. Compared to civilian cars, garda vehicles going in for a tyre change were prone to needing an extraordinary number of replacement valves, wheel alignments and other chargeable extras.

In 2005 a court heard that four senior garda officers had been fined for "discreditable conduct" after the detective branch of the media established that they had been sumptuously wined and dined by Advance Tyres Limited. Over a number of years, Advance laid on quite a count of educational excursions for the upholders of law and order. On one field-trip, the firm spent €55,000 whisking senior policemen off to the Continent for an inspection tour of tyre factories. However, the businesslike schedule didn't quite run to plan and the disappointed voyagers only got to visit one factory on a tour which took in several countries. The majority of their time was spent soaking up sun and culture, and swinging the lead on world-class golf courses. In his 2006 report – which came out a full four years after the force was asked to hand over the maintenance of its fleet to a competent body – the Comptroller noted reproachfully that the necessary measures had been held in a state of arrested development.

Shortly before the 1987 general election, the stridently free-market *Economist* magazine lambasted Ireland for the "domestic indulgence" of spending too much social welfare on the country's recession-hit needy. Shortly before the 2007 election the same publication showered praise and congratulations on Ireland for pulling off a miraculous transformation. Using the best scientists working in the magazine business, the *Economist* measured the quality of life in Ireland against that of 180 other states worldwide. The boffins weighed up a diversity of factors such as earnings, disposable income, political freedom, annual rainfall, epic commutes, nervous exhaustion, toll-bridge log-jams visible from space, crushing crèche charges, soaring personal debt, rocketing gun crime, stealth taxes, Podge & Rodge fatigue, cocaine madness, crippling house prices and so on. When the *Economist* had computed the results from across the globe, it declared that the people of Ireland should be the most thankful folk in the whole wide world for their lot in life.

I Punch The Wall

During his campaign which secured a Fianna Fáil landslide in the 1977 election, Jack Lynch toured the country billed as 'The Real Taoiseach'. In 2006, John Gormley of the Green Party dubbed Bertie Ahern 'The L'Oreal Taoiseach', in reference to Ahern's alleged €480 a week make-up habit. Months later, Ahern strengthened his persuasive claim to the all-time title of 'The Surreal Taoiseach', when he proudly declared to the nation: "The boom times are getting even more boomer."

Different citizens responded in different ways to the jagged ups and downs of this new, boomer Ireland. For the mother of one troubled tearaway who had fallen through the porous social safety net, the glass remained half-full rather than half-empty. On RTE's *Liveline* show, host Joe Duffy asked her: "Was your son sleeping rough?"

"*Oh no*," came the miffed reply. "He was sleeping in a phone box."

That mother may have been the living embodiment of the spirit Michael McDowell sought to galvanize, when he said: "I want to argue the subversive notion that the weak and the vulnerable in our society are better off with the Progressive Democrats in government than with Labour in government."

On the radio station Newstalk 106 vox-popper Henry McKean encountered a youngster who was finding the best country in the world a tricky and thorny place.

McKean: "How do you deal with your anger?"

Youth: "I punch the wall."

McKean: "That must hurt."

Youth (indignantly): "It does – but it's still dealing with your anger."

On another of his walkabouts, McKean encountered someone who'd come up with a coping mechanism more practical and a lot more popular than punching walls. It was still only mid-morning but the man on the street was thoroughly and unapologetically plastered. Asked to account for his drunken condition so early in the day, he offered the sobering thought: "I've had a few because I'm so distressed by the performance of Bertie Ahern and this government." Somewhere, it had all gone horribly right.

Selective Glossary

Ahern, Bertie
Real name Patrick Bartholomew Ahern. Elected leader of Fianna Fáil in 1994 and of the country 1997-2002, 2002-07. Dubbed the Teflon Taoiseach after a synthetic fluoropolymer with non-stick and non-reactive qualities and a high melting point. Technical manuals say that, because of its chemical inertness, Teflon (PTFE) has "no memory" and is associated with "a little creep".

Anti-Treatyites
In January 1922, 64 Sinn Féin Dáil deputies voted in favour of the Treaty with Britain granting limited independence to a partitioned Free State. Fifty-seven Sinn Féin TDs voted against. Later that year, the anti-Treatyites went to war against their former colleagues, now "Free-Staters".

Arms dumps
When Fianna Fáil entered the Dáil in 1927 the party resisted government calls to surrender its illegal arms. Séan Lemass said the secret dumps were "harmless".

Ballsbridge Complex, The
The 1920s form of "the Dublin 4 set". Used to describe a well-heeled rump of Cumann na nGaedheal which coexisted, sometimes uneasily, with the party's former gunmen.

Blueshirts, The
A force established in 1933 to protect "free speech" amid

fears that the Fianna Fáil government intended to overturn the Free State from within.

Browne, Noel
Medical doctor who became Minister for Health on his first day in the Dáil, 1948. Made great strides against the scourge of TB. Vilified by the medical profession and Catholic Church for trying to improve the health service.

Browne, Vincent
Publisher of enormous gusto. Founded *Magill* in 1977. Editor of the *Sunday Tribune* 1983-94. Thorn in the side of Charles Haughey.

Bruton, John
Elected to the Dáil aged 22 in 1969. Leader of Fine Gael 1990-2001. Became Taoiseach, without a general election, as head of Rainbow Coalition 1994-97. Appointed EU Ambassador to the US in 2004.

Burke, Ray
Taoiseach Bertie Ahern looked "up every tree in north Dublin" before appointing Burke to Cabinet in 1997. Burke didn't keep his large pots of funny money up trees. Served four months in jail in 2005 for tax evasion.

Childers, Erskine
The son of an executed anti-Treatyite, Childers held several Fianna Fáil ministries before election as fourth President of Ireland in 1973. Died in office 1974.

Childsex
Term coined by the self-styled Children's Protection Society in 1987 to attack candidates supporting more liberal contraception, which would allegedly lead to ten-year-olds fornicating with each other.

Clann na Phoblachta
Founded in 1946 as a younger, more republican and more virtuous alternative to Fianna Fáil. Entered government in 1948 in a five-party coalition.

Clann na Talmhan
Sought preferential treatment for small farmers 1938-65. 1944 manifesto stated "the farmer has a God-given right to complete overlordship of the land he inherited". Took part in the Inter-Party governments of 1948-51 and 1954-57.

Cluskey, Frank
Trade unionist first elected to the Dáil in 1965 for the Labour Party. Elected party leader in 1977, but stepped down from that post after losing seat in 1982. Died 1989.

Coalition
Fianna Fáil's first act in Dáil Eireann in 1927 was to try to oust the government by forming a coalition. With greater Dáil strength, opposition to coalition became a "core value" of FF, until 1989 when Charles Haughey sought the help of the despised PDs to stay in power.

Collins, Michael
Signed Treaty agreeing to a partitioned Free State in 1921. Quipped that he may have signed his own death warrant. Killed August 1922 by anti-Treaty forces in Civil War.

Communist
Comically absurd term of abuse levelled by just about every party at just about every other party from 1920s to 1990s.

Cosgrave, Liam
Son of Fine Gael founder WT. Party leader 1965-77 and Taoiseach 1973-77. Voted down his own government's Bill to permit married couples to access contraceptives.

Cosgrave, WT
William Thomas Cosgrave (1880-1965). Fought in 1916 Rising. First leader of the Free State from 1922 to 1932. Ensured the survival of the fledgling Irish democracy.

Costello, John A
Twice compromise Taoiseach at the head of coalition governments (1948-51, 1954-57), but never leader of his own Fine Gael Party. In 1948 announced that Eire would become a Republic in 1949.

Cumann na nGaedheal
The first government of the Free State (1922-32), originally made up of the pro-Treaty TDs of Sinn Féin. The name, adopted in 1923, meant League of the Irish.

Democratic Left
Split from The Workers Party in 1992 to become New Agenda, then Democratic Left. Shared power in Rainbow Coalition of 1994-97. Merged with Labour in 1999.

De Rossa, Proinsias
Interned in Curragh in 1950s for Sinn Féin activity. Elected TD 1982 and leader of The Workers Party 1988. To break link to Official IRA, he led 6 TDs out of WP to found Democratic Left in 1992. Labour MEP from 1999.

Desmond, Barry
Labour Minister for Health 1982-87. MEP 1989-94. European Court of Auditors 1994-99.

De Valera, Eamon
Fought in 1916 Rising. Led Sinn Féin until 1926. Founded Fianna Fáil in 1926. Taoiseach through most of 1930s, 1940s and 1950s. President of Ireland 1959-1973.

Dictatorship
In 1927, Fianna Fáil accused the Cumann na nGaedheal government of plotting to create a dictatorship. Over the following 20 years, FF were accused of plotting the same.

Dukes, Alan
Became Minister for Agriculture on first day in Dáil, 1981. Leader of Fine Gael 1987-90. Implemented "the Tallaght Strategy" in 1987 which supported CJ Haughey in power "in the national interest".

Dillon, James
Son of John Dillon, last leader of the Irish Parliamentary Party. Founder of National Centre Party. Founder of Fine Gael 1933. Expelled 1942 for advocating support of Britain in World War II. Rejoined FG 1954. Party leader 1959-65.

Economic War
When FF gained power in 1932, Eamon de Valera stopped paying annuities to Britain. In retaliation, Ireland's biggest export market blocked trade, damaging the Irish economy. Dispute resolved in 1938.

Emergency, The
Neutral-speak for World War II.

Ex-Unionist
In the years after the establishment of the Free State, this term was widely used to refer to members of the Protestant community.

Farmers Party, The
Won 15 seats in the 1923 general election. Backed the pro-Treaty Cumann na nGaedheal government of WT Cosgrave.

Fianna Fáil

Founded in 1926 by Eamon de Valera to allow Anti-Treatyites participate fully in Free State politics. Described by future Taoiseach Séan Lemass as a "slightly constitutional party". Currently favours "a fairer, stronger Ireland".

Fine Gael

Founded in 1933 from pro-Treaty groups Cumann na nGaedheal, the National Centre Party and the National Guard (The Blueshirts). Very attached to law-and-order.

Fitzgerald, Garret

Minister for Foreign Affairs 1973-77. Leader of Fine Gael 1977-87. Taoiseach July 1981-February 1982, December 1982-March 1987.

Flanagan, Oliver J

Fine Gael TD. Minister for Defence 1976-77. Mad.

Ghandi, Mahatma

Champion of Indian independence and of Fianna Fáil from beyond the grave.

Giles, Patrick

Army Captain. Fine Gael TD for Meath. Opposed to sissies.

Goodman, Larry

Powerful Beef Baron whose companies were the focus of the Beef Tribunal which uncovered disturbing irregularities in the meat trade. Said: "We don't like the word 'power'. That is a sort of Leninist idea."

Green Party, The

Founded in 1981 as the Ecology Party of Ireland. Became Green Party in 1987.

Griffith, Arthur
Founded Sinn Féin (Ourselves Alone) in 1905. Negotiated the Treaty of 1921. Died suddenly 1922.

Hannafin, Des
TD and Senator. Chief fundraiser for Fianna Fáil until relieved of duty by Charles Haughey. Staunchly anti-divorce and "pro-life".

Harney, Mary
Appointed Fianna Fáil Senator 1977. Elected TD 1981. Founder member of Progressive Democrats 1986. First woman Tánaiste 1997.

Haughey, Charles
Kleptocratic four-time Taoiseach.

Inter-Party Government, The
Fianna Fáil had succeeded in turning 'coalition' into a dirty word, so the two coalition governments of the 1940s and 1950s used the term 'inter-party'.

Irish Parliamentary Party, The
Led initially by Charles Stewart Parnell, the IPP was the first modern European parliamentary party to impose a strict whip voting system. Wiped out by Sinn Féin in the 1918 general election.

Irish Press, The
Fianna Fáil house organ established by Eamon de Valera in 1931 while defrauding the newspaper's shareholders. Shut down 1995.

Irish Republican Army
The army of the first – outlawed – Dáil Eireann which was

constituted by the Sinn Féin MPs elected in the 1918 Westminster general election.

Irish Times, The
Ireland's "newspaper of record". Formerly the voice of the Protestant community.

Irish Volunteers, The
A military organisation infiltrated by members of the Irish Republican Brotherhood, including Padraic Pearse. Staged 1916 Rising. The IRA claimed their mantle.

Irregulars, The
Government name for anti-Treaty forces in the Civil War.

Jinks Affair
Sligo TD John Jinks disappeared from the Dáil in 1927 when his vote was required to topple the government of WT Cosgrave. Drink was reportedly taken.

Kevinmander
Just before the 1969 general election, Fianna Fáil's Kevin Boland adjusted the constituency boundaries in the best interests of the democratic process, and not anything else.

Labour Party, The
Founded in 1912 by James Connolly, James Larkin and William O'Brien as the political wing of the Irish Trade Union Congress. Shot itself in the foot by opting out of the 1918 and 1921 general elections.

Lemass, Séan
Fought in the GPO in 1916. Founder member of Fianna Fáil. Taoiseach from 1959-65.

Lenihan, Brian
Fianna Fáil Minister for Justice, Education, Agriculture and Foreign Affairs. Failed Presidential candidate in 1990.

Lynch, Jack
Winner of six consecutive All-Ireland medals, five in hurling and one in football. Elected leader of Fianna Fáil and Taoiseach in 1966.

MacBride, Séan
Left post as IRA Chief of Staff to pursue career as lawyer. Founded Clann na Phoblachta and entered coalition government in 1948. Founder of Amnesty International.

MacEntee, Séan
Fought in the GPO in 1916. Founder member of Fianna Fáil. Minister for Finance, Industry & Commerce, Health, Local Government etc. Grandmaster of blather.

McCreevy, Charles
First elected to Dáil 1977. Fianna Fáil Minister for Finance 1997-2004. EU Commissioner 2004-present.

McDowell, Michael
Left Fine Gael to become founder member of PDs 1985. Attorney General 1999-2002. Minister for Justice, Equality, Law Reform and Announcements 2002-07. Became leader of PDs and Tánaiste 2006.

Mulcahy, Richard
Fought in 1916 Rising. Elected for Sinn Féin 1918. Elected leader of Fine Gael 1944.

National Centre Party, The
Founded 1932 as a party not entirely hostile to Britain.

Joined Cumann na nGaedheal and the Blueshirts to form Fine Gael.

National Labour Party, The
Split from the Labour Party in 1944, accusing Labour of being too left wing.

Noonan, Michael
Led push to depose Fine Gael leader John Bruton in 2001, taking over post. Resigned after FG wipe-out in general election of 2002.

Norton, William
Leader of the Labour Party 1932-60. Tánaiste in coalitions of 1948-51 and 1954-57.

Oath of Allegiance
The terms of the Treaty of 1921 provided for a 26-County Free State where members of the parliament took an Oath of Allegiance to the British monarch.

O'Brien, Conor Cruise
Minister for Posts and Telegraphs 1973-77. Lost seat 1977. Coined the phrase GUBU (Grotesque Unbelievable Bizarre Unprecedented) as a reflection on the leadership of Charles Haughey.

O'Connor, Pat, Pat O'Connor
Charles Haughey's election agent charged with attempted double-voting in 1982.

O'Higgins, Kevin
Hardline minister in early Free State governments. Introduced curbs on public disorder and drinking hours. Party to executions of IRA men. Gunned down 1927.

O'Kelly, Séan T
Jailed after 1916 Rising. Elected Sinn Féin MP 1918. Founder member of Fianna Fáil 1926. Second President of Ireland 1945-59.

O'Leary, Michael
Leader of Labour Party 1979-82. Tánaiste and Minister for Energy 1981-82. Joined Fine Gael 1982. Arranged meetings between disaffected FF and FG members, leading to formation of the PDs.

O'Malley, Des
Minister for Justice 1970-73, Industry & Commerce 1977-80, 1982. Expelled from Fianna Fáil 1985 for "conduct unbecoming", he founded the Progressive Democrats. Minister for Industry & Commerce 1989-92.

O'Moráin, Micheal
Hothead Mayo Minister for Justice opposed to "Left Wing political queers from Trinity College and Telefís Eireann".

Personation
Impersonating another voter at a polling station.

Progressive Democrats
Party founded in 1985 by Des O'Malley after his expulsion from Fianna Fáil. In 1993 he was replaced as leader by Mary Harney, who was replaced in 2006 by Michael McDowell.

Proportional Representation
Electoral system imposed by the British. In 1930 the Cumann na nGaedheal administration complained that it hindered strong government. FF twice tried to abolish it in referenda, without success.

Quinn, Ruairí
Minister for Labour 1983-86, Public Service 1987, Enterprise & Employment 1993-94, Finance 1994-97. Leader of the Labour Party 1997-2002.

Rabbitte, Pat
President of Union of Students in Ireland (USI) 1972-74. Elected to Dáil in 1989 for the Workers Party. Succeeded Ruairí Quinn as leader of the Labour Party 2002.

Rainbow Coalition
Administration of Fine Gael, Labour and Democratic Left 1994-97.

Reynolds, Albert
Ballroom owner and pet food manufacturer first elected to the Dáil for Fianna Fáil in 1977. Minister for Post & Telegraphs 1979-81, Energy 1982, Industry & Commerce 1987, Finance 1988-91. Taoiseach 1992-94.

Robinson, Mary
Senator 1969-89. President of Ireland 1990-97. United Nations Commissioner for Human Rights 1997-2002.

Royal Irish Constabulary, The (RIC)
Ireland's armed police force 1822-1922. Dublin had its own unarmed Metropolitan Police from 1836-1925. RIC replaced by the Garda Síochána in 1922.

Shatter, Alan
Fine Gael TD first elected to Dáil Eireann in 1981. Lost seat 2002.

Sinn Féin
Founded by Arthur Griffith in 1905 to press for the return of

an Irish parliament under a British monarch. In 1917 became a republican party.

Spring, Dick
Took his father's seat in the 1981 general election. Became leader of the Labour Party in 1982. Tánaiste 1982-87, 1993-97. Retired from politics 2002.

Treaty, The
Signed in London by a Sinn Féin delegation in December 1921, providing for a limited form of self-government for a partitioned Free State. Sinn Féin split over the issue.

Treatyites
Supporters of the Treaty.

Tullymander
In 1973, the newly-installed coalition decided to massage the constituency boundaries to their future advantage. Minister Jim Tully got the job. The operation backfired, and FF won by a landslide in 1977.

Workers Party, The
Began as political wing of the Official IRA. In 1977 became Sinn Féin – The Workers Party. In 1982 became The Workers Party. In 1992 six of the party's seven TDs left to become Democratic Left, and subsequently joined the Labour Party.